MW01055731

THE

PRINTER

AND THE

PREACHER

THE

PRINTER

AND THE

PREACHER

BEN FRANKLIN, GEORGE WHITEFIELD,
AND THE SURPRISING FRIENDSHIP
THAT INVENTED AMERICA

RANDY PETERSEN

NELSON
BOOKS

An Imprint of Thomas Nelson

Published in Nashville, Tennessee, by Nelson Books, an imprint of Thomas Nelson. Nelson Books and Thomas Nelson are registered trademarks of HarperCollins Christian Publishing, Inc.

The author is represented by the literary agency of Alive Communications, Inc., 7680 Goddard Street, Suite 200, Colorado Springs, Colorado 80920, www.alivecommunications.com

Thomas Nelson, Inc., titles may be purchased in bulk for educational, business, fund-raising, or sales promotional use. For information, please e-mail SpecialMarkets@ThomasNelson.com.

Library of Congress Control Number: 2014957204

ISBN-13: 9780718022211

Printed in the United States of America

15 16 17 18 19 RRD 6 5 4 3 2 1

CONTENTS

1. The Friendship That Invented America 1
2. England and America 11
3. The Inn and the Candle Shop 19
4. Casting Characters 28
5. The City of Brotherly Love 38
6. Hoodwinked 45
7. Next Stage: England 50
8. The Play's the Thing 59
9. The Education of George Whitefield 66
10. The Continuing Education of Ben Franklin 73
11. Boy, Interrupted 82
12. The Leather Aprons and the Bible Moths 89
13. Conversion 100
14. A Better Place 110
15. Doppelgängers 123
16. Georgia on My Mind 131
17. Face to Face 143
18. Cooling Off 155
19. The Awakeners 165
20. Love, Maybe 172
21. Fireside Chats 183
22. The Arc of Friendship 196
23. Death and Taxes 205
24. Special Effects 217

Acknowledgments. 227

Appendix A: Before They Met. 229

Appendix B: George Whitefield's Amazing American Tour . . 239

Appendix C: Encounters 243

Notes 247

Bibliography 263

About the Author. 267

Index 269

ONE

The Friendship That Invented America

They were the two most famous men in America. Both had enormous impact on the colonies that would become the United States. In the decades before George Washington came to fame, while Jefferson and Adams were still in school, the strands of American DNA were being twirled together by a printer and a preacher: Benjamin Franklin and George Whitefield.

With his dramatic preaching, Whitefield led the "Great Awakening" that established a spiritual groundwork for the American colonists. They were no longer merely Anglican, Presbyterian, or Baptist, but *Christian*— freed from the old establishment and united in an exciting new experience of faith.

With his wry writing and thirst for knowledge, Franklin helped to forge a uniquely American personality. His *Poor Richard's Almanac* set the tone. Americans could revel in their homespun humor, their hardscrabble common sense. Franklin's own life trajectory—from laborer to entrepreneur to politician to scientist to diplomat—proved his point. In this new world, no one had to bow to nobility. Success was available if you were willing to work for it. With this in mind, Franklin created a stunning array of social structures—a library, a fire brigade, a hospital, and many others—that knit together the citizens of the emerging country. Long before any talk of independence, he was already building a nation.

These two celebrities, George and Ben, knew each other, liked each other, supported each other, and challenged each other. Through conversations, letters, business projects, and meetings in Philadelphia and London, the two men carried on a meaningful friendship for more than thirty years.

The Odd Couple

They were an odd couple, to be sure. George was fully committed to his faith, and he openly shared the gospel of Jesus not only in his evangelistic meetings, but also in personal conversation and correspondence. More than once, he tried to get his friend Ben into a personal relationship with Jesus.

Franklin wasn't buying. He had constructed his own faith from various raw materials: the rough-hewn rocks of the Cotton Mather Puritanism he had learned in his boyhood Boston; the intricate machinery of the deism he had flirted with as a young man; and the sturdy timbers of his lifelong devotion to self-improvement. He believed in God, and he expressed a personal humility before his Creator, but he had difficulty accepting claims about the divinity of Jesus or his sacrificial death. Jesus was a good example of human behavior, as Franklin saw it. "Imitate Jesus and Socrates," he once included in his rules for living.[1]

Of course, Whitefield called for more than just imitation. He preached Jesus as God incarnate, the Savior, the sacrificial Lamb through whom God offered salvation to his chosen ones. With power and passion, this orator urged his hearers to respond to the Spirit's call and be "born again." Thousands did just that—but not Ben Franklin.

Besides their religious differences, the two men also had very different styles of communication, at least in public. Whitefield was highly dramatic in his sermons, with a booming voice that could be heard a city block away, theatrical gestures, and emotional pleadings that were the envy of the best professional actors of that day. Franklin addressed relatively small groups, not crowds. His most effective communication was one-on-one or in writing.

The differences go on. George was an Oxford graduate, Ben a grammar school dropout. In spite of this, Ben was universally acclaimed for his brilliance (and got honorary degrees from some of the world's best colleges), while George was often disparaged for a dearth of scholarly content in his sermons. Some felt he lacked the intellectual ability to go beyond popular puffery.

George was an Englishman who loved America, crossing the ocean thirteen times in a period of thirty-two years (all the more stunning when you consider that each trip took two to four months). Ben was an American who loved England. He fell for London on one trip as a young man, and he spent most of two decades there later, representing American interests.

Ben became known for his flirtation and sexual affairs, while George had trouble romancing his own wife. It might be true that Ben's reputation was more fancy than fact, but he never seemed to be troubled by it. Meanwhile, George was a traveling man with thousands of female admirers, yet he knew that any hint of sexual impropriety would doom his ministry.

How on earth did these two very different men become friends?

Just Business?

It began as a business partnership. In 1739, Franklin was one of several printers to publish Whitefield's journals and sermons. Early letters between them refer to some of these projects. In a short time, Ben became the primary printer for George, joining his keen business sense with the preacher's knack for public relations to make a great deal of money for both of them. Franklin also edited a weekly newspaper, the *Pennsylvania Gazette*, which often reported on Whitefield's public appearances throughout the colonies. Whatever their personal differences, they helped each other to stunning success.

Their friendship had some ups and downs, however. After Whitefield's first American tour, his critics became more vocal, and Franklin published their attacks. This has led some historians to suggest that there was no deeper friendship between the two men, that it was all just business. But a deeper look at their correspondence, which continued for more than two decades, reveals evidence of a growing relationship. Perhaps in the early 1740s Ben was asserting his editorial independence, proving he was more than Whitefield's publicity flack, but he later wrote powerful editorials defending George's reputation. And on a later tour of the colonies, when George needed a place to stay in Philadelphia, Ben opened his home.

In their letters over the following years, we find George sending regards to Ben's wife, not in a perfunctory way, but with a charm that suggests he was a frequent guest in the Franklin home, and Ben offering "cordial salutations" to "good Mrs. Whitefield." On a trip to Boston, George apparently met Ben's sister Jane. In a letter from London in the 1760s, Ben wrote to his wife that Mr. Whitefield had stopped by, with a casual air that implied both that George was a regular visitor and that Deborah Franklin would care about her old guest.

In another letter, written to George, Ben mused about starting a new colony with him in the wilds of Ohio, where the two of them would model the best of humanity—faith and philosophy together. Whatever distancing had occurred in their early acquaintance was now long gone. Even Ben's gentle rebuffs of George's proselytizing have the flavor of a conversation they'd had many times.

A Good Influence

While Franklin didn't agree with everything Whitefield was preaching, he did recognize the valuable effect Whitefield had on society at large. Ben was a champion of personal discipline, good citizenship, and charitable deeds. That was exactly what he saw in the behavior of Philadelphians, as more and more of them experienced the "new birth" that Whitefield was promoting. Critics could knock George's undignified delivery, but Ben was satisfied with the results—a better society.

Despite their religious differences, George and Ben shared a disdain for the rigid, sectarian, power-hungry, and often hypocritical church establishment. Though George was ordained as an Anglican minister, he was strongly opposed by many Anglican leaders in England and America. His theatrical style was popular with a lower-class crowd, and he encouraged emotional responses to his message. As a result, many traditional church folk were scandalized by the unchurchlike behavior of Whitefield's audiences, and some churches closed their doors to him. This forced him outside, where he could draw even larger crowds, free from church control.

Though Franklin supported and occasionally attended a couple of different churches in Philadelphia, he himself had experienced a few run-ins with church authorities. Especially troubled by rancor between different Christian denominations, Ben dreamed of setting up an academy in which different churches would share equally, and he did so. George supported this vision and actually helped him with this project. Ben would have loved seeing people from many different denominations thronging to George's outdoor services. In his sermons, George sometimes included a joke about searching in vain for particular denominations in heaven. Later in life, Ben was quoted telling a very similar joke.

This was more than a matter of religious taste. When Whitefield, with Franklin's support, broke down these denominational walls, he was clearing the way for the invention of America. Neither George nor Ben would have described it like that, but they both recognized the danger of religious division. George sensed that the gospel of Jesus had to break out of its ecclesiastical confinement. No single sect owned the truth about Jesus. The new birth was available to all who would receive it, regardless of their church loyalties. As a spectator viewing sectarian squabbles from the sideline, Ben understood that a strong American society would never be built unless Anglicans and Presbyterians and Quakers and others could all get along.

In a Class All Their Own

Another factor that might have drawn Ben and George together was social class—not only where they were, but also where they were going. Both came from working-class roots to find enormous fame, but neither was fully welcomed into the upper class.

We don't think much about class in America today. Any kid can grow up to be president, we say. If you apply yourself to your endeavors with pluck and grit, you can succeed, no matter what family you were born into.

It was Ben Franklin who taught us that. But in the early 1700s, those assumptions could not be made. "Gentlemen" lived in a different world, enjoying a different level of respect and receiving different privileges. A centuries-old vassal system lingered on, with nobility being a matter of money and manners. There were a few opportunities for upward mobility, and a constant danger of *downward* mobility, but to a great degree these castes still segmented society in England and, to a lesser degree, in America.

Gentlemen didn't work; they *owned*. Money came in through their holdings. They paid others to work their fields or run their businesses. They might occasionally inspect how things were going, but in general they were "men of leisure." If you worked for a living, that was proof you weren't a gentleman—no matter how rich or successful you were.[2]

Ben Franklin was dyed-in-the-wool working class, born into the home of a common candle maker (and dyer). He learned the trade of printing and became phenomenally successful at it. Yet he still wasn't a gentleman. As he got more involved in civic affairs and then academic pursuits, he rubbed shoulders with many gentlemen, but he was never entirely included in their ranks. This was a sore spot for him.

George Whitefield was at a similar point on the nobility grid, though he got there a different way. His grandfather had been a gentleman, but the family had fallen on hard times, and George grew up in an innkeeper's family. He attended Oxford College as a "servitor," earning tuition by doing menial tasks for upper-class students. This humiliating work led to a college degree, which led to his ordination, which (he hoped) would restore his family's status. But Whitefield squandered any social-climbing opportunity with his insistence on preaching to those on the lower rungs of society. Still, he had supporters among the nobility, especially Lady Selina Hastings, Countess of Huntingdon, who hired him as her personal chaplain and promoted him among her genteel friends.

Both Ben and George, then, had risen greatly from humble beginnings but still found themselves on the outside of the upper class looking in. Thanks to their fame, both moved among the gentlemen of America and Europe without being entirely welcomed into those ranks. Both of them saw the inadequacies of this class system but also felt the shame of being excluded, being denied the respect they deserved. Though both were fully ensconced in their class-based society and probably had trouble imagining a world without such structure, they still worked to break this chauvinism and empower common citizens.

Perhaps this is what led Ben to make that startling proposal to George: *let's make a new colony with the Indians in Ohio.* No kings, no "gentlemen," no artificial divisions, just people working hard to build a society and honor God. Maybe George would understand that dream better than anyone else.

This is essentially the America they invented, with Ben calling citizens to take responsibility for their own society and George calling souls into a personal relationship with God. No governor, no bishop, no monarch, no minister could establish a person's value, temporal or eternal. In their own ways, George and Ben invited Americans to act as if class distinctions did not exist, and while such distinctions were never completely eradicated, they mattered less and less.

Celebrity and Loyalty

George and Ben would have respected each other for gaining success through hard work rather than inherited status, and they might have commiserated about the rejections they both received from the higher-born. But there was yet another factor they would have understood about each other more than anyone else: *celebrity.*

Franklin and Whitefield were quite simply the biggest celebrities in the colonies. Some have suggested they were the *first* American celebrities. There simply was no previous publicity machine that came close to what Franklin and Whitefield created. Newspapers had existed, but it was Ben who harnessed their power. George employed advertising techniques that were cutting-edge for business enterprises and absolutely revolutionary in the church. As George conducted tour after tour in America, through town after town, up and down the coast, virtually everyone knew who he was. Whoever didn't get to see him in person could read about him in Franklin's newspaper, or in any number of publications from Franklin's sprawling network of printers. Ben's own fame grew steadily through the decades—first as a best-selling author, then as America's leading scientist, and then as a diplomat representing the interests of various colonies in Europe. For a century, the disparate colonies had pursued their own isolated interests. Why should Virginians care about Boston? But now, suddenly, they were all united in their fascination with this astonishing preacher from England, and over time they got to know their own printer-thinker-statesman, Dr. Franklin.

How would this unprecedented celebrity affect George and Ben? Both struggled to keep their own hubris in check, and they did fairly well with that, despite a few glitches. But how would celebrity alter their relationships with others? Both faced vilification as well as adulation. Both experienced betrayal from people close to them. Was this the price of fame? Were all friendships now twisted, poisoned by duplicity and opportunism?

Despite their differences, these two men could understand each other as no one else could. They could be authentic with each other because they had attained the same level of celebrity. Neither worshiped the other. Neither was angling for some sort of advantage. Early on, they had helped each other achieve their phenomenal success, but as the years went on, they didn't really need anything from each other anymore. No pretense was necessary.

And the letters that passed between them indicate a remarkable authenticity. Ben didn't try to be religious to impress the great preacher. George didn't dial back his evangelistic impulses. They said what they felt. With this level of openness in their correspondence, we can imagine that their personal conversations had an even greater honesty.

Of course, their friendship didn't start with such soul-baring intimacy. Journaling about their first meeting in November 1739, Whitefield didn't even mention Franklin's name. He was just "one of the printers" with an idea for selling books. Clearly George didn't recognize that Ben had been producing the wildly popular *Poor Richard's Almanac* for six years already. On his slow trajectory, Ben had achieved a modest height of fame, but George was already stratospheric.

Within the next year, George returned to Philadelphia several times, probably met with Ben about several publishing projects, and must have inquired about Ben's faith, because in November 1740 he wrote him a letter, saying, "I do not despair of your seeing the reasonableness of Christianity."[3]

After a cooling-off period of several years, during which Franklin published pieces both for and against him, Whitefield took another preaching tour to the colonies and faced stronger opposition than ever. Especially damaging were accusations about misuse of charitable funds. Ben's support proved crucial to George, as he published a financial report, praised his ministry, and affirmed his "unspotted character."

About twenty years later, it was Franklin who needed support. Representing several American colonies, he appeared before Parliament in February 1766 to argue for the repeal of the hated Stamp Act. While that measure was repealed, Parliament passed another act giving itself broad powers to tax the colonies in the future. After initial glee, many Americans realized that the new measure might be worse than the old one, and many blamed Franklin for failing them.

This time George rushed to Ben's defense, putting out a letter to be copied and distributed through the vast network of his American supporters, saying that Franklin had done very well in his testimony before Parliament and "did honour to his country."[4]

We must note not only the loyalty shown in this friendship but also its longevity. George and Ben knew each other for more than thirty years, from George's first visit to Philadelphia in 1739 to his death in 1770. Both were very busy men, but they stayed in touch with each other, meeting on both sides of the Atlantic and sending occasional letters. Some of this correspondence has surely been lost, but the letters that remain provide a fascinating slideshow of a relationship-in-progress between two extraordinary people.

Franklin devoted about six pages of his autobiography to his recollections of Whitefield, but he has baffled some readers by concluding, "Ours was a mere civil friendship, sincere on both sides, and lasted to his death."[5]

What was he saying there? He wrote that in 1788. Whitefield had died eighteen years earlier, but was still widely remembered and much loved. Maybe Franklin was demonstrating his characteristic humility, under-playing his connection with Whitefield to avoid poaching the dead man's glory. More likely he was indicating that he never became one of Whitefield's converts. Their friendship wasn't a religious one, but "merely civil."

What he *couldn't* have been saying, given the strong evidence of three decades of correspondence, was that they were just business acquaintances. We get further verification of their relationship in a 1747 message Franklin sent to his brother. Hearing that Whitefield had arrived in Boston safe and well, Ben wrote, "He is a good man and I love him."[6]

Each of these men individually had a major influence on the emerging American society. The Great Awakening that Whitefield carried through the colonies set a tone of personal religious commitment that endures today. Yet Franklin's humanism also endures. The ideals he promoted, the civic responsibilities of citizens banding together for the common good, took root in the founding documents of this nation. But the two men also helped each other exert that influence. Years before the Declaration, long before the shot heard 'round the world, Ben and George were teaching the colonists to think, act, and believe for themselves. Their parallel messages created social and spiritual infrastructures for the nation that came to be.

TWO

England and America

It was the Wild West.

Long before George and Ben captivated the colonies with their preaching and pragmatism, America was an idea, a dream, a sacred hope. For centuries Europeans had imagined following the setting sun to parts unknown, sailing the great ocean to mysterious new lands. The prospect was exciting—and terrifying. Did this ocean wrap around the earth and reappear in the East, or was there something else out there?

For thinkers of old, these uncertainties sometimes gave birth to religious notions, grand apocalyptic theories. Would the mysterious West be the promised land for true believers? Would human history "set" there, like the sun, as it had risen in the East?

Poets waxed lyrical about the possibilities. In Dante's *Inferno*, Ulysses tells a tale of sailing through the Strait of Gibraltar and out into the western sea. Urging his crew not to "deny the knowledge . . . of the unpeopled world," he pressed westward, "following the sun," until he reached the afterlife.[1] Scholars found hints in the Bible and other ancient literature suggesting that God had great plans for a new land to be found beyond the sea. Christopher Columbus was an avid student of end-times prophecy, and saw himself fulfilling those predictions by journeying to the new world.

It didn't hurt that the great explorers were braving the western ocean about the same time that the great reformers were crafting a new faith. In 1492, while Columbus was "sailing the ocean blue," another Italian, the fiery Savonarola, was pronouncing judgment upon the Roman church. Balboa looked out over the Pacific Ocean from the Isthmus of Panama just as Luther was getting settled into his teaching post at the University of Wittenberg, where he would soon post the ninety-five complaints that launched the Protestant Reformation. Magellan's crew was sailing around the world as Zwingli was beginning to stir up the Reformed movement in Zurich.

There was a new world to be found. This was the message of both groups of seekers. That world was "out there" and "in here," across the sea and within the soul. *Don't remain behind rock-hewn walls of ignorance that have stood for centuries. God is doing something new here.* Whitefield's message of the new birth fit right in with the spirit of discovery that had motivated European settlers from the start. *Take a chance on a new existence, a life of freedom, where you can commune with your God in a new way in a new land.*

English Spin

As the exploratory 1500s gave way to the 1600s, the English took the lead in exploring North America. (Their 1588 defeat of the Spanish Armada had shifted the balance of power in Europe and freed up the seas for English travel.) A number of English writers put their own apocalyptic spin on the new settlements. The poet-preacher John Donne rallied one group of settlers (the Virginia Company) in 1622 after they had received word of a massacre in America. Expounding Acts 1:8, he urged them to share the gospel in this uttermost part of the earth and not just worry about their business enterprises. And he looked forward to a day when the youngest of those settlers would feel at home in a fully settled America. "You shall have made this island, which is but as the suburbs of the old world, a bridge, a gallery to the new, to join all to that world that shall never grow old, the kingdom of Heaven."[2]

The English had often considered themselves the great western hope of Europe, but now those hopes were transferred farther west, across the ocean. Perhaps no one expressed this more clearly than George Herbert, an Anglican poet, priest, scholar, and member of Parliament. *The Temple*, his landmark book of religious poetry published in 1633, included a sprawling poem that surveyed Christian history, "The Church Militant." Here Herbert referred with great anticipation to the westward direction of God's plans. "Religion stands on tiptoe in our land / Ready to pass to the American strand."[3] He saw the world hurtling to a conclusion, and the church's last act would be written in America.

A century later, the writings of George Herbert would have great influence on the life of a college student named George Whitefield. He too was convinced that God had great plans for America, and he was eager to be part of them. Days after he met Ben Franklin, George included Herbert's "tiptoe" quote in his journal, adding that this "prophecy is now being fulfilled."[4]

Mission: America

From the start the discovery of America was seen as a religious mission, but it was also an economic venture. Spanish conquistadors gathered gold for the royal coffers, and English settlers sought to establish lucrative trade in the rich resources of this new continent. These two motives worked side by side. The natives of America were a new people to evangelize. An assortment of priests, ministers, and missionaries journeyed alongside scouts, soldiers, and entrepreneurs, bringing the gospel of Christ to those who had never heard it. Columbus himself focused on evangelism as his role in fulfilling prophecy (and he was actually collecting gold to fund the rebuilding of Jerusalem, another part of his end-times vision).

There is much to condemn about the methods of these early missionary enterprises in America. In general, there was too much conflation of God's ways with European culture and a wanton disregard for the welfare of the native population. But we must not ignore the fact that the settling of America was a religious mission as much as it was a business opportunity.

It was also a quest for religious freedom.

The Protestant Reformation, beginning in the early 1500s, created chaos in Europe for at least a century and a half. Not only were there violent conflicts between Catholics and Protestants, but there were several different types of Protestants in the mix—Lutherans, Calvinists, Anglicans, and various independent groups. These were often political power plays more than religious disagreements, but still, in many places it was dangerous to follow the wrong religion. Many of those who could emigrate did so. Eventually, many of these religious refugees landed in America.

As Thomas Paine would write later in his *Common Sense* pamphlet, "The reformation was preceded by the discovery of America, as if the Almighty graciously meant to open a sanctuary to the persecuted in future years."[5]

England had its own religious free-for-all, from the time that King Henry VIII wrested the Anglican church away from Roman Catholic control in 1534. For the next century and a half, tensions continued between Catholics and Protestants, often erupting in violent measures and brutal reprisals. Presbyterian and Puritan groups were also jockeying for position *within* the Church of England, though some left that church. In general, Puritans sought to purify the church of Catholic excesses—robes, genuflection, musical instruments, and also the immense power given to bishops. Believing it was more biblical to give power to the church body, they sometimes were known as Congregationalists. And there were also many independent churches (notably Baptists and later Quakers) that found the Anglicans too corrupt, too restrictive, or still too Catholic. Independents who left the Church of England were known as Separatists, Dissenters, or Nonconformists. They were often arrested and jailed, and some sought refuge in the much more tolerant Netherlands and eventually in America.

The Jamestown colony in Virginia was settled in 1607 as an enterprise of the Virginia Company, primarily for business purposes but also with some stated evangelistic aims. It soon began paying off, producing tobacco and other resources. Beginning in 1620, America also became a haven for England's religious exiles, as the *Mayflower* landed in Massachusetts, bearing a group we know as the Pilgrims. They had obtained a royal charter to settle in northern Virginia but were blown off course.

Many of the *Mayflower* passengers were Separatists seeking a new home after a brief exile in Holland. Though some took the *Mayflower* voyage for business purposes, this was a religious quest for many of them; these pilgrims hoped to find freedom to practice their faith in the new world.

Forty-one men aboard that ship signed the Mayflower Compact, an agreement setting out expectations for an independent, faith-based community. It read in part: "Having undertaken for the Glory of God, and Advancement of the Christian Faith, and the Honour of our King and Country, a Voyage to plant the first Colony in the northern Parts of Virginia; Do by these Presents, solemnly and mutually, in the Presence of God and one another, covenant and combine ourselves together into a civil Body Politick, for our better Ordering and Preservation."[6]

This occurred just four score and six years before Ben Franklin was born—and less than fifty miles from his Boston birthplace.

The Great Migration

Meanwhile, back in England, political events were unfolding that created a huge wave of religious emigration. With a number of Catholic-leaning measures, King Charles I alienated the Puritans. Thousands of them sought a new life in America. Happy to get rid of them, Charles granted a charter for the Massachusetts Bay Colony, situated next to the Pilgrims' Plymouth Colony. Over the next decade or so, more than twenty thousand Puritans made that journey. Historians call it "The Great Migration."

This was a grand experiment, a chance to create a society from scratch based on truly Christian principles. The Puritans had bought into the highly structured theology of John Calvin, who was a lawyer before he became a religious leader. Just a century earlier, Calvin had tried to create a similar society in Geneva. Now his spiritual heirs had a new colony on a new continent. Its first governor, John Winthrop, called it "a city upon a hill,"[7] invoking Jesus' comment from Matthew 5:14, which begins, "You are the light of the world."

All those lofty descriptions of the westward expansion of God's redemptive activity were once again in play. The Puritans were not just building a new home; they were creating a new Israel, a nation run by God's principles. This would indeed be a light to the world, showing everybody on earth how to live God's way. "The eyes of all people are upon us," Winthrop announced.[8]

Of course, it didn't work out so well for everyone. The Puritans had their own discontents. In 1638 Anne Hutchinson was banished from the colony for daring to teach her Bible study group about God's grace and thus disparaging God's law. Mid-century, several Quakers found their way to Boston and were severely punished for their charismatic and egalitarian ways. And 1962 saw the start of the Salem witch trials, in which the fear of devilry caused the colony to act in devilish ways—arresting dozens on dubious evidence and executing nineteen of them.

This is the irony of religious freedom. All too often, we want freedom for *our* religion, but we fail to grant it to others. Puritans rejoiced in the opportunity to break free from the Church of England and to worship in the ways their own consciences dictated, but then they established a colony that imposed religious restrictions on others.

Benjamin Franklin was born into this religious culture, just thirteen years after the end of the witch trials. As a young man, he knew Cotton Mather, who had inspired and advised the Salem prosecutors. While there were a great many positive aspects to Puritan teaching, and we see some of them in Franklin's character, with the speckled history of the previous century it's no surprise that Ben became a skeptic—especially with regard to sectarian Christianity.

The Puritans reflected the duality of the European mission to settle America—both religious and economic. Their "city on a hill" was designed to enlighten the world from this new western position, but it would also function as a *city*, a society, an economic entity in which everyone pitched in for mutual benefit. These two goals were inseparable for those early Puritans as they sought to build a righteous community. They became known for their "Puritan work ethic," in which citizens served God by doing their part in the local economy.

We see the same duality in Ben and George, except the two strands had come apart. Whitefield bought heavily into the Calvinist theology of the Puritans, with a strong sense of God's calling. While Franklin rejected Puritan theology, he embraced the idea of a well-functioning society, with each citizen contributing to the economic success of the community.

The Forces at Work

As Puritans and others were settling Massachusetts in the mid-1600s, there was more fighting in England. Parliament, led by Puritans and Presbyterians, deposed Charles I but ruled for only eleven years before giving way to the exiled Charles II. A backlash followed, targeting Puritans and Dissenters. This is why the independent minister John Bunyan was in prison when he wrote his 1678 classic *The Pilgrim's Progress*. And a few years later, a Congregationalist tradesman from Northamptonshire named Josiah Franklin decided to escape England's religious repression by moving his wife and three children to Boston. Over the next three decades in America, he would father fourteen *more* children, including Benjamin—and he faithfully took his growing family to the Congregationalist Old South Church. America was a haven for the Franklins, a place to work and worship freely.

Ben grew up in an environment shaped by three major forces: faith, freedom, and fortune. Those forces were still strong when George Whitefield visited America, and they still characterize the United States today.

We have seen that some settlers were motivated by business opportunities in the new world. Jamestown held the promise of new resources and new trade, and the Virginia Company eagerly financed the project. Even aboard the *Mayflower* there were seekers of fortune side by side with the religious refugees. As the colonies grew, the economic bounties became more apparent. There was land aplenty, and it grew good crops. As Ben Franklin continually expounded, anyone could make a good living here through ingenuity and hard work—and he modeled that in his own life many times over. Even Georgia, the last of the original thirteen colonies to be settled (and the first visited by Whitefield), was largely populated by those freed from debtors' prisons in England, seeking a chance to start new accounts.

Freedom surely felt sweet to those debtors, but it was religious freedom that beckoned to many. Those who had to worship secretly back in England, who had to cut back on their evangelizing, who had to pay lip service (and taxes!) to a church they didn't agree with—these believers risked their lives on rickety ships to enter a land where they could be honest before God and their neighbors. Others sought political freedom, where their prospects weren't determined by the whim of a king. Freedom is always tricky in its application, as Franklin found out in his statecraft and Whitefield in his soulcraft, but liberty's lure is strong and its rewards are rich.

And finally, there was the powerful faith that flowed through the hearts of many colonists. Some crossed the ocean in order to share their faith with the natives of this new land, or (like Whitefield) with the colonists who preceded them. But the steady migration westward was also fueled, in some way, by a belief that God's plan was moving in this direction. Poets and philosophers had been hinting at this for some time. Follow the setting sun and a new light would rise there, in the wilderness across the western sea. Deep in their souls, these faithful colonists sensed that the Creator was creating something new in this new land.[9]

THREE

The Inn and the Candle Shop

They were born about nine years and one ocean apart. For children growing up in working-class homes in the early 1700s, England and America
weren't all that different. Both Ben and George were sent to school, but they
also helped out in the family businesses. Ben cut wicks, poured wax, and
ran errands for his father's candle-making shop. George assisted at the inn
his mother owned. Fortunately, both saw fit to write accounts of their lives,
and so we can gather a number of details regarding their upbringing—at
least as they remembered them.

Benjamin was born on the sixth day of 1706, or so he thought. There
is some confusion about many dates in that era, because the British
Empire switched from the Julian calendar to the Gregorian in 1752, essen-
tially erasing eleven days from the calendar. September 2 was followed
by September 14 that year, to realign the year with the solar seasons.
As a result, many important dates from the early 1700s have both "Old
Style" and "New Style" numbers. Ben was born January 6, 1706 (OS), or
January 17 (NS). George Whitefield was born December 16, 1714 (OS), or
December 27 (NS).

Meet the Franklins

The Franklins had a huge family. Ben's father, Josiah, sired seven children with his first wife, Anne Child—three before moving to America and four afterward. After Anne died, he married Abiah Folger and fathered ten more. Benjamin was the third youngest child in the clan, with two kid sisters. Not all of the children survived to adulthood, but Ben remembered a moment, probably when he was nine, with thirteen Franklin progeny sitting around the dinner table.[1] Imagine the challenges of growing up in that kind of crowd. How do you find your place in such a family? How do you get the attention you need?

Young Benjamin was smart, an avid reader, and precocious. "I was generally a leader among the boys," he recalled, "and sometimes led them into scrapes."[2] On one occasion, at Ben's instigation, the boys raided a construction site and carried off stones, which they used to build a wharf for their own fishing hole.

This is a remarkable story, which is why Ben included it in his autobiography half a century later, noting that "it shows an early projecting public spirit, tho' not then justly conducted."[3] We see him gathering his playmates in a massive public works project, inspiring them to work hard to build something that would benefit them all. This is the sort of thing he did all his life. Library, fire company, hospital—he had a knack for building society, and apparently it started early. Of course, in his youth, he overlooked the fact that he was stealing the materials from someone else. The boys' thievery was discovered, and their fathers "corrected" them. Ben "pleaded the usefulness of the work," but his father convinced him that "nothing was useful which was not honest."[4]

Because of Ben's unique intelligence, Josiah Franklin had special plans for this, his tenth and youngest son, "intending to devote me as the tithe of his sons to the service of the Church."[5] As the ancient Israelites brought a tenth of their produce to the tabernacle—their *tithe*—so this tenth son would be dedicated to the church. That was the plan, anyway. Church ministry would require education, and so, while his older brothers were apprenticing with various tradesmen, Ben was sent to grammar school, where he excelled. He rose to the head of his class and jumped to the next grade, and he was about to jump to the next when his father realized there was no money for advanced education. He would never be able to send Ben to college, and so the dream of making his son a clergyman vanished. Ben was enrolled in a different school for more practical training in writing and arithmetic. (He did well in the writing—not so well with math.) But then, at the age of ten, he was finished with his schooling. Since college would never be an option, Ben would need to learn a trade. For the next few years, Ben stayed home to work in his father's candle-making business—when he wasn't getting into "scrapes" with his pals.

Ben hated candle making. He didn't want to do this all his life. Because the sea had always fascinated Ben, Josiah feared that the boy might run off to be a sailor, so he became increasingly desperate about finding a trade his youngest son would like. "He therefore sometimes took me to walk with him, and see joiners, bricklayers, turners, braziers, etc. at their work, that he might observe my inclination, and endeavour to fix it on some trade or other on land," Ben wrote.[6]

This turned out to be a great education in how a society works. Benjamin Franklin never became a professional bricklayer or joiner (carpenter), but he saw how each of these craftsmen contributed to the civic enterprise. "It has ever since been a pleasure to me to see good workmen handle their tools," he commented years later, adding that he himself had since used some of the skills he had observed in that walkabout.[7] But there was a larger education going on here. Twelve-year-old Ben was watching democracy in action, long before it became a political reality. All his life, he would respect the work of the common laborer. Hobnobbing with "gentlemen" who looked down on those who got their hands dirty, Franklin would always keep quite a different opinion.

As it happened, Josiah had a nephew who was setting up shop as a cutler, and he made arrangements for Ben to apprentice with him. When they couldn't agree on the financial arrangements (the family was expected to pay for the apprenticeship), this experience was cut short. Ben was back to square one. Would he have to make his living on the high seas?

One of Josiah's older sons, James, had recently returned from London with a printing press and was setting up shop in Boston. Noting Benjamin's love of books, Josiah sought to arrange an apprenticeship there. Though Ben resisted at first—the sea still beckoned—this was where he ended up. Papers were signed that committed Benjamin to work for his brother until he was twenty-one.

Room at the Inn

Across the pond, George Whitefield was still a toddler. He too was a youngest son, in fact the youngest of seven children born to Thomas and Elizabeth Whitefield, who ran an inn in Bristol, Gloucestershire, England. It took his mother fourteen weeks to recover physically from this birth, and George notes that she "used to say, even when I was an infant, that she expected more comfort from me than any other of her children."[8] This sense of specialness, as the baby of the family, seeps through Whitefield's journals and through his life. There was a sense that he was destined for great things.

The family was not especially religious, though they participated in the generic Anglican faith of that region. George's great-grandfather had been an Oxford-educated Anglican rector, but the family's status had dropped a few pegs in the succeeding generations. Elizabeth's dreams for her youngest son may have been more social than spiritual, that he might attain a respectable church post and thus lift the whole family's fortunes. The fact that he was born in an inn often prompted George to "make good my mother's expectations, and so follow the example of my dear Saviour, who was born in a manger belonging to an inn."[9]

Thomas Whitefield died suddenly at age thirty-five, when George was just two. The inn was left in Elizabeth's care, with her children to help. Yet she wouldn't let young George work there. His education came first.

As you might expect from a Calvinist, Whitefield described his childhood in terms that fit with the concept of total depravity. "I was so brutish as to hate instruction. . . . Lying, filthy talking, and foolish jesting I was much addicted to, even when very young. Sometimes I used to curse, if not swear." He stole money from his mother's pocket, broke the Sabbath, and indulged in "common entertainments" like play going, card playing, and reading romances. "Often have I joined with others in playing roguish tricks, but was generally, if not always, *happily detected*."[10]

Compare this with Franklin's story of stealing stones. In both situations, "roguish tricks" were "detected" and lessons learned. But Ben reveled in his impish boyhood, not to mention the leadership ability shown in the wharf-building episode, while George berated himself for his innate wickedness. Ironically, it would seem that the Franklin home was religiously stricter than the Whitefield home, and yet each man looked back autobiographically and analyzed the sins of his youth in a way that matched his adult mind-set. Boys will be boys, and yet Ben looked back at a lesson learned in good citizenship while George saw his desperate need for a Savior.

After eight years of widowhood, George's mother remarried—and it nearly destroyed her. Her new husband tried to take over the inn, failed, left her, stole as much as he could, and filed for divorce. At that point, the family's fortunes plummeted. Though George had done well in school, especially in speech making and theater, it became clear that the family would not be able to send him to college. So, in a situation similar to Ben Franklin's, George dropped out of school as a teenager and worked full-time at the inn for a year and a half—and for a time he even worked for an older brother who had taken over the inn.

Father Figures

Psychoanalyzing historical characters is always presumptuous, but it's worth noting that Ben Franklin grew up with a strong father and George Whitefield did not.

It's really quite touching to read Ben's tribute to his father in the early pages of his autobiography, especially when we remember that this was written to his own son. "I think you may like to know something of his person and character," the sixty-five-year-old Ben wrote to William, who was in his early forties. After describing Josiah's appearance, singing voice, and mechanical genius, Ben added, "his great excellence lay in a sound

understanding, and solid judgment in prudential matters, both in private
and public affairs." Though the man never had time for any governmental
post, Ben remembered that he was "frequently visited by leading people,
who consulted him for his opinion in affairs of the Town or of the Church
he belonged to and showed a good deal of respect for his judgment and
advice."[11]

Ben went on to talk about the family dinners, where Josiah often invited
friends to converse with (though surely the table was already crowded) and
"always took care to start some ingenious or useful topic for discourse, which
might tend to improve the minds of his children. By this means he turned
our Attention to what was good, just, and prudent in the conduct of life."
With such food for thought, no one talked about the quality of the meal.[12]

We've already seen the care Josiah took in finding the right direction
for Ben, acquainting him with different trades and seeking to negotiate a
suitable apprenticeship. He seemed to be a gentle giant in Ben's life. Ever
after, in all his relationships, this son prized the qualities he had seen in his
father, and he sought to be that kind of father to his own son.

Whitefield, on the other hand, had a single mom who doted on him.
Like Josiah Franklin, Elizabeth Whitefield had high hopes for her gifted
youngest son, only to be limited by economic realities. As much as she tried
to care for George, she herself needed the care of her family, in her own
recuperation from George's birth, her grieving over her first husband, the
practical difficulties of running a respectable inn as a single woman, and
dealing with the fallout of her catastrophic second marriage. We get the
idea that for much of his youth, George was pretty much rearing himself.

Still, he wrote about her with great appreciation, and he maintained a
relationship with her throughout his life. He made her very proud.

Yet we can't help but wonder what effect his upbringing had on his
adult relationships. With a father he hardly knew and a rogue for a step-
father, how did he learn about being a man? What sort of models did he
have for marriage? In his youth, George had some trouble deciding what
sort of person he would be. He would surely have benefited from more
attentive parenting. And there are two details from his adult life that take
on greater significance when we consider the fractured home he grew up

in. First, the charitable cause to which he devoted his life was an *orphanage*. He did all he could to provide a stable home for children in need. And second, when he visited the renowned theologian Jonathan Edwards, he came away with a profound respect for his *marriage*. Perhaps he had never seen such a loving relationship up close, certainly not in his boyhood home.

Work and Words

As Ben grew up in Boston and George in Bristol, both quickly found their places in a world of *work* and *words*.

Both of them learned the value of hard work in the family business—and they acted on that knowledge the rest of their lives. Ben would write about it; George, with his remarkable preaching schedule, would practice it. Remember, too, that the wider culture didn't always support this principle. The mark of a true gentleman was that he didn't *have* to work. But the world was beginning to change its mind about this—especially in America—and both Ben and George would contribute to that change.

There was plenty of work to do in America. The growing society needed people who rolled up their sleeves and pitched in. The founders of the new colonies had been workers, not royals. The Puritans hallowed work as God's calling. The Quakers celebrated the value of community by working together. This was a land of brawn and sweat, where people burned the candle at both ends. While making some of those candles, young Ben gained an appreciation for common laborers. Tending bar and making beds at his mother's inn, young George began to see his own value in serving others.

In different ways, both men incorporated this work ethic into their religious views as they grew older. For Franklin, the measure of a man was his contribution to society. Vices impeded productivity. Even today, we quote his mantra—"Early to bed and early to rise / makes a man healthy, wealthy, and wise." This wasn't just a catchy rhyme. It embodied an ethic that was very important to Franklin.

As a young man, Ben constructed for himself an elaborate plan of self-improvement, with thirteen virtues he would work at developing, one a week, four times a year. His autobiography explains it in words that seem almost Methodist: "I conceived the bold and arduous project of arriving at moral perfection. I wished to live without committing any fault at any time." He's looking back at his youthful ardor with a smile, adding, "I soon found that I had undertaken a task of more difficulty than I had imagined."[13]

So maybe his Thirteen Weeks to Self-Actualization was a bit too ambitious, but Franklin worked at improving himself in various ways all his life, and his wit and wisdom helped others do the same.

For Whitefield, on the other hand, the role of good works in a person's life became a critical issue. Like his friends John and Charles Wesley, he threw himself into religious disciplines—including prayer, fasting, meditation, and Bible study. This was the "method" of attaining holiness that earned them the nickname "Methodists." But, in separate events, all of them reached basically the same conclusion that Franklin did: the task of attaining moral perfection was more difficult than they imagined. The breakthrough for Whitefield and the Wesleys was the acceptance of God's grace. They could never be righteous enough on their own; they needed the atoning sacrifice of Jesus. Whitefield had this conversion experience in 1735, after he had already been meeting with the Holy Club at Oxford for a couple of years.

Good works came afterward. God did his work of sanctification in the believer's heart, and this resulted in works of righteousness, love, and service. Along with the other Methodists, Whitefield reclaimed a methodical approach to righteous living—not as a way of earning God's favor, but as a way of letting God improve him. George worked tirelessly in God's service because, frankly, he didn't deserve a day off. He was a depraved sinner, saved by grace, and he owed God every moment.

A number of books provided guidance for young Whitefield in this spiritual journey—besides the Bible, of course. These included two instructive and devotional works by English scholar William Law: *A Serious Call to a Devout and Holy Life* (1728) and *A Practical Treatise upon Christian Perfection* (1726). Earlier he read works by Anglican bishop Thomas Ken and medieval devotionalist Thomas à Kempis. To get the books that fascinated him,

George would beg, borrow, and steal. Literally. He saved up money to buy some books, and sometimes friends would lend him reading material. From Charles Wesley, he borrowed *Nicodemus, or A Treatise Against the Fear of Man* by German August Hermann Francke. In the mea culpa that begins his journal, he confessed that he even stole a few books as a child. They were devotional writings.

But Whitefield's early reading was not confined to religious works. He loved to read plays until religious conviction compelled him to give up the theater. For a time he found his "heart's delight" in "reading romances"[14]— not the sex-obsessed novels of today, but adventure stories featuring heroes of old. Clearly he understood the power of language from a young age. As an orator, actor, or preacher, he would find a way to make words work for him.

Ben Franklin wrote: "From a child I was fond of reading, and all the little money that came into my hands was ever laid out in books." He loved John Bunyan's *The Pilgrim's Progress*, so he bought a collection of Bunyan's works. Plutarch's *Lives* was a classic set of biographies "in which I read abundantly," and there were works by Daniel Defoe and Cotton Mather he found helpful.[15]

A friend introduced him to poetry, and as a young teen he began dabbling in verse. He wrote two ballads on recent events, one about a lighthouse keeper who drowned, and the other about the killing of Blackbeard the pirate. "They were wretched stuff," Ben admitted.[16]

Over the next few years, Ben engaged in several writing exercises to develop his own ability, and he continued to read widely. As a printer's apprentice, he was perfectly situated, with access to books and newspapers that gave him a window on the wider world. Like George Whitefield, he began to realize that he would impact that world with *words*.

FOUR

Casting Characters

The working day is done, but the teenage boy sets himself to a new task. Disguising his handwriting, he pens a letter, introducing himself as a writer in the area and beginning to tell his life story. Except it's not his own story. He's making up a new character. He employs his own ample wit within the letter, but he disguises this as well, trying to write in the manner of a middle-aged woman. He signs the letter "Silence Dogood" and slips it under the door of the print shop where he works.

Benjamin Franklin is at it again, but there's a purpose to this prank. He's beginning to realize that he's a gifted writer, at least as intelligent as most of those who contribute to the newspaper his brother publishes. But his brother, who is also his boss, won't give him a chance. James Franklin sees Ben as his errand boy, an indentured servant, *not* a colleague. So Ben has to disguise his voice to let it be heard.

James finds the letter from Mrs. Dogood, and he loves it. He talks with his friends about it, those other writers who come by the shop with their news items and editorials. Ben overhears them voicing their approval, and he's bursting with pride. The first letter has promised updates every two weeks, and the letters come through on schedule, under the door of the print shop. The writers who gather there make guesses about the true identity of the author. The suspects they mention are among the smartest folks in town.

Can you imagine the smirk that Ben tries to hide as he sweeps up around this conversation? Yet he keeps his silence, through a third Dogood letter, and a fifth. Over the next six months, fourteen such letters are surreptitiously submitted.

At first it's just a very entertaining autobiography, rolled out bit by bit. "Silence" says she was born on a ship crossing to America, but the moment her father learned of her birth, a wave swept him overboard. "Thus was my disconsolate mother at once made both a parent and a widow."[1] After her mother died, she went to work as a housekeeper for a bachelor minister and eventually married him. So goes the comic melodrama that Ben invents for his unlikely alter ego. But then the letters branch out to social issues, tackling education, government, religion, and even the status of women.

In Letter 4 she relates a lengthy dream about a "Temple of Learning," filled with symbolic characters like something out of *The Pilgrim's Progress*. Her minister-husband quickly interprets it as a fair depiction of Harvard.[2]

By Letter 9 she's talking about religion, wondering whether society "suffers more by hypocritical pretenders to religion, or by the openly profane?" She thinks that "the hypocrite is the most dangerous person of the two, especially if he sustains a post in the government."[3]

There is great fun in the writing, a constant winking at the reader. The language is a bit flowery, but it remains clear. Ben's cleverness is apparent in multiple ways. He has created an effective character here, and he has mastered her language. It's a great way to prove himself as a writer and social commentator. But, further, he has discovered a rather safe way to deal with controversy: *put your critical thoughts in the mouth of a lovable character.*

Finally the game is up. Ben admits to the ruse, gaining the instant respect of his brother's friends but causing irritation to his brother.

———

Decades later, Ben told the story in his autobiography. "I kept my secret till my small fund of sense for such performances was pretty well exhausted."[4]

He was still smirking about it. But this was far more than a childish prank. Young Ben Franklin learned several things through the Silence Dogood charade. First, he was a good writer. Moving well beyond doggerel about Blackbeard, his prose was good enough for the newspaper. Second, he learned that life is often a performance, and sometimes you can choose the part you play.

Later he would use pseudonyms to great effect in his own Philadelphia newspaper. When he wanted to stir controversy, or to express opinions that might get him in trouble, he could invent a character to say what needed to be said. No one would have to know that the byline on the page was just a figment of the publisher's imagination. And of course Franklin made the most of his most popular pen name, Poor Richard, whose series of almanacs turned out to be best sellers.

Escape

Ben was just sixteen when the Dogood letters were printed, not yet halfway through his appointed apprenticeship. Though he loved the world of words—many nights he borrowed books from the shop and returned them the next morning—he found James a difficult master. When the Dogood hoax was revealed, James worried that Ben might grow vain. And the fact was he didn't need another writer; he needed someone to deliver papers. Ben seemed to be outgrowing his position, and there were still five years to go.

At that time, an apprentice was essentially an indentured servant. The contract that committed a worker to a certain number of years of service was legally binding. The boss had great power over the apprentice, even to the point of corporal punishment. ("My brother was passionate and had often beaten me," Ben wrote later.[5]) The Franklin situation involved family, so Ben could rely on his father for some mediation, and he did, but he still longed to be free from his brother.

James was just nine years older than Ben—an adult, yes, but still making his own way. He had bought his printing press in London when he was just twenty-one, and two years later he started his paper, the *New-England*

Courant, only the fourth regular newspaper ever established in the colonies. In many respects, James was a slightly older and less brilliant version of Ben. He was beginning to make a name for himself in Boston. People in high places were taking notice of his little publication. He didn't need a little brother tagging along.

Until he did.

In 1722, James ran a piece in the *Courant* criticizing government authorities for colluding with pirates in raids near Boston Harbor. Some assemblymen took offense and had James jailed for nearly a month. (America was still six decades away from freedom of the press.) Ben took over the operation of the newspaper in that time. The court released James on the condition that he no longer publish the *Courant.*

What to do? Friends suggested a name change for the paper, but the *Courant* was gaining a reputation in town and James didn't want to lose it. Could he just list Benjamin Franklin as the publisher and continue running it himself? Well, the authorities would see right through that sham. They would assume the apprentice was under the control of his master. But what if Ben were officially released from his commitment as an apprentice? He would then be a free agent in publishing the *Courant*, at least as the public saw it. This was the solution James chose. The official apprenticeship contract was dissolved and replaced with a secret agreement that had the same terms. James resumed calling the shots with Ben as his apprentice, but as far as anyone else knew, the sixteen-year-old Benjamin Franklin was the sole publisher of the *New-England Courant.*

So once again we find Ben Franklin advancing his career through fiction. He faithfully played the role of publisher for several months, with James actually in charge, until the brothers had a major disagreement. At that point Ben realized he had blackmail power. James could never go public with their new, secret apprenticeship contract, because he might be thrown back into jail for publishing the paper again. The fiction had become the reality. With this leverage, Ben was in effect a free agent. He began applying for posts with other printers in town, but no one wanted to offend the older brother by hiring the younger.

It became clear that Ben needed to skip town, so he sold a few books to pay for passage and slipped away quietly on a sloop to New York. He was just seventeen.

Ben's Great Adventure

At the time, New York was the third largest city in the colonies, behind Boston and Philadelphia. The only printer in town, Bradford, already had all the help he needed. But Bradford's son, a printer in Philadelphia, happened to have a vacancy on his staff, and so Ben set his sights about another hundred miles southwest. He caught a boat across the channel, walked across New Jersey, and hopped a rowboat down the Delaware River.

It was his Robinson Crusoe adventure. Out of New England for the first time in his life, with barely enough money in his pockets but brimming with confidence, the young man made his way through colonial America, wondering what the future would hold.

Franklin's autobiography holds a fascinating anecdote from this leg of his journey. His boat had some difficulty crossing from New York to Perth Amboy, New Jersey. A sudden squall caused some turbulence, and a drunken passenger fell overboard. Ben managed to pull him up. As this passenger, a Dutchman, sat recovering in the boat, he emptied his pockets and handed Ben a beautiful little book, asking him to dry it as best he could.

It was a Dutch translation of *The Pilgrim's Progress*, "finely printed on good paper with copper cuts [copperplate engravings], a dress better than I had ever seen it wear in its own language [English]."[6] It's no surprise that the young printer-in-training would remember the details of this finely produced book. In his autobiography, the elderly Franklin took the opportunity to comment on the immense popularity of *The Pilgrim's Progress*, how it had been "translated into most of the languages of Europe," and on its unique writing style, mixing narration and dialogue.[7]

Scholars sometimes question how accurate Ben Franklin was trying to be in his autobiography. We can forgive occasional slips on the historical details from a sixty-five-year-old man recollecting his youth, but was he carefully crafting this account, intentionally tweaking and positioning the stories to leave the reader with a certain impression? The stormy waters, the rescue, the beautiful book restored from its "baptism"—it all reads more like fiction than history. Some critics think Franklin was intentionally creating the character of Young Ben as he related the tale of his own pilgrimage, in the same way that author John Bunyan created the character of Christian in *The Pilgrim's Progress*.[8]

Crafting a Life

In a chapter entitled "The Arts of Seeming Truthful: Autobiography," historian Daniel Boorstin suggested that, along with his other inventions, Franklin invented a new literary form in this book: the success saga.[9] Many other writers would follow in this train, but Franklin was the engineer. This doesn't necessarily mean Ben was making up these events, just that he was consciously packaging them in a success-focused narrative.

There had been a few other autobiographies published before Franklin's, but not many. The first great one was *The Confessions of St. Augustine*, in which the bishop traced his spiritual journey, recounting events from his childhood, youth, and young adulthood that led up to his conversion. There was a clear through line as Augustine recognized God's hand shaping his life. Franklin had a through line, too, but no particular spiritual agenda. The eighteenth-century autobiography that most closely followed Augustine's was not Franklin's, but George Whitefield's, published in 1738 (and later republished by Benjamin Franklin). In its opening pages, Whitefield noted that many biographies had "partial" authors. "They have given us the bright, but not the dark side of their character." He promised to be impartial, as biblical accounts were about their subjects. "I have simply told what I was by nature, as well as what I am by grace."[10] Augustine would have been pleased.

But Franklin had a different kind of journey, a rags-to-riches story that celebrated the rags as well as the riches. There was no particular conversion he led up to, just a series of lessons learned, changes made, and feats accomplished. He rejected the sense of total depravity that we'd find in

Augustine, Whitefield, or the Puritan teaching he grew up with. While he did refer to a few regrets along the way (always a printer, he called them "errata," like a newspaper's typographical errors), he focused on how basic human virtues lead to success.

And he wrote with a disarming charm. As soon as the reader is tempted to think the story's too good to be true, Franklin displays some seemingly authentic humility. "By my rambling digressions I perceive myself to be grown old. I used to write more methodically."[11] This appears early in his autobiography, when he first stopped to reread his early, breathless pages. That sort of apology recurs throughout the text—somewhat reminiscent of the delightful self-deprecation we first found in the Silence Dogood letters. If he was intentionally inventing a fictional image of himself, he was doing a brilliant job of making it seem *unintentional*.

Maybe he wasn't crafting his literary character any more than he crafted his personal character. Ben Franklin was extremely conscious of the person he was and the person he wanted to be. He understood the importance of image in business, in statecraft, and in relationship. This awareness helped him broadcast his dangerous ideas to all of Boston in the guise of letters from the devout Dogood. He knew that the image of "Benjamin Franklin" as publisher of the *Courant* would set him free from his apprenticeship, no matter what the secret reality was. As Boorstin noted, "In his inward battle between Appearance and Reality, Appearance always wins."[12] Throughout his life, he played roles that brought him success—from the hardworking young printer ostentatiously carting paper down Market Street to the coonskin-capped American diplomat wowing the French aristocrats. And so, whatever image creation Franklin did in his autobiography might just be an extension of the images he was creating in life.

He wasn't writing fiction. He was living it.

The Pilgrimage

Returning to the beautiful edition of *The Pilgrim's Progress* pulled out of the water, one might wonder whether Ben was playing novelist there, dropping in a meaningful symbol at a key moment, or whether God was the true trickster, offering the young pilgrim a tangible (and beautifully printed) reminder of divine providence.

The Pilgrim's Progress, by John Bunyan, was one of the first books Ben ever read. It's an allegory of a character, Christian, who journeys from his home in the City of Destruction to the Celestial City. Various characters—including Pliable, Mr. Worldly Wiseman, Civility, and Good Will—help him, hurt him, pull him backward, or get in his way. He passes through the Slough of Despond and the Village of Morality and cowers before Mount Sinai before (with the help of Evangelist) he gets on the King's Highway.

In the fourteenth century, the medieval play *Everyman* had presented a similar allegory, but with a very Catholic vision. *The Pilgrim's Progress* teemed with evangelical theology, and it struck a chord in a post-Reformation world. It wasn't only a best seller—it was *the* best seller. As Franklin's autobiography notes, "It has been more generally read than any other book except perhaps the Bible."[13]

As a boy, Ben was so taken with this book that he bought a collection of John Bunyan's works. These were readily and cheaply available throughout the English-speaking world. While this collection probably had other allegorical works, such as *The Holy War* and *The Life and Death of Mr. Badman*, it would have also included Bunyan's autobiography, *Grace Abounding to the Chief of Sinners*. This latter work, published in 1666, long before *The Pilgrim's Progress* (1678), also told of a spiritual journey, a step-by-step movement toward God, toward forgiveness, and toward ministry. (Its deep introspection bears similarity to that of Augustine's *Confessions* and Whitefield's autobiography.)

John Bunyan was a commoner with limited schooling, though he clearly learned to write well. As a youth he enjoyed sports and dancing, he says, but also cursing and other wild behavior. "I was the very ring-leader of all the youth that kept me company, in all manner of vice and ungodliness."[14] The only dowry his wife brought into the marriage consisted of two religious books, but John found these quite transformative. Trying to get rid of his bad habits, he started going to church. Bunyan worked as a tinker, mending pots and pans, and then began preaching in

an Independent church in Bedford, drawing crowds. This was during the
Restoration period, with Charles II on the throne and a strongly Anglican
Parliament. Non-Anglican church meetings were illegal, and their leaders
were often jailed—as was John Bunyan. But in prison he wrote *The Pilgrim's
Progress*, which rapidly became a hit.

Along with nearly every other literate person in the English-speaking
world of that time, George Whitefield also read *The Pilgrim's Progress*. He
revered John Bunyan, preached once in Bunyan's old church, and even
wrote a preface to a 1767 edition of Bunyan's works. The different ways
George and Ben viewed this book and its author are instructive.

Like Bunyan, Whitefield mourned the sins of his youth. In both
Bunyan's allegory and life story, Whitefield saw a process of spiritual
discovery—first a commitment to righteous living, then a despair over his
own inability to live that way, and then the acceptance of Christ. In that
1767 preface, Whitefield wrote that Bunyan "was of the meanest occupa-
tion, and a notorious sabbath-breaker, drunkard, swearer, blasphemer, etc.
by habitual practice: And yet, through rich, free, sovereign, distinguishing
grace, he was chosen, called, and afterwards formed, by the all-powerful
operations of the Holy Ghost, to be a scribe ready instructed to the kingdom of God."[15] Whitefield found here a model for his own ministry. Though
George was ordained an Anglican, the evangelical gospel he preached was
very similar to that of John Bunyan, the Dissenter.

Ben's approach to Bunyan was quite different. Like Bunyan, Franklin
was a commoner with little formal education but a keen mind and a knack
for writing. Books would transform Ben's life, as they had for Bunyan. A
tradesman like Ben, Bunyan turned tragedy to triumph. In prison, under
the same persecution that Ben's father had fled, Bunyan found phenomenal
success by writing for the common people. His simple but deeply meaningful allegory engaged the masses in the same way that Franklin would later
with his own best seller, the simple but wise *Poor Richard's Almanac*.

As Whitefield's preface noted, "*Pilgrim's Progress* . . . is read with the
greatest pleasure, not only by the truly serious, of divers religious persua-
sions, but likewise by those, to whom pleasure is the end of reading."[16]
That might be a nod in Franklin's direction. Yet Ben might have found

inspiration not only in Bunyan's pleasurable prose, but also in his ability to parlay common origins and the misfortunes of life into stunning success.

In *Grace Abounding*, Bunyan recalled some close calls of his youth: "Once I fell into a creek of the sea, and hardly escaped drowning. Another time I fell out of a boat into Bedford River, but, mercy yet preserved me alive."[17] In a fascinating poetic connection—either by Franklin's design, pure coincidence, or the Creator's wry providence—Ben remembers a key moment of his own life when he pulled a drunkard out of a river and "preserved" Bunyan's *book* from "drowning."

Ben Franklin was on a pilgrimage. He wasn't sure where he was ultimately headed, or what his "Celestial City" would look like, but he was definitely on the move.

FIVE

The City of Brotherly Love

Philadelphia is still Ben Franklin's city. You can cross the Benjamin Franklin Bridge from Jersey, exit the expressway onto the Franklin Parkway, and visit the Franklin Institute (the local science museum). Stay in the Franklin Residences on Chestnut and take a tour of the Franklin Mint, or perhaps you'd rather see a game at Franklin Field (at the University of Pennsylvania, which Ben sort of founded). Head back to Old City and tour the newly renovated Franklin Museum on the site where he lived and worked. Walk along those streets—Market, Chestnut, Walnut—and you're likely to pass the locations of several outfits he had a hand in: the post office, a branch of the Free Library, the American Philosophical Association. You'll even pass the Benjamin Franklin Beer Distributors.

Stroll through the courtyard behind Independence Hall, where Ben did some of his best work. You might actually see a Ben Franklin impersonator walking beside you, with the classic spectacles, pudgy face, white hair, and balding pate. At Fourth and Arch you can see his final resting place, shared with his wife, father-in-law, daughter, and son-in-law. Across the street is a fire company, established by, well, you can probably guess.

William Penn founded this town, but Ben Franklin *made* it. Penn laid out its streets, but Franklin knit them together. Penn christened the city with its Greek name, meaning "brotherly love," but Franklin loved it like a brother—even more so.

Philadelphia was also sort of a base of operations for George Whitefield. This preacher was always on the move, so it's hard to think of any American site as his home (except possibly the orphanage he founded in Georgia). Yet Whitefield preached repeatedly to huge crowds in Philadelphia, and he kept coming back to the city. This was where most of his literature was printed (by Franklin), and this was where citizens constructed a building for his converts—a project Franklin helped to fund and manage. (This became the institution that became the University of Pennsylvania.)

The City of Brotherly Love was a good fit for Whitefield. At the time of his first visit, it was the second-largest city in the colonies, and before his last visit it surpassed Boston as the largest. It was also more centrally located than Boston or New York. For the promotion-conscious Whitefield, there was no better place to make a splash. Word of his preaching would travel fast, north and south. In fact, Franklin eventually set up a network of printers throughout the colonies to publish and distribute Whitefield's sermons and journals even more efficiently.

After a brief trip to Georgia in 1738, setting up his orphanage, Whitefield felt called to conduct a preaching tour of the colonies. So in 1739 he headed straight for Philadelphia, like an arrow shot into the heart of America. He couldn't wait to get there. When the boat entered the Delaware Bay and docked temporarily at Lewes, George got out and rode north on horseback (later meeting his shipmates in the city), greeting well-wishers along the way and preaching to them.

Ripe for the Picking

Philadelphia was ripe for Whitefield's message. William Penn had founded the city in 1682 on the concept of religious tolerance. A Quaker, Penn had been jailed in England for his non-Anglican faith. In America, he was

determined to set up a haven for all sorts of believers. The colonial constitution Penn drew up explicitly guaranteed freedom of religion. As a result,
the Philadelphia area had several different denominations well represented.
Quakers remained plentiful, but there was a strong group of Presbyterians
in town, as well as some Baptists and a growing number of German immigrants with Mennonite, Moravian, or Lutheran backgrounds. And of course
there was Christ Church, the Anglican house of worship on Second Street,
just north of Market. It's still there today.

Whitefield himself was nearly as religiously diverse as the city.
Ordained an Anglican, he was part of the brand-new Methodist movement, but he had adopted Calvinist theology, which put him closer to the
Presbyterians. Yet his message wasn't about any of those sects—just about
Jesus. He invited people from every religious persuasion to make a personal
connection with Christ. His indifference to denominations played very well
in tolerant Philadelphia.

And for a few days in 1739, it was very clearly Whitefield's city.
An estimated six thousand people came to hear him the first night he
preached in Philadelphia—at a time when the metropolitan area had
maybe thirteen thousand people.[1] To get that percentage of the area's
residents to attend any event today, you'd need fifty stadiums. And
there were a couple thousand more the next night. Whitefield preached
Thursday, Friday, and Saturday nights from the courthouse steps to
growing crowds, and then a few times on Sunday. In a nine-day span,
he visited the sick and imprisoned, entertained visitors in his lodging,
met with church leaders, dined with William Penn's heir, and prayed
with troubled individuals. Then he took his preaching up to New York
City and back again, through New Jersey and the northern suburbs of
Philadelphia. Whenever he lifted his voice in this area, he drew a crowd.
And this went on at regular intervals over forty years, as he kept coming
back to the City of Brotherly Love.

Whitefield's ministry made a deep impact on the lives of Philadelphians.
"It was wonderful to see the change soon made in the manners of our
inhabitants," Franklin wrote. "From being thoughtless or indifferent about
religion, it seemed as if all the world were growing religious; so that one

could not walk through the town in an evening without hearing Psalms sung in different families of every street."[2]

"Blessed be God, for the great work begun in these parts," Whitefield journaled as he left the city in late November 1739. He went on to quote a Bible verse from Revelation addressed to believers in an ancient city also known as Philadelphia: "Behold, I have set before thee an open door, and no man can shut it."[3]

On one of George's trips to Philadelphia, probably an early one, Ben conducted an experiment of sorts. He had doubts about reports from England that Whitefield had preached to twenty-five thousand people in an open field. Was it even possible for a man's voice to carry that far, to be heard by so many? As Ben's scientific mind began whirring away, he decided to test it out. George was preaching from the top steps of the courthouse, which then stood in the middle of Market Street, on the west side of Second. Ben began walking through the crowd, away from the preacher, toward the Delaware River. How far could he get before he would lose the sound of George's voice? He got as far as Front Street, a full city block away. Then, computing the number of people who could fit in that area (and apparently they were jam-packed), he did the math and ascertained that in fact *thirty* thousand people could stand within earshot of this powerful preacher.

You could pace that out yourself. There's no courthouse there anymore, but you could stand at Whitefield's preaching spot on Market at Second (not for long, though—there's always traffic). You could walk to Front Street, as Ben did. You could imagine that street thronged by Philadelphians and visitors eager to hear a life-changing message—or maybe just eager to see what all the fuss was about. You could let your mind drift back to a time when this city belonged to both the printer and the preacher.

Yet there's no Whitefield Pizza Palace there. No bridge with George's name on it. No Whitefield impersonators giving sermons on street corners. There's a statue of him at the University of Pennsylvania, but most of the students who walk past probably don't know who it is.[4] Philadelphia is now, and always will be, Ben's town.

Day One

On October 6, 1723, Benjamin Franklin walked into Philadelphia as a stranger. In his autobiography, he fondly recounted stepping into the city for the first time. The seventeen-year-old runaway cut a less-than-impressive figure. "I was dirty from my journey; my pockets were stuffed out with shirts and stockings . . . I was fatigued with travelling, rowing and want of rest. I was very hungry, and my whole stock of cash consisted of a Dutch dollar and about a shilling in copper."[5]

The boat put in at Market Street Wharf, and the hungry boy found a bakery just a block away, on Second. Asking for a "three-penny loaf," a type of bread common in Boston, he received three huge "puffy rolls," so he walked the streets of Philadelphia "with a roll under each arm, and eating the other."[6] Continuing on Market up to Fourth Street, he passed the house belonging to John Read, whose daughter Deborah was standing by the door and saw him. She later became Ben's wife.

This is a detail that gives historians pause, for it seems too convenient that Deborah sees him walking past the house in his first *hour* in town. Ben doesn't remark on the oddness of the coincidence; he just notes that she "thought I made as I certainly did a most awkward ridiculous appearance."[7]

But maybe it's not as far-fetched as it first seems. It's no surprise that Ben passed the Read house—Market Street was Philadelphia's main drag then as now. And is it all that unusual that a young woman might be looking out her door as people passed—or that she might remember a strapping young man with shirts in his pockets and bread under his arms, especially when he came to lodge in her home a few days later?

Ben Franklin has proven himself capable of spinning a yarn, and maybe that's what he was doing with his "first day in Philadelphia" story. But he was also recalling the events nearly half a century later, and it's possible that the details morphed in his memory. Additionally, *appearance* was very important to him. In this case, he emphasized the oddness of his look and manner as he first entered his city and compared it to the far more respectable presence he had later. Maybe he exaggerated some things for effect, but maybe it really happened that way.

Ben walked past the Read House, turned left on Fourth, walked south one block to Chestnut, and turned back toward the river. At some point he moved down one more block to Walnut, ending up at the wharf again, where he gave his extra bread to a woman and child who had been on the boat with him. Then he headed back into town.

It was Sunday. Ben noticed well-dressed men and women walking along Market Street, and he followed them to the Quaker Meeting House at Second Street. He took a seat and, "after looking round a while and hearing nothing said," he fell asleep.[8] There's a joke here: Quakers are known for their silence. Often there's no particular preacher at their meetings. They wait for the Spirit to move someone to speak, and sometimes they wait a long time.

So the elderly Ben painted himself as an ignorant kid, intruding on a service he knew nothing about, and falling asleep. Wryly he noted that this was the first house in Philadelphia he ever slept in. Then he set out to look for the second—lodging for the night. He was about to enter one inn when a concerned Quaker stopped him on the street and warned him that it was a disreputable place. The Quaker redirected Ben a few blocks south to the Crooked Billet, where he got food and a bed before seeking a job with the local printer the next morning.

Walk of Fame

If you ever get to Philadelphia, you could take this walking tour yourself. The Quaker Meeting House has moved and the Crooked Billet is gone, but those streets are still there and pocked with history. You might find a certain thrill from walking the old grid. A great deal of history happened within an area about six blocks square, and Ben Franklin was involved in most of it. You could cross the streets he crossed, turn the corners that he turned, look out on the Delaware River just as he did. You could go on the same three-block "commute" that Ben took each day when he met with the Continental Congress at Independence Hall. If you let your mind drift back in history a bit, it might just give you goose bumps.

Maybe Ben felt the same way about this area. Maybe that's why he wrote about it with such care. The history hadn't even been fully written yet. When he wrote this first part of his autobiography in 1771, the Liberty Bell was just another bell. But he had poured his life into that city. He knew every inch of that grid intimately. On those streets he had sold papers, conducted experiments, held business meetings, rallied troops, and listened to a preacher from England stirring the hearts of thousands.

What's more, as he wrote this early part of his autobiography Ben was across the ocean, representing Pennsylvania's interests in London. He had been away from Philadelphia for nearly seven years. So why wouldn't he take delight in the details of his first foray into Philadelphia all that time ago?

But it's more than a trip down memory lane; it's also a success story. He explains to his main reader, his son, that he's being especially "particular" in his description of "my first entry into that city, that you may in your mind compare such unlikely beginnings with the figure I have since made there."[9]

So Franklin uses all his literary skill to show himself as a Boston bumpkin, clueless at a bakery, looking idiotic when his future wife sees him, and falling asleep in church. It's the "before" picture.

He liked to quote a Bible verse his father taught him, Proverbs 22:29: "Seest thou a man diligent in his business? He shall stand before kings" (KJV). Ben felt he was living proof of this promise. A lifetime of self-improvement made a huge difference, crafting an impressive "after" picture. The city that first baffled him eventually counted on him to "stand before kings" on its behalf.

SIX

Hoodwinked

Young Ben Franklin settled nicely into Philadelphia, getting a job with one of the two printers in town, connecting with a group of young friends, and even courting Deborah Read.

Three friends in particular formed a sort of literary club with Ben. One of these, James Ralph, wanted to become a full-time poet, though he was currently working as a merchant's clerk. Franklin thought Ralph's writing was quite good, but he discouraged his friend from making a career of it, especially since he had a wife and child. (Even then, Ben's business sense was evident.)

On one occasion, this quartet decided to have each member write a poem based on Psalm 18 and present it to the group for feedback. James Ralph asked Ben to help him play a trick on the others, who were usually very critical of Ralph's work. Franklin would present Ralph's work as his own, while Ralph would pretend he didn't have any poem to share. As they suspected, the others were lavish in their praise of "Ben's" poem. In a delicious bit of irony, only Ralph found fault with it, but Ben defended "his" work, and the others kept praising it. The following week, the trick was revealed.

As with the Silence Dogood letters, here Ben saw the power of a byline.

He didn't need to be an actor on a stage to play different roles. He could change public opinion by changing a name, by adopting a character, by playing a trick. The image of the author could be as important as the content of the writing. This is a modern concept—we think of Marshall McLuhan, the growth of advertising, and today's image-crazy culture. But Ben Franklin was, as usual, ahead of his time. The power of image was a concept he would return to throughout his life, and he would bring it into his work with George Whitefield.

The Governor

Soon after that, Ben got hoodwinked by a villainous character who first played the role of a hero. Sir William Keith, the governor of Pennsylvania, happened to see a letter Ben had written and was impressed with his maturity. Stopping by Ben's print shop, he took the young assistant out for a drink (leaving Ben's boss staring "like a pig poisoned").[1] Several dinners followed, and a secret plan unfolded in which Keith would set Ben up in his own printing business.

This was all very exciting. Of course Ben would have to hide this from his boss, who would not only lose a capable assistant but also gain some fierce competition. This secrecy kept Ben from getting wise counsel from anyone else in town—which would have been helpful.

Unfortunately, Governor Keith didn't have much capital to offer, just his name—but he was willing to use that name to promise the moon. He sent a letter of recommendation to Josiah Franklin, and Ben returned to Boston to see if he could get some funding from his father. The elder Franklin, ever wise, believed Ben was still too young to run his own business. He promised to invest later, if Ben could save enough money for a start-up at age twenty-one. Yet, despite his doubts about the business project, Josiah was pleased that his son had made such a high-level contact—with a governor!—and so he sent Ben back to Philadelphia with his blessing.

On that quick trip back to Boston, Ben also stopped in at his brother's print shop, where he had been employed less than a year earlier. James wanted nothing to do with him, but the other workers gathered around to hear Ben talk about his new life in Philadelphia. This former apprentice had made good. He wore a new suit, flaunted his new pocket watch, and bought them a round of drinks. Ben was playing the role of a gentleman, and his hardworking brother was deeply insulted.

Apparently Ben made one more visit on this trip, dropping in on the renowned Puritan minister Cotton Mather. Now sixty-one, Mather had pastored Boston's North Church for nearly forty years, a position he inherited from his father, Increase Mather. In 1724, Cotton Mather was probably the most influential man in Boston. Early in his ministry, he had supported the Salem Witch Trials. More recently, he had taken a controversial stand in favor of inoculation to prevent the spread of smallpox. The *New-England Courant*, edited by James Franklin, assisted by Ben, had printed opposing views and, in the process, lampooned Reverend Mather.

It's not clear why Ben stopped in to see him. The minister may have been an old family friend. While the Mathers had higher status than the candle-making Franklins, Ben's mother was the daughter of Peter Folger, one of the first settlers in the area, who was mentioned by Cotton Mather in his history of New England (*Magnalia Christi Americana*). Although it was the largest city in the colonies, Boston was still a small town by modern standards, so it's likely that the Mathers would have known the Franklin family, especially since they were also Puritans (though they worshiped at the Old South Church, not the Mathers' Old North). Many years later, Ben would write a couple of letters to Cotton's son, Samuel Mather, mentioning that he had once run an errand for Increase Mather and describing this 1724 visit. So Cotton Mather might have been very familiar with the youngest son of the Franklin brood. And he would have certainly been aware of the attacks against him published by James Franklin in the *Courant*.

So why did Ben go to see Cotton? To apologize for the paper's attacks? Maybe, but James would be blamed for the paper's content, not Ben. To pay homage to the religious leader of Boston? Maybe, but Ben was already discarding the faith of his youth. Perhaps it was Mather's writing, rather than his religion, that attracted Ben. Cotton was a prolific author and a respected scholar, having written on history, philosophy, and science as well as theology. In fact, Ben cited Mather's 1710 book, *Essays to Do Good* (published as *Bonifacius*), as one of the early books he read and a major influence on his life.[2] And maybe Ben was feeling his oats as a successful young ladder-climber. He was already pals with the Governor of Pennsylvania. Could he add the great Cotton Mather to his network of powerful friends?

In this light, the story Ben told about this visit makes a lot of sense. After they met in Mather's personal library, the reverend showed Ben a shortcut out of his house. Ben went first through a narrow passageway, with Mather behind him, still talking. Suddenly Mather said, "Stoop! Stoop!" Turning back to hear, Ben didn't see the low crossbeam. "I did not understand him till I felt my head hit against the beam," Ben wrote later.[3]

But there was more to the story. Cotton Mather was "a man that never missed any occasion of giving instruction,"[4] and this was no exception. "Let this be a caution to you not always to hold your head so high," he told young Franklin. "Stoop, young man, stoop—as you go through the world—and you'll miss many hard thumps."[5]

In his 1773 letter to Samuel Mather, Ben cleverly commented, "This was a way of hammering Instruction into one's head: And it was so far effectual, that I have ever since remembered it, though I have not always been able to practice it."[6]

We might surmise that he learned this lesson *after* he played the dandy in his brother's print shop.

London Calling

Back in Philadelphia, Ben and the governor continued making plans. Keith asked for a wish list of equipment Ben would need in order to set up shop. Total cost: 100 pounds sterling, a huge sum. Most of this equipment, including the printing press, would need to be purchased in London. Ben would have to go there and get it. Governor Keith promised to give Ben letters of credit, which could be paid back after the business started turning a profit.

So young Ben Franklin, not yet nineteen, set off across the Atlantic in early November 1724, accompanied by his poet friend, James Ralph. Among the other travelers was a Quaker merchant named Thomas Denham, who would turn out to be a great help.

During the voyage, Ben assumed that the letters of credit from Governor Keith were in a mailbag on board. The ship's captain would only give Ben those letters when they reached England. But at that point, the naïve Philadelphian discovered that the letters didn't exist. As he bemoaned this fact, his new friend Thomas Denham confirmed his worst suspicions about the governor. Sir William Keith was famously unreliable. He had no credit to give. There would be no hundred pounds, no printing press, no business to set up back in Philadelphia. Ben's future had evaporated.

This time, Ben was the victim of a false persona, but it was no mild prank. Governor Keith had played the role of benefactor, raising Ben's hopes and sparking his dreams. "He wished to please everybody," Franklin suggested later, "and having little to give, he gave expectations."[7]

Did the governor really see potential in his young friend? Did he think his "expectations" would be enough to get Josiah Franklin to bankroll his son in a new venture? Did Keith ever intend to provide letters of credit, or did he expect that the power of positive thinking would get Ben started in a new business, and that the boy would forever feel indebted to Keith for believing in him?

Surely Ben wrestled with all these questions. In retrospect, years later, he was amazingly charitable toward this backstabber. Apart from Keith's damaging duplicity, Ben wrote, "He was otherwise an ingenious sensible man."[8]

Still, in the closing days of 1724, Ben Franklin found himself homeless, jobless, and poundless in the most exciting city on earth.

SEVEN

Next Stage: England

It was Christmas Eve, 1724, when Ben Franklin stepped off the boat in England, just shy of his nineteenth birthday. About 120 miles to the west, George Whitefield had just turned ten. It was probably not the Best Christmas Ever for either of them.

After eight years of widowhood, George's mother had just remarried. George's new stepdad was Capel Longden, a hardware dealer. (The term at the time was *ironmonger*: he sold iron objects.) Life in the new family would turn sour very soon.

As we might expect, George had difficulty with this remarriage. He was the baby of the bunch, pampered through his whole life, and groomed for greatness. His older siblings helped out at the family inn, but Elizabeth Whitefield wouldn't let George get involved in the business. He was destined for greater things—college, perhaps the ministry. Several of their ancestors had been respected clergymen. Now it was up to George to lead this family back to its former greatness. In his memoirs, George compares himself at one point with the Old Testament Joseph, and it's an apt analogy.[1] Jacob's favorite son ultimately delivered his family from a famine. Would George restore the Whitefields' social status?

But now there was a different savior in the house. George suddenly had to share his mother's attention with a new, strange man. That would have been difficult even if Capel Longden turned out to be a good guy.

He didn't.

"Longden appears to have been an unpleasant personality," wrote one historian.[2] In his memoirs, Whitefield crisply commented that the marriage proved to be "what the world would call an unhappy match."[3] It seems that Longden tried to take over the operation of the Bell Inn, and he hurt the business considerably. George's older siblings opposed their new step-father, and Longden left after a few years.

George's description of his own childhood shows an odd combination of mischief and piety, as if he was trying equally hard to pursue his holy calling and sabotage it. Even when we assume that his memoirs probably overstate the extent of his childhood depravity, we still find a curious juxta-position of good and bad. He said he stole money from his mother *and gave some of it to the poor.*[4] Some of the books he pilfered were *devotional* writings.

He wrote: "I remember, when some persons (as they frequently did) made it their business to tease me, I immediately retired to my room, and kneeling down, with many tears, prayed over that Psalm wherein David so often repeats these words—'*But in the Name of the Lord will I destroy them.*'"[5]

The passage is Psalm 118:10–12, which indeed repeats that phrase, and it's an apt reference. "They compassed me about like bees," the Psalmist complains (v. 12 KJV), and we can imagine a schoolboy being surrounded by taunting classmates. Maybe they were teasing him about his squinty eye, the legacy of a bad bout with measles when he was four. As an adult, he was sometimes mocked as "Dr. Squintum." Younger mockers might use even more hurtful terms.

We can certainly understand the anger stirred by such bullying, but it's interesting that this future evangelist uses the Bible as his defense. Brandishing the Psalter as a weapon, summoning divine destruction upon his foes, he was like James and John, those "Sons of Thunder," who wanted to call fire from heaven to punish a village for bad hospitality (Luke 9:54).

Whitefield told another story about a dissenting minister in Gloucester by the name of Cole, whom he and his friends loved to ridicule. As a prank, George would run into this man's church, shouting, "Old Cole! Old Cole!

Old Cole!" Someone in that congregation asked George what business he was planning to go into when he grew up. Perhaps this was a friend of his family, someone who already knew the answer and wanted to get George to think twice about his irreverent behavior. George replied that he wanted to be "a minister, but I would take care never to tell stories in the pulpit, like the old *Cole*."[6]

This smart aleck felt no dissonance here. He wasn't rejecting his faith with his bad behavior; he was *practicing* it. Old Cole had the audacity to tell stories from the pulpit rather than stick to the Scriptures. Young Whitefield felt this was wrong, and in the simplistic judgment of a ten-year-old, he could justify his own disruption of Cole's service. Some years later, Cole happened to hear the adult Whitefield preach—and what did he hear? Stories. George had become a master of the anecdote, the parable, and the hypothetical case. The veteran preacher laughed, "I find that young *Whitefield* can now tell stories, as well as old *Cole*."[7]

Sometimes kids pretend to be good in order to satisfy their religious parents, and they become holy terrors when they're out of sight. But George's family was not especially religious. Yes, he bore the messianic expectations of his mother, but these appear to be more social than spiritual. He was being shoved toward the Anglican ministry, but it was up to him to find his own faith.

George might have been exploring more than rebelling. "I was always fond of being a clergyman," he noted in his memoirs, adding that he would "frequently . . . imitate the ministers reading prayers, etc."[8] So maybe he was pushing the borders of what religious devotion meant. Could he be a Robin Hood, taking the money his mother earned at the inn from adulterers and drunkards and redistributing it to the poor? Could he use the psalmist's own words to invoke God's wrath on his tormentors? Could he interrupt a Dissenter church service because they were worshiping the wrong way?

The fluctuating nature of his youthful behavior suggests that George was struggling through a significant period of identity formation. It's not unusual for children to work through identity issues from ages ten to thirteen, but the combination of high expectations and lack of guidance from his mother made it more of a struggle. What kind of person was he going to be? Could he find a character that worked for him? We see a glimmer of the kind of identity games Ben Franklin was playing as a writer. Could he get ahead in the world by pretending to be someone else? Yet George's identity crisis was deeper, more personal. He wasn't just finding a character to play in public. He was finding a character he could *be*.

London Bridges Falling Down

In London, Ben Franklin, just turned nineteen, faced an identity crisis of his own.

Aboard the ship, he and his companion, James Ralph, were first treated as "ordinary persons," and sent to the steerage section. But just before departure, a friend of Governor Keith came on board and showed Ben some respect. This raised his status, and when there was extra room in the Great Cabin, Franklin and Ralph were invited to stay there with the more esteemed folks. This certainly made for a more pleasant voyage, and it must have given Ben a taste of the good life. At that point he expected to do his business in London, buy the equipment he needed, maybe splurge a little on the governor's line of credit, and head home to start a great new life as a businessman. This trip was a bridge to his own celestial city.

The shock of the governor's betrayal wasn't just a disappointment; it forced a reimagining of all Ben's hopes and dreams. Would he ever be able to travel in the Great Cabins of life again, or would he always be consigned to steerage? Would he ever be his own boss, or would he always be someone else's errand boy? Would he even be able to survive in this strange city?

As with his entry into Philadelphia, it was a Quaker who helped him find his way: the merchant Thomas Denham, who explained that Governor Keith was notoriously untrustworthy and laughed at the notion that Keith's credit would be worth anything. He suggested that Ben seek work with a printer in London, which Ben did. A year and a half later, Denham would hire Ben as his own assistant and bring him back to Philadelphia at his own expense.

In the meantime, Ben lived and worked in London, getting to know himself better. You might call this his college experience, though he never enrolled in any institution of higher learning. Still, he was always learning. He had a roommate who liked to party, and Ben went along with that for a while before buckling down and hitting the books.

James Ralph was a wastrel. Full of creative ideas, he chased after them with abandon, leaving any sense of responsibility behind. A merchant's clerk in Philadelphia, Ralph had told Ben he was coming to London to set up relationships for his own future mercantile business. Once they got there, Ralph confessed he was really just escaping from his wife and child. He had brought no money along, so they lived off Ben's meager savings, renting a cheap apartment in Little Britain.

Ralph promised to pay Ben back once he found the right job, but that proved difficult. At first, Ralph thought he might become an actor, and he auditioned at a nearby playhouse for Robert Wilks, one of the giants of the London stage at that time. Wilks, who was famous for being gruff and temperamental, "advised him candidly not to think of that employment, as it was impossible he should succeed in it."[9] Then Ralph decided to be a writer, proposing to a publisher that he could churn out a weekly newspaper, but was rejected again. He couldn't even get a job as a hack writer of legal documents.

Meanwhile, Ben was working away at Palmer's print shop and supporting both of them. "I was pretty diligent," Ben wrote later, "but spent with Ralph a good deal of my earnings on going to plays and other places of amusement."[10]

Ben's autobiography doesn't tell us what plays and amusements Franklin and Ralph attended, but the history of entertainment in London is well documented. There were four main theaters in town at the time. The King's Theatre specialized in opera, usually Italian opera, for which there was a big craze in London in that era (one that George F. Handel helped to satisfy). Little Haymarket Theatre was offering a series of French plays. Lincoln's Inn Fields and Drury Lane Theatre had a good competition going, fighting for market share with new English plays and pantomimes in the Commedia style.

Maybe Ben Franklin and James Ralph caught a performance of *Caesar in Egypt* at Drury Lane. They would have seen London's premier actor, Colley Cibber, in a play about a tyrant extending his power to a land across the sea.

In January 1725, perhaps Ben saw *Harlequin Sorcerer* at Lincoln's Inn Fields, a pantomime featuring dance and music, with noted impresario John Rich in the lead. "Let the thunder crack and roll . . ." sings the character known as Air. "Nature shall yield to your great skill: / Your art, with ease, shall, when you please, / Transform all things to what you will."[11] Young Ben may have gained some inspiration here for his later scientific attempts to "transform" nature to the service of humanity—even developing the lightning rod, so that we needn't worry when the thunder cracks and rolls.

Besides these plays, pantos, and operas, there were other "places of amusement" available to these two young men. Just four years later, a writer commented caustically on the various entertainment options in London, lampooning not only the plays, operas, and pantomimes, but also prize fighting, Italian strollers (minstrels), mountebank stages (magic shows), cockpits, puppet shows, fairs, and public auctions—not to mention the bear gardens. Yes, there were arenas set up for fights between bears and other animals, and crowds showed up to watch. In full satire, the writer said, "Who can view dogs tearing bulls, bulls goring dogs, or mastiffs throttling bears, without being animated by their daring spirits! And what is brutal fierceness in them, may produce true human courage in us!"[12]

The satirical writer was none other than James Ralph, who stayed in England after Ben left and apparently attended many more amusements. With his biting critique of London's entertainment scene, published in 1728, he finally made a name for himself. He became a friend of the writer Henry Fielding (author of *Tom Jones*), and had the dubious honor of being mentioned in Alexander Pope's *The Dunciad*, a poetic blast at the entire arts community of London. Pope likened Ralph to a wolf howling at the moon. The wastrel eventually found his niche: howling at other works of art.

But in that watershed year of 1725, living hand to mouth, holed up in a cheap apartment with a buddy whose debt kept rising, spending all his pay on fairs and bears, Ben had a decision to make. Who was he going to be? James Ralph or James Franklin? Would he use his quick wit and creative mind to chase impossible dreams, to tear down everything around him, and to use people for his own benefit? Or would he work night and day, refusing fun, to build his career and to contribute something to society? Or was there some option in between?

One of the first things Ben did in this self-identification process was to decide what he thought about God.

Very early in his employment at Palmer's print shop, he was asked to typeset a philosophical work by William Wollaston. This clergyman-scholar had embraced the emerging Enlightenment and produced some very modern-minded books. Could God be known through nature, he wondered, without the special revelation of the Bible? Could we find religion, moral-ity, and even faith just by observing the created order? Even today, scholars disagree on whether Wollaston was pushing a variation of Deism or just exploring the biblical notions of, say, Romans 1:18–20. Maybe Wollaston wasn't sure about that himself—sometimes he had second thoughts about his writing and destroyed it. In 1722, he had written his masterwork, *The Religion of Nature Delineated*, but he kept it to only a small print run and pri-vate distribution. When Wollaston died in late 1724, many printers rushed to republish the book—including Ben's employer, Samuel Palmer.

Page by page, line by line, young Ben pored over Wollaston's naturalistic philosophy, and he formulated his own thoughts in response to it. The result was Ben Franklin's first book—more of a pamphlet, really—*A Dissertation on Liberty and Necessity, Pleasure and Pain*. In it, he deconstructed the Puritan faith of his youth, taking it to its logical extreme, or so he thought.

If God is infinitely wise, good, and powerful, Ben determined, then everything that happens is God's will. As he put it, "Nothing can exist or be done in the Universe which is not agreeable to His Will, and therefore good." Elsewhere he noted, "Evil doth not exist." Since we cannot thwart the divine will, he said, our behavior is always good; there is no distinction between vice and virtue. He acknowledged that people might not like these ideas, but "Truth will be Truth though it sometimes prove mortifying and distasteful."[13]

If this time in London was Ben's "college experience," then this was his sophomore project. Though there were glimmers of brilliance and immense bravado, it was ultimately pretty foolish. He later regretted printing it, though he repackaged some of the ideas in more mature writings to come.

Ben dedicated the work "to J. R."—James Ralph. As it turned out, he might have regretted that too. They had a falling out over a woman whom James Ralph had loved and left. Ben made a pass at her, which she rebuffed and reported to Ralph, who was very upset (or claimed to be) and decided that now he would never repay Ben the money he had borrowed.

The story becomes more interesting in light of Ben's "dissertation." If there's no such thing as evil, then why *shouldn't* a young man try to bed a woman he fancies—even if it might hurt his best friend? If there's no distinction between vice and virtue, then how can you expect anyone to pay back a loan? Once you've stripped the universe of morality, then all that's left is cause and effect, action and reaction. Ben flirts, James reneges, and a friendship is scuttled.

As the smoke cleared, Ben realized that this breach actually set him free, and he began to think about saving money for a trip home. To that end, he found a new job at a larger print shop.

Fortuitously, one of his sophomoric pamphlets got into the hands of another author in town, who befriended Ben and introduced him to other authors and thinkers. Soon the young printer was hobnobbing with the literati in clubs and coffee houses—when he wasn't working to earn money. One of these new friends hinted that he might introduce Ben to Sir Isaac Newton, but it never happened.

The dissertation was not Ben's first or last attempt to create a religion of his own. With the soul of an inventor, he kept tweaking the status quo, looking for a better way. Seeing the shortcomings in the philosophies of others, he kept trying to fashion his own set of values—beginning on the voyage back to Philadelphia as he crafted his "Plan . . . for regulating my future conduct in life."[14]

The James Ralph experience had taught him a great lesson, and he would build on it for decades to come. The two roommates shared many qualities—quick minds, keen insight, biting wit—but Ralph lacked *responsibility*, and Franklin decided he couldn't live without it.

As Ben was boarding the boat for America, George was not too far away, nearly twelve years old, preparing to go to the school that would prepare him for college and a life in the clergy. This was his destiny, and he knew it. But something deep inside him wanted to invent his own way.

EIGHT

The Play's the Thing

Everybody missed Shakespeare. By the 1720s, when Ben attended plays and George studied them, it had been more than a century since the Bard of Avon had put down his quill. Writers like Kit Marlowe and Ben Jonson had helped William Shakespeare create a golden era for theater around the year 1600, and rival companies competed to catch the imaginations of their audiences. New stages were built. Rich and poor alike flocked to see the latest offerings—the rich got seats, while the poor paid a penny for standing room.

There were always concerns about morality. Playwrights and directors had to dance around the demands of censors. Many of Shakespeare's bawdiest puns reflect this tension. Those who have ears to hear will get the joke, but there's nothing explicit to offend the authorities.

While some upper-class citizens patronized the theater, others avoided it as a haven for lowlifes. In 1597, the Lord Mayor complained to the Queen's Privy Council that theaters "are the ordinary places for vagrant persons . . . thieves, horse stealers, whoremongers . . . contrivers of treason, and other idle and dangerous persons to meet together and to make their matches to the great displeasure of Almighty God and the hurt and annoyance of her Majesty's people." He went on to suggest that the plays encouraged idleness in the unemployed, enticed apprentices away from their work, and kept people from attending "sermons and other Christian exercises, to the great hindrance of trades and profanation of religion."[1]

A few years later, Thomas Dekker railed against the theaters in similar terms:

> Do they not induce whoredom and uncleanness? Nay, are they not rather plain devourers of maidenly virginity and chastity? For proof whereof, but mark the flocking and running to Theatres and curtains, daily and hourly, night and day, time and tide, to see plays and interludes; where such wanton gestures, such bawdy speeches, such laughing and fleering, such kissing and bussing, such clipping and culling, such winking and glancing of wanton eyes, and the like, is used.[2]

And he wasn't just talking about what happened *on* stage. People paired up at the theater and went home to do disgraceful things. "Theaters are snares unto fair women," he charged.[3]

These attitudes became even more prominent as Puritan power grew in the mid-1600s. Theaters were shut down after Parliament deposed Charles I, but when Charles II returned from France in 1660 to restore the monarchy, it also meant a restoration of the artistic life of London. Playwriting had its next great heyday, with the "Restoration comedies" of Sir George Etherege, William Wycherley, Aphra Behn, William Congreve, and others. For the most part, these were plays about the English upper class. Comedy was found in the characters' hypocrisy, their over-attention to manners, and the need to hide their affairs. Behavior that Puritans found scandalous was now back in the open. And for the first time, women were permitted on stage (previously, female roles had been played by men or teenage boys). It was no secret that many actresses supplemented their income with prostitution. In fact, it was widely known that Charles II's main mistress was an actress, Nell Gwyn.

The old opposition to the theater's immorality didn't vanish. It just lacked clout. As long as the dissolute Charles II was on the throne, London theater had free rein. But when William and Mary took over in the

"Glorious Revolution" of 1688, the nation seemed ready to find a sensible middle course. In 1698, clergyman Jeremy Collier published *A Short View of the Immorality and Profaneness of the English Stage*, in which he critiqued specific plays for their immodesty and negative themes. "Here is a large collection of debauchery," he observed. "Sometimes you have it in image and description; sometimes by way of allusion; sometimes in disguise; and sometimes without it."[4] Collier seemed especially upset with how "smuttily" the actresses talked.[5]

Other writers responded, defending the theater. As much as they wanted to dismiss Collier's criticisms, they recognized that he had captured the public spirit. The party was over. There was less and less of a market for Restoration excesses. William Congreve, Richard Steele, and others began writing softer plays, with restrained language and even some lessons in morality.

So when Ben Franklin and James Ralph arrived in London late in 1724, they found a theater world in flux, waiting for the next heyday. Shakespeare was long gone, and the Restoration comedies had run their course. No wonder some theaters turned to Italian opera and French farce. English playwriting was still trying to find its way. There were a few prominent actors worth following—Colley Cibber and, in the next generation, David Garrick—and there were some producers creating impressive spectacles, but the new plays being produced were hit or miss, mostly miss. (That also explains why the booming literary genre in the following decades was satire. When entertainment quality is poor, make fun of it. This is how James Ralph eventually succeeded, as well as Henry Fielding, Alexander Pope, and Jonathan Swift.)

Three Plays

In English society in the 1600s and 1700s, theater was *the* lively art, revealing the popular spirit of the time. This is the culture that Ben and George grew up in, participated with, and changed.

We've already seen that Ben was watching plays in London at a critical time of his life, and we'll soon see that George was impacted by theater in England, mostly as a student in Gloucester. Moreover, as his career developed, Whitefield *replaced* theater in England, Scotland, and America, wherever he went on his preaching tours. He was the best show in town. Everywhere, people commented on his dramatic delivery and the emotional power of his presentation. By studying the state of theater in England and the dearth of theater in America, we can get a sense of the cultural hole that Whitefield filled, with Franklin's help.[6]

Three plays hit the London stage, with considerable popularity, between 1722 and 1731—from the time just before Ben came to London to the time George went to Oxford.

The Conscious Lovers by Richard Steele exemplified the new, softer style of theater—less offensive, more moral. Produced in 1722, it enjoyed a run of eighteen nights, lengthy for its time. The play's prologue made it clear that a new ethic was being followed. "No more let ribaldry, with license writ, usurp the name of eloquence or wit." This playwright's aim was "to chasten wit and moralize the stage."[7]

Some critics, still mourning the demise of the edgy humor of Restoration comedy, panned this sentimental story. It had all the ingredients of the old style—high-born characters, couples in and out of love, mistaken identity, and so on—but the passions were muted. At the play's climactic moment, the main character chose *not* to have a duel with his rival. In true comedic form, there was a happy ending with multiple marriages, but this was the result of good choices made by the characters, not the whimsy of fate.

This play had come and gone by the time Ben got to town, but its lessons had seeped into the culture (or perhaps the culture had seeped into the play): Happy lives are the results of wise decisions. Don't count on a whimsical universe to provide you with a happy ending just because you say clever lines. You need to work for what you get. James Ralph belonged in a Restoration comedy—clever, lusty, little sense of moral responsibility; all he lacked was the social status. Ben almost followed him into that kind of life, up to the point where he tried to steal Ralph's mistress. In so doing, Ben created his own little morality play. He learned that choices have consequences. Betray a friend, and you're likely to lose that friend. Success in life comes through responsible decision making, not untamed passions. This was the new spirit of London. It formed the moral foundation of *The Conscious Lovers* and a whole new slate of sensible plays to follow, and it became Ben's gospel.

If he had stayed in London another year and a half, Ben would have seen *The Beggar's Opera*, a musical satire unlike anything that had ever been done. Opening at Lincoln's Inn Fields on January 29, 1728, it smashed the box-office records and became the talk of the town. Part of its popularity came from its mockery of Italian opera, a genre many Londoners might have been growing weary of. It was also a thinly veiled commentary on political corruption—and critics kept guessing about who the targets were. Yet *The Beggar's Opera* made its greatest splash by being about, well, beggars: thieves, tramps, and hookers. The "hero"—if you can call him that—was Macheath, a notorious robber. Much of the play took place in lairs and brothels. London's ugly underbelly was taking center stage.

The city had grown steadily as the capital of a burgeoning empire, but its underclass was growing faster than its upper class. Crime was becoming a problem. Certain sections of the city were being written off as slums. Magistrates had their hands full, and public hangings were common. In 1724, a burglar named Jack Sheppard was finally caught and executed, but not before becoming one of London's foremost celebrities. Books were written about him. The Drury Lane Theatre produced a panto about him. He had a portrait painted.

With *The Beggar's Opera*, playwright John Gay capitalized on this public fascination with crime. He broke new ground in setting a play among the lower class. Most previous plays—going back to the Greeks—had featured aristocrats. Slaves and servants occasionally appeared, but in support of wealthier masters. Restoration comedy was thoroughly an upper-class affair. But this play turned everything upside down. *Look, lowlifes are human too!*

This had two major consequences that affected the life and work of Ben Franklin and George Whitefield. In biblical terms, you might say it exalted the humble and humbled the proud. The play carried a powerful satirical message that *everyone's* a crook. Scene 1 began:

> *Through all the employments of life,*
> *Each neighbor abuses his brother;*
> *Whore and rogue they call husband and wife,*
> *All professions be-rogue one another.*[8]

That was played out in the course of the story, but it was the dirty little secret that every Londoner knew. *We're all corrupt! Jailer, judge, priest, politician. At least the burglars are honest about it.* At the tender age of nineteen, Ben had already been shafted by the crown-appointed governor of Pennsylvania. Young George was dealing with the greed and duplicity of his stepfather. "There is none righteous, no, not one," the Scriptures thundered.[9] The London stage was a strange place to hear that message, but there it was.

By tearing down the pretensions of the ruling class, *The Beggar's Opera* lifted up the dignity of the lower class. By charging that aristocrats are no more righteous than anyone else, the play put all citizens on an equal footing. This played into a new populism emerging in England and growing in the colonies.

Ben Franklin was returning to an America with a strong working class and a limited aristocracy. Over the next half century, important decisions would be made about the value of persons in different classes, and Ben would be involved in many of those decisions. This growing awareness of human depravity, among rich and poor alike, would lead to the implementation of checks and balances, of regular elections, of local militias. You couldn't just count on aristocrats to do the right thing. Ben had learned that the hard way.

There was also a religious revolution brewing. The Methodist movement would grow in England by reaching out to coal miners, common workers, and servants. George Whitefield and the Wesley brothers would reject the aristocratic spirit of the established church and preach in public squares and fields. Lowlifes were welcome to repent and receive God's blessings. Macheath himself could be reborn through God's grace.

The third play of note in this period was *The London Merchant*, by George Lillo, opening at Drury Lane in 1731 and performed often in the following decade. Nearly as popular as *The Beggar's Opera*, it was a cautionary tale about a young apprentice who falls for the wrong woman and descends into a spiral of theft, murder, and punishment for those crimes. "Be warn'd ye youths, who see my sad despair," the man intones. "Avoid lewd women, false as they are fair. . . . By my example learn to shun my fate; (How wretched is the man who's wise too late!)"[10]

This play was as moralistic as *The Conscious Lovers*, only tragic. The apprentice was a good guy who made bad choices, letting his passions override his good judgment. Penitent at the end, he still had to pay for his crimes.

And *payment* is an important theme here. This play lives in the world of the middle class. What *The Beggar's Opera* did for the underclass, *The London Merchant* did for the bourgeoisie, putting it on stage for everyone to see. Socially, the middle class—and especially the merchant class—was growing in numbers, wealth, and influence. Many land-rich aristocrats were cash poor, while the merchants were flush. Lillo's play reflected this new reality, and it wove a fabric of middle-class morality that had seldom been seen on stage before. Every action has its consequence; every sin has its cost. The scales always balance out.

It's worth noting that it was little more than a year after the opening of this play when Ben Franklin, back home in Philadelphia, published the first volume of *Poor Richard's Almanac*, which began celebrating this same sort of morality in the colonies. Franklin himself embodied the rising middle class as a tradesman whose business grew through hard work and good decisions.

George Whitefield had his own rise to prominence during the 1730s, though his route was more circuitous. As a student, an actor-in-training, a barkeep, a collegian, a servant to other collegians, a small-group participant, a minister, a missionary, and an evangelist, he would grapple with many of the themes that the London stage had introduced in the previous decade. He served aristocrats; he preached to paupers; and he became a phenomenally successful merchant of the gospel. Along the way, he learned about guilt and grace and good decisions, and he taught what he learned.

The London theater didn't give him his message, but it readied the population for what he had to say.

NINE

The Education of George Whitefield

"I would give a hundred guineas if I could say 'Oh' like Mr. Whitefield."[1] So said David Garrick, London's greatest actor in the mid-1700s. He wasn't the only one raving about George's powerful delivery. Regarding Whitefield's preaching style, Ben Franklin himself wrote that "every accent, every emphasis, every modulation of voice, was so perfectly well turned and well placed that without being interested in the subject, one could not help being pleased with the discourse, a pleasure of much the same kind with that received from an excellent piece of music."[2]

Where did George learn to speak like that? Though he was certainly practicing on his own from an early age, his formal training would have begun at age twelve at St. Mary de Crypt grammar school in Gloucester. Working-class children generally learned trades and entered apprentice-ships, as Ben Franklin had done. Upper-class children often had private tutors. But for those families in between, those who hoped to send children to college but lacked the resources for private instruction, the "grammar school" was generally the best option. This was the course of study Ben Franklin had started and stopped when it became clear that his family couldn't afford college. The grammar school was a pathway toward college that involved several years of learning Latin, Greek, the classics, and some mathematics. Most likely, the curriculum would have included a thorough study of Cicero's writing on rhetoric and oratory. In his memoirs, George mentioned that he had "good elocution and memory" and that he was sometimes asked to give speeches to the student body.[3]

The most famous of the ancient Roman orators, Cicero had divided speech making into five parts: *inventio*, developing arguments; *dispositio*, arranging the arguments; *elocutio*, choosing techniques of wording; *memoria*, memorizing the speech; and *actio*, using voice and gesture.

"The orator takes all those things that are commonly thought to be evil and troubling and frightening, and with his words makes them even more so," Cicero wrote. "And whatever seems desirable and valuable in ordinary life, he amplifies and embellishes by speaking about it."[4]

This serves as an apt description of Whitefield's preaching, as he extolled the virtues of faith and repentance and warned against the sin that would keep someone from responding to God.

Cicero hailed the orator "who speaks distinctly, explicitly, copiously, and luminously, both as to matter and words; who produces in his language a sort of rhythm and harmony; who speaks, as I call it, gracefully. Those also who treat their subject as the importance of things and persons requires, are to be commended for that peculiar kind of merit, which I term aptitude and congruity."[5] Rhetoric was a whole-person discipline, not just a matter of slick speech. A good speaker needed something to say, as well as the mental capacity to organize ideas and communicate them in ways that would connect with the audience.

George learned these lessons well, but apparently he also developed a love of acting. And why not? He had already been reading plays (surprisingly, many plays of the time found more of an audience in print than on stage), and it's likely that he saw some theatrical productions in the large meeting room at his mother's inn. Bristol's community theater didn't start up until about 1740, but there were various traveling troupes ("strollers") that might bring their shows around.

At school, George's elocution and memory would enable him to learn parts and recite them clearly. As he got more involved in theater at school, he would sometimes cut other classes for several days in order to learn his role.

Obviously, acting was more important to him than the rest of his studies. A teacher at the school recognized George's ability and interest, as well as his effect on his classmates, and wrote some new plays for them to perform.

A few years earlier George had been bullied by his peers, but now he was respected and admired, at the head of his class in oratory and drama. Whitefield's own report of his childhood reveals some confusion about what kind of person he wanted to be, yet for a few years at St. Mary's grammar school, he put things together. He could speak well. He could act well. When he was on stage, people liked him. Though his attitude toward theater drastically changed in the following years, he never lost this sense of fulfillment. He loved being in front of people.

Acting Lessons

Whitefield doesn't record much about the lessons he learned at St. Mary's. Cicero would have been in the curriculum, and possibly Quintilian's *Institutes of Oratory*, but some theater instructors of that time were trying to find new approaches to acting, going beyond the Latin classics to find techniques that would bring life to the stage.

In 1710, Charles Gildon published *The Rules of Oratory Applied to Acting*, in which he suggested that the actor stand in front of a mirror and try to experience the emotion of his character. The mirror would show him how those feelings looked. "You must lift or cast down your eyes according [to] the nature of things you speak of. Thus if [you are speaking] of Heaven, your eyes naturally are lifted up; if of Earth or Hell or anything terrestrial, they are naturally cast down."[6]

Gesture was widely studied and catalogued. Certain feelings called for certain movements. Increasingly, acting teachers were going back to Aristotle's writings on the arts, focusing on the "passions" he listed: anger, calm, friendship and enmity, fear and confidence, shame, favor, pity, envy. There were different lists of these passions, usually including six to ten. Each of these human emotions had a particular look and feel to it, which the successful actor would attempt to master.

One of the leading theorists of acting in the 1700s, Aaron Hill, put out a newsletter called *The Prompter*. The first thing you should do as an actor, he said, is:

> To consider the nature of the thing of which you are to speak and fix a very deep impression of it in your own mind before you can be as thoroughly touched with it yourself, or able by an agreeable sympathy to convey the same passion to another. Let a man, for instance, recollect some idea of sorrow; his eye will, in a moment, catch the dimness of melancholy; his muscles will relax into languor and his whole body sympathetically unbend itself into a remiss and inanimate lassitude.[7]

As early as 1724, Hill was writing about "acting the passions."

It's possible that George's teacher in Gloucester, who was enterprising enough to write his own plays for the class, was familiar with Charles Gildon's 1710 book, and he might have kept in touch with Hill's ideas, too, passing them on to his students.

In any case, we see the results of George's training in his lifetime of ministry. You would expect oratory. Any successful speaker would certainly apply the Ciceronian values of preparation and style. There were plenty of preachers doing that, from the Wesley brothers in England to Gilbert Tennent and Jonathan Edwards in America. But George Whitefield brought something very different to the pulpit. It was clearly his theater training that taught him to embody the passions.

We can read reports from two continents about Whitefield's emotional displays. One listener remarked on his "unreserved use of tears," saying that the preacher was "frequently so overcome, that, for a few seconds, you would suspect he never could recover." Whitefield refused to apologize for the waterworks. "You blame me for weeping, but how can I help it when you will not weep for yourselves, though your immortal souls are on the verge of destruction?"[8]

In the dramatic action of his sermons, he sometimes interrupted himself. "Once, when preaching on eternity, he suddenly stopped his message, looked around, and exclaimed, 'Hark! Methinks I hear [the saints] chanting their everlasting hallelujahs, and spending an eternal day in echoing forth triumphant songs of joy. And do you not long, my brethren, to join this heavenly choir?'"[9]

Whitefield's storytelling skills were much in evidence, and he knew how to find the passions in any scene. "Once, when he described a storm at sea, his description was so vivid that a sailor in the audience actually cried out, 'To the lifeboats! To the lifeboats!'"[10]

Eyewitnesses (and ear witnesses) described his gestures and gyrations, his thundering tone, and the characters he assumed while telling those stories. He was not just speaking. He was *acting*, in an Aaron Hill sense. He was experiencing the passions of his subject and conveying them to his audience. That's what made him special. Some of his antics might have lost him a few points in Ciceronian oratory, but they gained him a vast following. His style engaged people enough so that they heard the message of God's redemption.

Critics, then and now, have assumed that Whitefield's dramatic delivery was phony, put on, or manipulative. In so doing, they reveal an ignorance of the craft of acting. Whitefield himself addressed this in a story he told about an actor conversing with the Anglican archbishop. "We actors on the stage speak of things imaginary as if they were real, and you in the pulpit speak of things real as if they were imaginary."[11] Remember that Whitefield had a running battle with the established church. Using this actor's words as an indictment of the insipid triviality too often heard from Anglican clergy, George renewed his own commitment: "I will not be a velvet-mouthed preacher."[12]

By that time, Whitefield was no friend of the theater either. He lambasted play going as a worthless diversion. Yet he himself used his acting skills, forged back in that grammar school, to create a new kind of ministry. He would speak of things that were alarmingly real, and he would use a full range of theatrical expression to focus attention on those realities.

Historian Harry S. Stout has explored this subject well. "At an early age . . . ," he writes, "Whitefield managed to fuse a public amalgam of preaching and acting that held audiences spell-bound. . . . At heart, Whitefield became an actor-preacher, as opposed to a scholar-preacher."[13]

Changing His Mind

George changed his mind about theater after he got to Oxford. It was part of his spiritual development to focus fully on God and cast aside such worldly diversions as play reading and card playing. And of course attending plays or acting in them was out of the question. That might seem to modern readers like an overly strict taboo, but at the time it was a clear choice, and Whitefield never wavered.

It wasn't just the idea that play reading (or play going) was an unproductive activity for the serious believer. The theater world existed on the opposite side of a great divide. It was a world of bawdy humor and drunkenness, loose morals and raw sexuality. Playwrights questioned authority and challenged accepted ideas about God. Plays often mocked religion.

The first psalm offers a blessing to "the man that walketh not in the counsel of the ungodly, nor standeth in the way of sinners, nor sitteth in the seat of the scornful. But his delight is in the law of the LORD; and in his law doth he meditate day and night" (Psalms 1:1–2 KJV). As an Oxford student newly convicted by God, that's the man George Whitefield wanted to be. It meant giving up theater.

One curious detail of his scholastic acting experience is related in his memoirs tersely, somewhat painfully. As he acted various roles in the plays written by his teacher, he sometimes had to dress in girls' clothes, as was common. Only in 1660 were women first allowed to perform on London stages, and so there was a long-standing tradition of boys in female roles. In an all-boys school, it would be a matter of necessity. *Somebody* would have to play Juliet. In fact, it might have been an indication of George's acting ability that he could play a girl's role well. Still, he commented, "The remembrance of this has often covered me with confusion of face, and I hope will do so, even to the end of my life."[14]

He wrote that more than a decade later, in 1739, as an ordained minister sailing to Philadelphia for the first time. And in a further addition, he felt compelled to repudiate his theatrical training even more, noting that "this way of training up youth has a natural tendency to debauch the mind, to raise ill passions, and to stuff the memory with things as contrary to the

Gospel of Jesus Christ, as light to darkness, Heaven to Hell." But even then a bit of ambivalence enters in. While he "had to repent of . . . my education in general," he still had to thank his teacher for taking great pains to help him to "speak and write correctly."[15]

Ships at Sea

About the time that George Whitefield was starting his studies at St. Mary de Crypt grammar school, Ben Franklin was on a ship from London to Philadelphia. He filled the three-month voyage by observing the ocean, conducting some scientific experiments, planning how he would live the rest of his life, and keeping a journal. After about two months at sea, his ship came alongside another ship, which was traveling from Dublin to New York. "There is really something strangely cheering to the spirits," Ben journaled, "in the meeting of a ship at sea containing a society of creatures of the same species and in the same circumstances with ourselves, after we had been long separated and excommunicated as it were from the rest of mankind." They had been feeling a bit like the passengers on Noah's ark, he said, as if they were alone in the world—but then this other ship appeared. "My heart fluttered in my breast with joy when I saw so many human countenances, and I could scarce refrain from that kind of laughter which proceeds from some kind of inward pleasure."[16] The two vessels sailed together for a while, and the two captains even met for dinner.

It's a delightful account, but also an appropriate image for us as we consider two lives. George Whitefield and Ben Franklin were making very different voyages through life, but their paths would cross in 1739 and at many points thereafter. They would "sail together" for a time and then move on to their own destinations. Was there a certain "joy" they found in each other? Did they recognize that they were of the same "species"? Perhaps each of them sensed that he was not quite as alone as he feared.

The Continuing
Education of Ben Franklin

As George Whitefield was attending his classics classes—or skipping them to work on plays—Ben Franklin was back in Philadelphia, getting an education of an entirely different kind. For a short time, he worked for the good Quaker merchant Thomas Denham, but then Ben came down with a serious illness—pleurisy, an inflammation of the lining of the lungs. He said it "very nearly carried me off." That doesn't seem to be an exaggeration. In his autobiography, he indicated that, in his great suffering, he made his peace with impending death and was actually "rather disappointed when I found myself recovering," as he remembered all the work remaining to be done.[1] As it turned out, this was probably the disease that killed him more than sixty years later.

The near-death experience might have shaken young Ben spiritually. In such situations we speak of life passing before one's eyes, and maybe that happened to Ben. But at age twenty-one (it was probably the spring of 1727 when he got sick), how much life did he have to review? A series of adventures and a string of broken relationships. He had wriggled out of a stifling apprenticeship, survived the governor's betrayal, and avoided the snare of

James Ralph's lazy hedonism. Ben was a promising young man—everyone said so. But if he was on his deathbed, would that promise ever be fulfilled?

Franklin said that he "gave up the point" in his own mind as he considered his own death.[2] It's an interesting term, used by a man who had been in plenty of debates. It means he conceded. He stopped arguing. With God? With himself? We can imagine that he had mustered plenty of arguments as to why he should keep living, but he got so sick that he gave them up. He accepted the inevitable.

And then he recovered.

You might expect some sort of "conversion" here. Shouldn't a trip to death's door result in a renewed commitment to make life count? But Ben had already been very intentional about living the best life possible. He had been making commitments all along. On his recent ocean voyage back to America, he had begun to set out his personal ethics. What more could a life-shaking illness do for him, except to confirm the direction he was already taking?

Unless we're talking about his relationship with God. It's true that, when people prepare to "meet their Maker," they often actually meet their Maker. Not in the afterlife, but in this earthly life. God becomes real to them, and they begin to live their lives for him. In a few years, George Whitefield would have an experience like that—not exactly from a life-threatening illness, but poor health would be a factor. Wouldn't this be a perfect time for young Ben to give up his resistance to the Puritan theology of his youth, to realize that Cotton Mather and John Bunyan and his parents were right all along, and to rely on Jesus for his salvation?

It didn't happen like that. In the aftermath of this serious disease, we don't see any particular religious devotion—and yet there is a suggestion of a new social awareness. Up to that point, Ben's life had been largely about Ben. How could he best use his own remarkable abilities? But in the next few years, he started to develop groups that would harness the abilities of a whole society. He learned to communicate with the city, with the colony, and with the movers and shakers. He swayed public opinion and worked cleverly to improve the collective life of America. How could he make the world a better place? That was the question that began to propel his activity. Skeptics, then and now, could point out that Ben never gave up his self-interest, and that's true. He profited greatly—in terms of reputation and business—from most of these early social efforts, but he never saw it as an *either/or* proposition. And in a world with plenty of selfish profiteers, Ben Franklin made a name for himself by working for the prosperity of the whole community. Was this a shift of life purpose that resulted from that deathbed moment when he "gave up the point"?

Ben's patron, Thomas Denham, also got sick about the same time, but he did not recover. The mercantile business was bequeathed to his children. The newly recovered Ben was out of danger, but also out of work (and out from under his debt of ten pounds to Denham from the ship trip home).

Fortunately, his old boss Samuel Keimer hired him as sort of a foreman at the old print shop. Ben now had responsibility over several workers and, with Keimer off managing a stationery store, he was free to improve the business. From his own account, he managed the workers well and made the shop more efficient. When the press needed new type, Ben arranged to mold the letters himself, rather than paying and waiting for a new set of press forms from England. When the shop got the job of printing paper currency for the colony, Ben fashioned a copperplate press to handle the intricate work necessary to protect against counterfeiting.

Yet Keimer and Franklin didn't get along. Gone were the days when they would debate for the fun of it or try to think up a new religion. When Ben had first come to Philadelphia, Keimer seemed to be a father figure—or at least the kind of friendly big brother that James Franklin had never been. But now the boss seemed threatened by Ben's ability and perhaps jealous of his convivial personality. Maybe that dated back to the situation with Governor Keith, when Keimer was surprised and humiliated that this illustrious personage was coming to call on his shop boy rather than Keimer himself. Now Keimer and Franklin traveled together to meet new clients, and it was Franklin who would dazzle them with his wit, his reading, and his travels. Keimer stewed in his jealousy. Ben suspected that his boss was just using him to train the workers, and when they could run the shop on their own, Ben would be sacked.

So there were several run-ins between boss and foreman, and Ben began making plans with one of the workers, Hugh Meredith, to open up their own print shop. Meredith said his father could put up the capital. So when Ben finally got fired from Keimer's shop, it was the perfect opportunity to fulfill a dream of starting his own business.

That didn't go quite as planned.

The new partners rented a place at 139 Market Street, installed their equipment, and began taking print jobs. But Hugh Meredith had a drinking problem. Overseeing Keimer's shop, Ben had managed to convince Hugh to keep his addiction under control. As a result, Hugh's father considered Ben a good influence on his son, which was one big reason he was willing to put up the money for this business venture. But once they went into business with Ben, both of the Merediths proved irresponsible. The father provided only about half the promised funds, and the son returned to his drinking. Always conscious of his public image, Ben suffered on both counts. Creditors were suing his company to get paid, and townspeople regularly saw Hugh Meredith gambling and tippling at the local taverns. Neither of these factors was good for business.

Through financial support from two affluent friends who insisted Ben sever ties with Hugh, he was able to buy out the Merediths and, for the first time, run his own shop. He quickly set about repairing his public image, working day and night to meet deadlines. People took notice of the fact that he was at work earlier and later than everyone else on Market Street. Ben made a point of purchasing paper himself, returning to his shop with a wheelbarrow full of it. People would see this hardworking young businessman and be impressed enough to give him their business.

As the third printer in a two-printer town (Keimer and Andrew Bradford, son of the printer Ben met in New York), Franklin had a tough task ahead of him. He was determined to succeed on the basis of hard work and high-quality output. He was also a great writer—perhaps the best in America at the time—and this gave him an additional edge, especially when it came to newspaper publishing.

Remember that Ben had already enjoyed a brief stint as a newspaper publisher, filling in on the *New-England Courant* when his brother was jailed. This had clearly been the high point of his apprenticeship, and it's no surprise that, soon after establishing his own printing business, he would want to start another paper. There was already one newspaper in Philadelphia, Bradford's *The American Weekly Mercury*, but Ben didn't think very highly of its writing, and he was sure he could find his own readership.

He made the mistake of mentioning his newspaper dream to a friend, who mentioned it to Samuel Keimer, Ben's old boss. In response (and possibly still nursing sour feelings against Ben), Keimer quickly launched a newspaper of his own: the *Universal Instructor in all Arts and Sciences: and Pennsylvania Gazette*. Consisting largely of reprinted encyclopedia entries, this paper was even worse than Bradford's. Recognizing that the town wasn't big enough for *three* papers, Ben Franklin embarked upon a shrewd and cold-hearted plan to drive his old boss out of the newspaper business. Employing strategies that bring to mind modern "hostile takeovers," Ben used the most devastating weapon available: his pen.

First he submitted a series of columns to Bradford's paper, the *Mercury*. These columns, printed under the pseudonym Busy-Body, openly criticized the shoddy quality of Keimer's rag. Of course these articles were also witty and delightful, far better than anything else in Bradford's paper. Keimer took the bait, publishing whiny responses that reduced the quality of his paper even further. In this exchange, Franklin—still writing under pseudonyms—began to describe his idea of what a newspaper could be. This not only disgraced Keimer, but it made readers disappointed in Bradford's paper, and it set the scene for Franklin's entrance into the market.

Eventually Keimer lost enough business that he sold the paper to Franklin, who shortened its name to the *Pennsylvania Gazette*. Finally Ben could publish his brilliant writing in his own newspaper, and its quality quickly exceeded that of the *Mercury*.

This episode may force us to revise our image of Franklin, who could be a shark when he needed to be. One might protest that Keimer brought this on himself, with his mistreatment of Franklin, from whom he stole the newspaper idea to begin with. In a way, Ben was just reclaiming his own intellectual property. Still, he was ruthless in his response to Keimer, who ended up deeply in debt and even imprisoned for a time.

Perhaps there was even more at stake here. Ben knew what a good newspaper could mean to a society. He had seen the power of the *Courant* in Boston, standing up to the political and social powers of the time, even the great Cotton Mather. Unfortunately, in his view, neither of the Philadelphia newspapers was worth the paper it was printed on. They were squandering their potential status in a society that desperately needed *informed* citizens. By rushing into print with regurgitated encyclopedia pages, Keimer wasn't just stealing an idea from Franklin, he was silencing the voice of a colony.

This was not the first time Ben would use a pen name to get his way. And it would not be the last time he would use the power of the press to sway public opinion. About a decade later, Franklin's coverage in the *Pennsylvania Gazette* would make George Whitefield a household name. Many of the same tricks that Ben used in his early days—such as phony letters to the editor to create controversy—would be used again with Whitefield, but to build him up rather than destroy him. By 1739, Ben Franklin had become a powerful star maker. That power began to be displayed here, in 1729.

Betrayal

In these crucial years, not only was Ben getting an education in business, but he was also learning more about relationships. He must have had remarkable social skills. With his wit, awareness, and humility, he made friends wherever he went. But with the Meredith fiasco, not to mention the implosion of the relationship with Keimer, we begin to see a pattern. People betrayed Ben. They used him. His closest friendships ended in bitter disappointment.

We could start with his brother James. As a precocious apprentice, Ben surely wanted more of a collegial relationship there, especially after he proved himself with the Silence Dogood letters and by taking over the paper while James was in jail. But this wasn't to be. Ben himself sabotaged the future of this relationship when he returned to Boston in show-off mode. *Of course* James would turn a cold shoulder.

Another relationship from Ben's Boston days later turned sour. John

Collins had been a boyhood friend. A "bookish lad," Collins used to debate social issues with Ben. It was Collins who arranged Ben's escape from Boston on the sloop to New York. Later, Collins came to Philadelphia and stayed with Ben for a time, borrowing more and more money, which he spent largely on liquor. That friendship sank on a rowboat ride with several other friends, when Collins refused to do his share of the rowing. After asking several times, Ben finally threw Collins overboard. He knew the guy could swim, so there was no danger there, just inconvenience and humiliation. When Collins finally dried off, moved out, and got a job elsewhere, he refused to repay the money he had borrowed.

Ben suffered through the James Ralph years and the Governor Keith disappointment, as well as the dismantling of once-promising working relationships with Samuel Keimer and Hugh Meredith. Was Ben a bad friend, or did he attract the wrong kind of people?

In his autobiography, Ben admitted to errors ("errata") with his brother and with Ralph, though each of them used Ben in his own way. Perhaps Ben was naïve in trusting the governor and entering into business with the Merediths. Perhaps Ben's affable manner, along with his desire to present a pleasing image, sent out the message, "Use me!" People seemed to appreciate what Ben could do for them, but when he demanded a reciprocal relationship, things fell apart.

There may be a hint of the passive-aggressive in Ben's behavior, the personality model commonly depicted in the phrase "I don't get mad; I get even." Ben put up with a great deal of mistreatment from all of these people without getting mad. Then he got even in a big way—running out on an apprenticeship, throwing this guy out of a boat, trying to steal that guy's girlfriend, and destroying someone else in print.

Things didn't get much better for Ben throughout the rest of his life. He had a lot of friends, but few soul mates. A lot of people tried to use him, and eventually he learned to recognize that. His affability remained, but he had some dark undercurrents that occasionally surfaced. Everybody liked Ben Franklin, except those who didn't. His friendships ran broad but shallow. He seemed to follow Poor Richard's advice: "Let all men know thee, but no man know thee thoroughly."[3] There are a few names that recur in his letters, people he seemed to connect with on a deeper level—a sister, some scientific colleagues, and for a time his son—but that's a rather small circle.

How close a friend did George Whitefield become? The easiest answer is *at least as close as most other friends.* If Ben had five people in his inner circle, then George was at least tied for sixth. If Ben was wary of people using him, then perhaps he could relax with a man who eventually matched him in fame, influence, and moneymaking ability.

Parenthood

At some point around 1730, Ben had an affair with a woman that resulted in the birth of a son, William. He never denied paternity and took William into the home he set up with Deborah Read. Historians have debated both the timing of William's conception and the identity of the mother. Franklin was strangely silent on the matter considering his attention to detail in the rest of his autobiography. He never divulged the woman's name.

This leads some to think it was Deborah herself. She had gotten married when Ben was in England, but her husband had run off in 1728. Divorce laws were strict, so Ben couldn't officially marry her until there was proof of the husband's death. Also, adultery standards were unfair to women, so Deborah would suffer socially for bearing a child out of wedlock, while Ben could get away with fathering an illegitimate child. As it turned out, Deborah raised William as her own child, which he might have been.

That theory has some holes, however. Why would Ben keep the secret all his life, even after Deborah's death? Why did Deborah show such resentment toward William? And there was a letter from a friend of the family, claiming that William's birth mother was someone else, a woman of low class and low morals, later sustained by occasional financial support from Franklin.

As for the timing, in a letter to his mother in 1750, Ben mentioned that William was nineteen, requiring a birth date of 1731—but he might have been fudging the data to make the boy seem legitimate. Other records show

William serving in a militia in 1746. If he had been born in 1731, he would have only been fifteen then, too young to serve. Most likely William was born around 1728 or 1729, before Ben settled down with Deborah. Since they didn't know the whereabouts of her first husband, or whether he was still alive, they entered a common-law marriage in September 1730.

As he turned twenty-five early in 1731, Ben Franklin was a successful printer, editor of one of two Philadelphia newspapers, and now a family man.

ELEVEN

Boy, Interrupted

Despite his love of acting, George Whitefield dropped out of school at about the age of fifteen. Apparently he used all his persuasive ability to convince his mother that this was best for the family. After being deserted by her second husband, she was suffering financially, and therefore couldn't afford to send George to college. In that case, he reasoned, he would just be "spoiled" as a tradesman if he learned too much Latin. As he wrote later in his memoirs, he thought he had made "sufficient progress in the classics" by this time, but in truth he was just "longing to be set at liberty from the confinement of a school."[1]

Mom was a hard sell, but George eventually got his way. At first he continued to study only writing, but then he stopped going to school entirely. Instead, he worked at the family inn, washing mops and cleaning rooms. This employment lasted a year and a half.

During this time he read the Bible often and would sometimes compose sermons as he worked. A friend would stop by as he tended the bar, urging him to go to Oxford University. "I wish I could," George replied.[2]

Things changed when his brother took over the inn. The brother's wife did not get along with George, and so George left the inn to live in Bristol with another brother. For the next two months, he experienced a new religious fervor, but then he moved to his mother's home in Gloucester and "all my fervour went off." Unemployed, he renewed acquaintances with some old school friends. He resumed reading plays and playing cards. "It was a proper season for Satan to tempt me," he later wrote.[3]

This sensitivity sounds strange to modern ears. *What's wrong with some mild diversion?* Yet for George it was all connected. A lack of spiritual discipline led to all sorts of bad behavior and bad thoughts. According to his memoirs, his friends in Gloucester were "debauched, abandoned, atheistical youths."[4] It was all too easy for George to try to fit in with them, to participate in their wanton activities. Already, we've gained a sense of George's need for acceptance, even applause. Did these accomplices goad George into shameful behavior? As he wrote about it a few years later, he answered unequivocally, "Yes!" Besides play reading and card playing, he reported getting drunk a few times and indulging in "secret sin." We can only guess what that might be, but George was deeply remorseful about it.[5]

Even in these times of sin, he would occasionally have a sense of God's calling: "One morning, as I was reading a play to my sister, said I, 'Sister, God intends something for me which we know not of. As I have been diligent in business, I believe many would gladly have me for an apprentice, but every way seems to be barred up, so that I think God will provide for me some way or other that we cannot apprehend.'"[6]

That way became clearer when a family friend, a young man a few years older than George, visited Mrs. Whitefield and told her about the "servitor" program that was paying his way through Oxford. A servitor worked as a servant of wealthier students, but also attended classes and earned a degree. "That will do for my son," said Mrs. Whitefield. George enthusiastically agreed.[7]

In short order, George applied for a servitor position at Oxford and returned to St. Mary's to complete his preparation in the classics. For the next year, he was back with his old classmates, and once again he reported his sinful behavior: "I took pleasure in their lewd conversation. I began to reason as they did. . . . In short, I soon made a great proficiency in the school of the Devil. I affected to look rakish."[8]

It was 1731. As Ben Franklin in Philadelphia was settling down into marriage, fatherhood, and business, in Gloucester the mercurial George Whitefield had another change of attitude. He received Communion on Christmas Day, just past his seventeenth birthday, and this seemed to mark a special moment for him. "I began now to be more and more watchful over my thoughts, words, and actions." During the following Lenten season he fasted Wednesdays and Fridays. He read devotional books. He went to public worship twice a day.[9]

Looking back on this extreme religiosity, he noted, "hypocrisy crept into every action. As once I affected to look more rakish, I now strove to appear more grave than I really was. . . . I often used to find fault with the lightness of others."[10] George was not a lot of fun to be around anymore. He even annoyed his mother.

Selling the Truth

Whitefield's preoccupations in this period—struggling to find his identity, weighing the merits of wildness and discipline, attending to his image— were all those of Ben Franklin in his own adolescence. Ben's circumstances were very different, his background was different, and his world was different, but parts of this pathway were much the same.

Both Ben and George left us with detailed accounts of their youth, and we would expect them to tag their younger selves with certain labels. But *within* these stories, we find each young man intentionally constructing and revising his own image. Ben pushes a wheelbarrow down the street to show potential clients he's a hard worker. George takes on a "rakish" appearance. Ben dandles his pocket watch at his brother's shop to show he's now successful. George practices preaching at the inn's bar. Ben remembers with some mock horror how bedraggled he was when Deborah first saw him on Market Street. George remembers with shame how he wore girls' clothing on stage.

In the following years, both would become masters of image crafting, each in his own way. On occasion, they would help each other do this. (Franklin's press coverage gave Whitefield a foothold in America. Later, during the Stamp Act controversy, Whitefield's support secured Franklin's image as a diplomat with America's best interests at heart.) Both understood the power of image to affect others, to find the most efficient use of their own abilities, and to change society. But even more than that, they seemed to understand *themselves* by these images.

In today's image-crazy age, savvy observers often try to separate image from reality. We assume that advertisers and politicians are lying to us as they display the pictures we want to see. The *true* identity of this product or business or person, we think, must be quite different. It would be easy to take the same approach with George and Ben, but what's at stake for them is a heartfelt question: *What kind of person do I want to be?*

Young George seemed to change his mind about that every other month. He would toy with a particular self-image and then radically redefine himself. He was not an eighteenth-century Eddie Haskell, smiling at the grownups while raising hell behind their backs. No, he was representing the reality of whoever he decided to be this month. In the same way, Ben Franklin pushed a wheelbarrow down the street to publicize the reality of his industrious nature. This was not a marketing gimmick. Well, it *was*, but he was backing up the image by actually working day and night. He was "selling" the truth about who he was.

Yes, Ben became a master of the pseudonym, the prank, the fake letter to the editor, but these could be seen as examples of the lie that speaks the truth. In his Busy-Body letters, for instance, he was telling the truth about Keimer's ineptitude as an editor and a businessman, and about his own vision of what a newspaper could be. What's more, most readers eventually knew that Ben was Busy-Body—yet the false name enabled people to see the true situation of Philadelphia's newspaper business. We don't need to defend Ben's tactics here, but deceit was not his crime. He brilliantly managed the imagery in this situation, but he was essentially "selling" the truth.

That might also be an apt description of George's preaching ministry as it developed. He was not playing the part of an emotional preacher. Well, he *was*, but it wasn't a false identity he put on. He was deeply dedicated to the truth of what he was preaching. His love for the gospel was stronger than any of Aristotle's passions, and so George used every stage tactic available to express himself. Surely he understood that his dramatic antics created greater interest in his message, but they sprang from his own dramatic self. He was "selling the truth" about himself—and about God.

Oxford Blues

In 1732, at the age of seventeen, George Whitefield enrolled at Oxford's Pembroke College. As a servitor, he paid most of his way by serving wealthier students. This was a humiliating position, but his time waiting on guests at the Bell Inn had prepared him well for the laundering, cleaning, and fetching he did there. His people-pleasing instincts were in full flower, and soon George's services were in high demand. "By my diligent and ready attendance, I ingratiated myself into the gentlemen's favour," he recalled.[11]

By comparison, it's interesting to note the experience of the great essayist Samuel Johnson, who also attended Pembroke College a year or two earlier. Johnson bucked against the class consciousness at Oxford. "I was miserably poor," he told his biographer. His feet were sticking out of his worn-out shoes, and he noticed the sneers of the "gentlemen" students. He described his attitude there as "bitterness." After about a year and a half, he dropped out, unable to pay tuition.[12] Such might have been the case with George Whitefield if it hadn't been for the opportunity to earn his tuition through serving—as well as his own accommodating spirit.

We've seen the ups and downs of George's spiritual life during his adolescence. He entered college at a time of strong commitment, and this helped him resist the peer pressure that might have brought him down. The other servitors who roomed with him were often going out at night, and they invited George to "join in their excess of riot." He said no, again and again, preferring to stay home by himself. Eventually they stopped asking. "When they perceived they could not prevail, they let me alone as a singular odd fellow."[13]

Good news: he was resisting temptation. Bad news: he was very lonely.

In a 1770 poem, Charles Wesley recalled his first impressions of George Whitefield at Oxford:

Can I the memorable day forget,
When first we by divine appointment met?
Where undisturb'd the thoughtful student roves,
In search of truth, through academic groves;
A modest, pensive youth, who mused alone,
Industrious the frequented path to shun.[14]

George "roved" through the halls of Oxford, "thoughtful" and "pensive." He wasn't chatting with friends, wasn't rolling a game of ninepin on the lawn. He was musing and very much "alone."

"I went to Oxford without a friend, I had not a servant, I had not one to introduce me," he said in a sermon years later.[15] His roommates were steering clear of him. He lacked the social status of the young gentlemen he was serving. There were no particular professors or tutors he drew close to. Of course, between classwork and servitor duties, he had plenty to do, and he doubled down on religious activities, observing a personal time of prayer and psalm singing five times a day, fasting every Friday, and taking Communion at a church near campus. Increasingly he withdrew from society, living a sort of monastic life in the midst of a bustling university.

A major influence on him at that time was a rather new book, *A Serious Call to a Devout and Holy Life*, put out by English churchman William Law in 1729. This book was also important to John Wesley, Samuel Johnson, and many others.[16] The title tells you what you need to know. William Law was calling Christians to get serious about their faith. It wasn't enough simply to show up at church. Christianity needed to affect one's whole life.

"Devotion signifies a life given, or devoted, to God," Law wrote. "He, therefore, is the devout man, who lives no longer to his own will, or the way and spirit of the world, but to the sole will of God, who considers God in everything, who serves God in everything, who makes all the parts of his common life parts of piety, by doing everything in the Name of God."[17]

The Church of England had, quite simply, grown cold. Sparks of authentic spiritual reformation had accompanied the political impulses of Henry VIII that birthed that church some two centuries earlier, but these sparks had long since died away. The bloody wrangling of the different politico-religious parties in England had given way to peace, with Anglicans in power and Catholics and Dissenters in a minority position. When any religious group gains power, you can look for other dynamics—an embrace of social rank, political issues, and financial growth; a freezing of spiritual development; the need to preserve the status quo. All of this was happening in England at the time. Also, Anglican leaders were buying heavily into the emerging Enlightenment. The church was all head and no heart.

"At that time, serious and practical Christianity in England was in a very low condition," wrote John Gillies in a 1772 biography of Whitefield. "Scriptural, experimental religion . . . was become quite unfashionable."[18]

It was exactly this "scriptural, experimental religion" that William Law was hawking. Faith needed to be lived out, a new experiment of devotion every day. He summoned Christians away from the empty diversions of entertainment, games, and gossip. Law's message: get serious about what's most important.

George had seen this book a year or so earlier, but now he was able to get a copy of his own and devour it. As a result, he wrote later, "God worked powerfully upon my soul."[19] A Serious Call seemed to give George a vocabulary for faith. He had previously felt bursts of passion for God, but now he had a reason. He answered this serious call. He determined to be a serious Christian.

Maybe too serious.

TWELVE

The Leather Aprons and
the Bible Moths

"Men and melons are hard to know."

This was one of the insights that appeared in *Poor Richard's Almanac*, the booklet Ben Franklin published annually (or nearly so) beginning in December 1732. Like any almanac, it contained basic data on practical matters—such as times of tides and sunrises, schedules and locations of public courts, recipes, and weather forecasts—along with historical trivia and sayings of what you might call "folk wisdom." What made Franklin's *Almanac* popular (and extremely profitable) was the originality of his folk wisdom. He didn't just gather hackneyed phrases and trot them out once again for public consideration—he made up new witticisms that were, in fact, witty. Many of them are still quoted today.

"Haste makes waste."

"No gains without pains."

"He that lies down with dogs, shall rise up with fleas."[1]

So, while George Whitefield was beginning to study the wisdom of the ages at Oxford, Ben Franklin was crafting wisdom of his own in Philadelphia. Once again, Ben used a pseudonym. Was he buffering himself against the possibility that this publishing venture wouldn't work? Possibly, but it's even more likely that he understood the marketing value of humility, so he used a humble persona to lower expectations and surprise his readers.

Those are modern, strategic terms for something Ben seemed to understand intuitively. He was at the top of his game, publishing (and also editing and writing) the best newspaper in Philadelphia, after some very public gamesmanship. Now it might backfire to offer an almanac of his personal outlook on life—at the ripe age of twenty-six. Readers might see this as hubris. The public might resist being oversaturated with Franklin's opinions. Remember: this was a Quaker-founded town. The spirit of Philadelphia was still communal rather than hierarchical. They would respond far better to the disarming wit of the bumpkin "Richard Saunders" than to the pronouncements of the powerful editor of the *Pennsylvania Gazette*.

And respond they did. Over the years, the *Almanac* became a runaway best seller, establishing Ben's printing business and enabling him to branch out. It also gave future readers a huge supply of maxims from Franklin's fertile mind.

Taken together, the Poor Richard sayings presented a simple worldview. Future success comes from present restraint. Ben learned many of these lessons the hard way—settling in with "dogs" like James Ralph and Hugh Meredith and emerging with the "fleas" of near disaster; failing to thump the "melon" that was Governor William Keith. We find a Solomonic progression in these sayings: A results in B, so avoid A. Lessons are drawn from nature—melons, fleas, and so on—so look for the true nature of things and act accordingly. Limit your foolish passions and save resources for the future.

"God helps them that help themselves," he also wrote, and this could sum up his religious thinking, at least at that point in his life.[2] He had gleaned enough from his Puritan upbringing to embrace the value of work, and he retained a basic belief in God. His scientific mind recognized the mechanical patterns of not only nature but also morality (A results in B). His own failings had taught him some humility, and so he knew that God was helping, and he was grateful. But this divine grace was granted to those who were disciplined enough to "help themselves." We launch the boat; God sends the wind.

In his autobiography, Franklin took some time out to discuss his religious development. He mentioned that, in his youth, he became "a thorough deist" after reading a book *against* deism and finding its arguments weak. (In short, deism has a mechanistic universe and an inactive creator, and thus a merely pragmatic morality. Do whatever works.) Later, after seeing the pain caused by such amoral "freethinking"—by Governor Keith, James Ralph, and himself (leaving Deborah to go to England)—he "began to suspect that this doctrine, though it might be true, was not very useful."[3]

So this inventor cobbled together his own faith from scraps of Cotton Mather and top deists of the day: "I grew convinced that truth, sincerity and integrity in dealings between man and man, were of the utmost importance to the felicity of life, and I formed written resolutions . . . to practice them ever while I lived." He rejected the revelation of God in the Bible, but began to think "that though certain actions might not be bad *because* they were forbidden . . . yet probably those actions might be forbidden because they were bad for us."[4]

Young Ben determined that there was a basic morality that just made sense, and as he entered adult life in Philadelphia, this belief gave him a "tolerable character to begin the world with."[5]

The Junto

Once again, Ben began blazing his own trail. Later in life he would become a successful inventor; now he was inventing a philosophy of life. He borrowed from other thinkers of the day, but he didn't wear anyone else's label. He wasn't exactly a deist, and he certainly wasn't a Puritan. Ben Franklin was his own man, going his own way. It was hard for anyone to keep up with him.

And here we find a major paradox in Ben's personality: it's lonely being the smartest guy in the room. His intelligence set him apart, and so did his keen sense of responsibility. As we've seen, he had been hurt several times by trusted friends who turned out to be irresponsible. You might think this would make him withdraw from others entirely, but he didn't. An inherently social being, Ben kept gathering groups of people around him. As biographer Edmund S. Morgan put it, "If it is true that he always held something of himself in reserve, it is also true that he could not get along without company."[6]

In 1727, he started one such group in Philadelphia. First known as the Leather Apron Club and later as the Junto, it included three coworkers from Keimer's print shop and a few other tradesmen Ben met around town. They convened every Friday night, first at local taverns and later in rented rooms, to discuss philosophy, business, and politics. While these gatherings teemed with laughter, friendship, and good ale, Franklin also organized them thoroughly. On a regular rotation, members were required to bring questions for discussion. They agreed to support one another in life and business.

This idea did not originate with Ben Franklin. In fact, he might have gotten it from his old friend Cotton Mather, who was probably adapting an idea that John Calvin had used in France in the 1500s. Mather wrote a book called *Religious Societies: Proposals for the Revival of Dying Religion, by Well Ordered Societies.* This was published in 1724, the same year young Ben visited Mather and bumped his head. As they met in Mather's library, did the old Puritan and the young printer discuss these "well ordered societies"?

Of course, religious "small groups" had been part of the Christian experience since the New Testament believers met "from house to house" in Jerusalem (Acts 2:46 KJV). It was part of the monastic movement in medieval times and revived by various groups (including Calvinists) during the Reformation. There is evidence of religious societies forming in the early 1700s in London and New England, specifically attempting to combat the "disorders" in the church and society—the growing immorality and corruption.

Mather's contribution to the idea lay in the breadth of its scope. For him, religious societies were not just extra church meetings or even splinter groups disaffected by the direction of the main church, but collections of people of diverse classes with different ideas exploring together how to apply their faith to everyday life. "Cotton Mather, in the organization of reforming and religious societies, brought the Church into the world," wrote one scholar.[7]

Franklin had problems with the Puritan faith that gripped Boston during his youth, but he never entirely repudiated it. Instead, we see him visiting Mather on that quick trip back home. We see him creating a kind of Puritan-deist hybrid as his personal way of life. And here we see him adapting Mather's idea for religious societies that discuss worldly matters (among other things) into a secular society that discusses religious ideas (among other things).

Mather had suggested ten specific questions that might be asked in religious societies on a regular schedule. Consider question 6: "Can any further methods be devised, that ignorance and wickedness may be chased from our people in general, and that household piety in particular may flourish amongst them?"

Or question 8: "Is there any matter to be humbly moved unto the legislative power, to be enacted into a law for public benefit?"

Or question 9: "Do we know of any person under sad and sore affliction, and is there anything we may do for the succor of such an afflicted neighbor?"[8]

So when Ben Franklin started the Junto, he came up with a similar list of questions. Of course this group wasn't so interested in "household piety," but it was still focused on social improvement and mutual "succor." Ben asked for reports on their reading "particularly in history, morality, poetry, physics, travels, mechanic arts, or other parts of knowledge."[9] Junto members were expected to share stories of fellow citizens who succeeded or failed in business.

Franklin's question 6 asked, "Do you know of any fellow citizen, who has lately done a worthy action, deserving praise and imitation? Or who has committed an error proper for us to be warned against and avoid?"[10] This wasn't mere gossip; it was a learning exercise. This group was studying human behavior and discussing what worked and what didn't.

Where Mather had sought to expose the dangers of "ignorance and wickedness" in the interest of greater "piety," Franklin asked, "What unhappy effects of intemperance have you lately observed or heard? of

imprudence? of passion? or of any other vice or folly?" (question 7). Both
sets of questions invited discussion on public policy. Similar to Mather's
eighth question, Franklin's fourteenth asked, "Have you lately observed any
defect in the laws of your country, of which it would be proper to move the
legislature an amendment? Or do you know of any beneficial law that is
wanting?"[11]

In both groups, members were invited to mention their own sickness
or that of neighbors. Always a pragmatist, Franklin pointedly asked, "What
remedies were used, and what were their effects?" (question 9).[12]

Through twenty-four questions, Franklin's Junto associates were considering ways they could offer practical help to one another and to their
community. Despite the similarities with Mather's groups, the Junto's goal
was not Christian fellowship, but social networking.

We see here the difference between the seventeenth century and the
eighteenth century, between old Boston and new Philadelphia. Despite his
attempts to bring the church into the world, Mather was coming from a
place where the church ruled society. It had been that way in Boston from
the start and was only now changing. It could be assumed there that the
solutions to society's disorders were religious in nature. Ignorance and
wickedness were the problem; piety was the answer.

In religiously diverse Philadelphia, Franklin made no such assumption.
His group had all the trappings of Mather's "religious society" but without
the religion. While some of its members were religious, the group did not
seek religious answers to social issues. Instead, they sought to improve themselves and society through hard work, good thinking, and mutual support.

Meanwhile, at Oxford University, a similar group was forming.

The Holy Club

John and Charles Wesley were sons of a Puritan minister in Epworth,
Lincolnshire. John received an MA from Oxford University in 1727, assisted
his father in parish ministry for two years, and then returned to teach
at Oxford in 1729. Four years younger, Charles also studied at Oxford.

Sometime during John's two years away from the school, Charles began meeting with other students for prayer, Bible study, and accountability. When John returned to Oxford, he joined the group, bringing his strong leadership skills.

At what point did this evolve from a casual get-together to an organized meeting? Even the Wesley brothers disagreed on that. But, starting with four or five members and adding a few more along the way, the group continued to meet about once a week. Besides prayer and Bible study (poring over the Greek New Testament), they also celebrated Communion and occasionally visited the sick or imprisoned. Other Oxford students derisively tagged them as the Holy Club, Sacramentarians, Methodists, or Bible Moths. (Presumably they fluttered around the Bible as moths around a flame, or they chewed on it as moths chewed cloth.) The name that stuck was "Methodist," a reference to their method of practicing the Christian faith.

Of course this small-group impulse did not arise in a vacuum. Like Cotton Mather, the Wesleys were continuing an ancient Christian tradition. They were possibly influenced by Mather's 1724 book, but it's even more likely that they learned from the Pietist movement that developed in Germany in the late 1600s. Pietist leader Philipp Jakob Spener had launched "piety groups" (collegia pietatis) within German Lutheran churches, in which serious Christians would pray, study, and encourage one another in spiritual growth. Professor August Francke, a Spener protégé, carried the Pietist movement into the universities at Leipzig and Halle in much the same way as the Wesleys were attempting at Oxford. The Wesleys might also have heard about a new community of Moravian Brethren forming in the 1720s at the German estate of Count Nikolaus von Zinzendorf, focusing on prayer, Scripture, and missionary outreach. (The Moravians would become very important to both John and Charles in later years.)

As an avid reader, John Wesley was challenged by works such as Jeremy Taylor's The Rule and Exercises of Holy Living (1650), the fifteenth-century Of the Imitation of Christ by Thomas à Kempis, and two new books by William Law: Christian Perfection (1726) and A Serious Call to a Devout and Holy Life (1729). All of these works urged a more disciplined approach to Christian faith, something the Wesleys wanted to share with their "Holy Club" at Oxford.

And just like Cotton Mather and Benjamin Franklin, the Wesleys created questions for the Oxford Methodists to consider, individually and together. Self-examination was crucial to personal development in holiness, so Wesley composed a "scheme" of six or seven different questions for each day of the week, including:

- "Have I duly meditated?"
- "Have I been zealous to do, and active in doing, good?"
- "Have I thought or spoke unkindly?"
- "Has goodwill been . . . the spring of all my actions toward others?"

Similar questions were part of the group meetings:
- "What known sins have you committed since our last meeting?"
- "What temptations have you met with?"
- "What have you thought, said, or done, of which you doubt whether it be sin or not?"[13]

While both Mather and Franklin asked about society and the group itself, the Wesleys' questions focused on the self, one's personal attitudes and actions. This doesn't mean that the Holy Club was entirely self-centered. On the contrary: its members were actively involved in helping the poor, visiting the sick, and going to prisons, yet they saw outward ministry springing from inward purity. The ultimate goal was not the improvement of society, but the improvement of the individual soul.

Joining the Club

Even before he entered Oxford University in 1732, George Whitefield had heard about the Holy Club. Once at the school, he often heard students mocking the Wesleys and their small group of devoted believers, and he would speak up in defense of these "Methodists." Yet he waited a year before connecting with them. He and Charles Wesley had seen each other in passing, but they hadn't met. (Remember the poem Charles wrote about seeing the "thoughtful" Whitefield as he "roved" about campus.)

We can't be sure why George waited so long, since he didn't elaborate on the point in his memoirs. We might imagine that he was nervous about joining up with such a disparaged group, since he already saw himself as an "odd fellow."

Here the young Whitefield displays a characteristic that he shared with the young Franklin: they were loners who needed people. The two men expressed this in different ways, certainly, but the contradiction can be seen in both of them. George had been playing out a personal drama in his soul, alternately striving to be the best and worst person possible. This had to be a lonely struggle, even though his good or bad actions often played out in public. He often connected with people by performing for them, whether in plays at school, practicing sermons at the inn, or running errands for his wealthy classmates. That satisfied some of his social needs, but it also kept an aesthetic distance around him.

At this point he was on his way to the goal of becoming an Anglican minister, like his great-grandfather, but he was also headed in a new direction. He was seeking spiritual discipline in his life, answering the call to be truly devout and holy. Was this a goal he could share with others, or would it be better for him to continue navigating his own path?

In his memoirs, George made his first meeting with Charles Wesley sound like a spy tryst. He sent a woman—an apple seller on campus—to Charles with news of someone in need. Though George wanted to remain anonymous, she revealed that he had sent her. Charles sent a message back with her, inviting George to breakfast the next morning.

"It was one of the most profitable visits I ever made in my life," George wrote about that breakfast. "My soul, at that time, was athirst for some spiritual friends to lift up my hands when they hung down, and to strengthen my feeble knees." Charles sensed this spiritual hunger in his newfound friend and lent George some books on spiritual matters. Those books changed George's life.[14]

The first was *Nicodemus, or A Treatise Against the Fear of Man*, by August

Francke, a leader in the German Pietist movement. "I do not offer this as a piece of great learning, or a thing extraordinary," wrote the professor in the opening pages of this 1701 work. "The plain truth of my God, set out in its natural lustre, and the least communication of his divine power lively affecting the heart, is infinitely more valuable to me, than all the polite arts and learning of this world. And my only boasting in the Lord is this, that I have betaken myself to that school, and, without any merit or worthiness of my own, have been received into it, wherein the highest wisdom is, 'to know Jesus Christ, and him crucified.'"[15]

This simple introduction served as a battle cry, one that rallied the impressionable Whitefield. There was a conflict in the Anglican church (as there had been in the German Lutheran church) between education and experience. Even in institutions with strong Christian heritage, like Oxford, the Bible was being openly doubted and dismissed. Professors were teaching natural philosophy rather than divine revelation, and preachers were being trained to deliver the same erudition to their congregations. When a group like the Holy Club sought to live by truly Christian principles, getting back to basics, and actually adopting a method of life prescribed by the university (but long neglected), its members encountered derision from their fellow students.

Francke's book spelled out the issues. The "plain truth" of God was enough, "affecting the heart." That personal experience of knowing Christ was worth far more than "polite arts and learning." Those who embraced this experience needed to get over their "fear of man," unlike the biblical Nicodemus, a secret disciple of Jesus. True believers needed to withstand mockery and expect mistreatment.

We can trace these themes through Whitefield's career. Despite his Oxford degree, he was never much of a scholar. He delivered a plain gospel, inviting his hearers to experience Christ. And he received strong opposition from religious leaders, many of whom thought he was dumbing down religion. Eventually he learned to expect this opposition and wear it with pride.

But for a young man of eighteen or nineteen, still figuring out who he was, this was an important challenge. Francke (like Charles Wesley) was throwing down a gauntlet. Would the people-pleasing Whitefield pick it up?

The second book George got from Charles was an anonymous 1680 work called *The Country-Parson's Advice to His Parishioners,* which put forth some basic evangelical theology and practical ideas for living righteously.

It's easy to see why the Wesleys would recommend this book to their Holy Club comrades. After challenging readers to commit to holy living, the Country Parson urged them to connect with other like-minded souls. "Thou wilt do well to seek out some good men that have taken up the same resolution and to acquaint thyself with them, and if possible . . . to make them . . . bosom-friends. Let them know thy design, and purpose of living holily, and Christianly. . . . Desire their prayers, their instruction, their reproofs, their encouragements."[16]

This was the game plan of the Oxford Methodists: mutual prayer, study, accountability, and exhortation. "I confess it will be no easy matter for thee to find such persons; the number of them is but small," wrote the Parson—and yet here was a group numbering maybe fifteen at the time Whitefield came along. The book also presented a future vision that proved downright prophetic:

> And let me tell thee by the way, that if these good men of the Church, will thus shew themselves, and unite together in the several parts of the Kingdom, disposing themselves into fraternities, or friendly societies, and engaging each other . . . to be helpful and serviceable to one another in all good Christian ways, it would be the most effectual means for restoring our decaying Christianity to its primitive life and vigour, and the supporting of our tottering, and sinking Church. . . . Be all as one man (thus it was with the primitive Christians, Acts 2) and so march forward in the good ways of God against all opposition.[17]

As they breakfasted together that Oxford morning, did Charles and George have any inkling of the immense role they and their tiny network of believers would play in restoring vigor to a decaying church?

THIRTEEN

Conversion

The Body of
B. Franklin
Printer;
Like the Cover of an old Book,
Its Contents torn out,
And stript of its Lettering and Gilding,
Lies here, Food for Worms.
But the Work shall not be wholly lost:
For it will, as he believ'd, appear once more,
In a new & more perfect Edition,
Corrected and Amended
By the Author.[1]

Ben Franklin composed this epitaph for himself at the ripe old age of twenty-two. Home in Philadelphia two years after his difficult London trip, he was setting up shop with the drunkard Hugh Meredith and meeting regularly with the Junto. Even as a young man, Ben had already stared death in the face—in his own nearly fatal bout with pleurisy and the passing of his mentor Denham—and emerged with his whimsical spirit intact.

Never actually engraved on Franklin's tombstone, this verse still displays not only Ben's unique wit but also his ostentatious humility. Yes, that's a contradiction in terms, but that is what made Franklin so charming—he expressed his humility in an artful way. These lines also reveal a somewhat Christian theology—the resurrection of the body to life everlasting—but, as usual, Ben was crafting his own system. The epitaph is often appended to his 1728 "Articles of Belief and Acts of Religion," a worship liturgy Ben created for his own use.

All of this confirms the impressions we've already been gathering: Ben Franklin was a very religious man—only he was making up his own religion. According to George Whitefield, that wasn't good enough.

"I have seen your *Epitaph*," George wrote to his friend Ben about twenty-six years later. "Believe on Jesus, and get a feeling possession of God in your heart, and you cannot possibly be disappointed of your expected second edition finely corrected, and infinitely amended."[2]

We can imagine that George appreciated Ben's humility. That was a fine Christian virtue, and also an essential way to approach the Creator. George would have no problem with Ben's dismissal of sectarian religion, since George himself wasn't pushing any particular denomination. And if he had picked up a copy of Ben's "Articles of Belief" with the epitaph attached, he would surely have loved a prayer that Ben had written there: "Thou art a Lover of Justice and Sincerity, of Friendship, Benevolence and every Virtue. Thou art my Friend, my Father, and my Benefactor. Praised be thy Name for ever."[3]

But there was one crucial thing missing: *Jesus.*

In 1752, the year that Ben flew his famous kite, George wrote, congratulating him on his scientific fame, but adding, "I would now humbly recommend to your diligent unprejudiced pursuit and study the mystery of the new-birth."[4] George was citing the third chapter of John's gospel, where Jesus conversed with Nicodemus, "Most assuredly, I say to you, unless one is born again, he cannot see the kingdom of God" (John 3:3).

This verse, with the idea of the new birth, became George Whitefield's battle cry as he built his preaching career. Over three decades, he issued the same challenge to rich and poor, men and women, free people and slaves, miners and actors, Anglicans, Presbyterians, Baptists, and even deists. No matter how moral you were, you needed to be reborn in the name of Jesus.

He had learned this himself as a lonely Oxford student in 1735.

Faith Breaks In

George had tried to be righteous. When his roommates went out to party at night, he stayed home. He was praying, singing psalms, fasting, studying Scripture, and receiving Communion on a regular basis. The "serious call" of author William Law found an answer in his own "devout and holy life." George was practicing discipline in his daily doings, striving to be the best Christian he could possibly be.

It was a great day when he finally connected with the Holy Club, joining Charles Wesley for breakfast. And the books Charles lent him—those had more of an impact than even Charles could imagine.

In *The Country-Parson's Advice to His Parishioners*, for instance, George would have read: "The Reward, which God intends for [his servants], shall not be proportioned to the little Merit of their Services, but to his own Infinite Goodness. . . . It is a Gift, as the Apostle tells us, Rom. 6:23, and such a gift as shall shew the Infinite Goodness and Beneficence of the Donor."[5]

The Bible verse cited by this anonymous author declared, "For the wages of sin is death; but the gift of God is eternal life through Jesus Christ our Lord" (Romans 6:23 KJV). Now any serious Christian, like George, would understand the first part. Sinners earned eternal death through their sin. That's why it was so important to avoid sin, so that you could earn God's favor and be welcomed into heaven rather than hell.

But that's not what the Bible verse was saying. As the "country parson" pointed out, eternal life was a gift. It had nothing to do with the "little merit" of striving people like George. It had everything to do with God's "infinite goodness."

Besides the country parson's book and *Nicodemus, or A Treatise Against the Fear of Man* by the Pietist August Francke, George received another volume from Charles Wesley: *The Life of God in the Soul of Man*, by Henry

Scougal. In his memoirs, Whitefield cited this book as the one that especially changed his life. "I never knew what true religion was, till God sent me that excellent treatise by the hands of my never-to-be-forgotten friend."[6]

Scougal was a Scottish minister who died in 1678. This short work was essentially a letter to a friend who had lost his faith.

"At my first reading it," George wrote, "I wondered what the author meant by saying, 'That some falsely placed religion in going to church, doing hurt to no one, being constant in the duties of the [prayer] closet, and now and then reaching out their hands to give alms to their poor neighbours.'"[7]

Falsely placed religion? This was what George's life was all about. What could possibly be wrong with these holy activities?

George's testimony continued: "'Alas!' thought I, 'if this be not true religion, what is?' God soon showed me; for in reading a few lines further that 'true religion was union of the soul with God, and Christ formed within us,' a ray of Divine light was instantaneously darted in upon my soul, and from that moment, but not till then, did I know that I must be a new creature."[8]

A new creature. The words come from another text written by the apostle Paul. "Therefore if any man be in Christ, he is a new creature: old things are passed away; behold, all things are become new" (2 Corinthians 5:17 KJV). Through his reading, George was discovering that no amount of effort would gain him salvation. He needed to be created anew. It was the work of the Creator.

Sometimes conversion is a process. Though Whitefield mentioned the ray of light that "instantaneously darted" upon him, his journal went on for a dozen pages describing a difficult period of intense (and unhealthy) religiosity that followed.

He blamed Satan for the ingenious temptation that would take godly impulses and push them to dangerous extremes. Increasingly, George withdrew from normal life, neglecting school assignments, becoming a laughingstock on campus, and even pulling away from Holy Club members. "Near five or six weeks I had now spent in my study, except when I was obliged to go out," he explained later. "During this time I was fighting with my corruptions, and did little else besides kneeling down by my bedside, feeling, as it were, a heavy pressure upon my body, as well as an unspeakable oppression of mind, yet offering up my soul to God, to do with me as it pleased Him."[9]

A severe Lenten fast sapped George's energy to the point that he could hardly climb stairs. His school tutor eventually called a doctor, and George was laid up for seven weeks. At the end of that convalescence, he returned to health not only physically but also spiritually. "After having undergone innumerable buffetings of Satan, and many months inexpressible trials by night and day under the spirit of bondage," he wrote, "God was pleased at length to remove the heavy load, to enable me to lay hold on His dear Son by a living faith."[10]

George's attitude was completely transformed. Where he was previously burdened by the pressure to attain a surpassing level of righteousness, now he seemed to relax in the work of God. "But oh! with what joy—joy unspeakable—even joy that was full of, and big with glory, was my soul filled, when the weight of sin went off, and an abiding sense of the pardoning love of God, and a full assurance of faith broke in upon my disconsolate soul! . . . a day to be had in everlasting remembrance."[11]

Versions of Conversion

Apparently George believed that this was the day he received the new birth—*after* the seven-week illness. His *understanding* of the new birth—that "ray of divine light" he saw after reading Scougal—was merely the beginning of a process that took him through a spiritual wilderness and into the arms of God. There was a highly emotional moment—joy unspeakable—that clinched it.

"Thus were the days of my mourning ended," he wrote, concluding this chapter of his journal. "After a long night of desertion and temptation, the Star, which I had seen at a distance before, began to appear again, and the Day Star arose in my heart. Now did the Spirit of God take possession of my soul, and, as I humbly hope, seal me unto the day of redemption."[12]

It is not unusual for people to go through such a process, even today. It often starts with a mental awareness of the story of Jesus, the validity of the gospel, or one's own need for a "new birth." The struggle can have various causes or take various forms. But then there is a release, an acceptance, a reception, often emotional in nature.

Notice the way Whitefield described it. The active verbs described the action of God—breaking in, taking possession. George was the *recipient* of these events. His role in the transaction was to stop struggling, to say yes, and to receive the blessing that God was dishing out.

Throughout his preaching career, George was accused of over-emotionalizing the gospel. His dramatic antics got people so excited, they might agree to anything, or so the critics said. But that was the whole point. Whitefield knew that the gospel broke into most people's lives through their emotions, not their minds—especially in a highly Christianized culture. People knew the Bible. They belonged to churches. They had a sense of Christian morality. What they lacked, George felt, was a transformation of the heart—and that would best happen not through logical argumentation, but through an emotional appeal. Those who hear the gospel "have more need of heat than light," he once preached. "Would to God we had as much warmth in our hearts, as light in our understandings!"[13] George knew this because it was his own story. He got it before he got it. He understood the mental concept of the new birth, and was even sharing it with others, months before he had the emotional experience of receiving it.

Strangely, George's mentors in this matter, John and Charles Wesley, trailed behind him. Both of them traced their moments of conversion to 1738, three years *after* George's, even though they were seemingly model believers long before that date. Not only did they start and lead the "Holy Club," but they also became ordained as clergy and even traveled to America as missionaries late in 1735.

On John's ocean voyage to the colony of Georgia, a fierce storm came up, and he feared for his life. But John noticed a group of Moravian Christians who remained calm through the danger, praying and singing psalms. Impressed by their faith, John struck up a friendship with them. His time in Georgia was difficult, and he came back to England in 1738 defeated and despondent. Then a Moravian friend invited him to a service, and he heard a preacher expound on Martin Luther's commentary on the apostle

Paul's letter to the Romans. In his journal, John said he went "unwillingly," but he went.

We might imagine that John Wesley did not learn anything new in that sermon. He himself had surely read Luther before, and he had studied the New Testament in its original Greek. Yet something happened that night that had never happened before. "About a quarter before nine, while he was describing the change which God works in the heart through faith in Christ, I felt my heart strangely warmed. I felt I did trust in Christ, Christ alone, for salvation; and an assurance was given me that He had taken away my sins, even mine, and saved me from the law of sin and death."[14]

Now it was personal. All of John's head knowledge had finally worked its way to his heart. The hard work of proving himself to God was finished. He was forgiven. He was accepted.

Just three days earlier, Charles Wesley experienced a similar conversion. He too had befriended some Moravian Christians, and they had been counseling him in their simple faith. "I felt a violent opposition and reluctance to believe," Charles wrote in his journal, "yet still the Spirit of God strove with my own and the evil spirit, till by degrees he chased away the darkness of my unbelief. I found myself convinced, I knew not how, nor when."[15]

Some theologians question whether these experiences were actually conversions. They were emotional moments, to be sure. They were epiphanies that brought these men closer to God—no one disputes that. But can we truly say that John and Charles Wesley, with all their personal devotion, were not *Christians* prior to these events? Some religious groups recognize these as "second blessing" experiences or "the baptism of the Holy Spirit." Perhaps that's what we have here—an attainment of a higher level of spirituality after an initial commitment to Christ. Given the amount of religious work the Wesleys did in the years before these epiphanies, wouldn't that explanation make more sense?

Yet it's pretty clear that John Wesley himself saw this as a saving moment for him. Three years later, he preached powerfully about the "almost Christian"—the person who does everything right *except* trust in Jesus:

I did go thus far for many years . . . using diligence to eschew all evil, and to have a conscience void of offence; redeeming the time; buying up every opportunity of doing all good to all men; constantly and carefully using all the public and all the private means of grace; endeavouring after a steady seriousness of behaviour, at all times, and in all places; and, God is my record, before whom I stand, doing all this in sincerity; having a real design to serve God; a hearty desire to do his will in all things; to please him who had called me to "fight the good fight," and to "lay hold of eternal life." Yet my own conscience beareth me witness in the Holy Ghost, that all this time I was but almost a Christian.[16]

Almost a Christian! By his own testimony, all John Wesley's religious work was not enough to get him into God's kingdom. Charles Wesley and George Whitefield would tell similar stories. For that matter, so would Martin Luther, whose writing was instrumental in John's conversion. It's quite appropriate that John on that fateful evening would hear a reading of Luther's commentary on Romans. Luther had grabbed the apostle's tag line "The just shall live by faith" and used it as an anchor for Reformation theology. As a monk, priest, and professor, Luther had tried to earn his way to heaven through religious works, but then he came face to face with this New Testament principle.

Even the apostle Paul had this experience. As a Pharisee, Paul had piled up plenty of good deeds before he saw the light (literally). Later he wrote about his impressive religious credentials, only to say, "these I have counted loss for Christ." He went on to use even stronger language, calling them "rubbish" (a relatively polite translation of the Greek word Paul used). Paul threw out all his religious accomplishments, he said, in order to "gain Christ and be found in Him, not having my own righteousness, which is from the law, but that which is through faith in Christ, the righteousness which is from God" (Philippians 3:7–9).

In the days of Whitefield and Franklin, many people assumed that the aim of religion was to make people behave better so they would be worthy of heaven. Many still assume that today. And that might be true for some religions, but it's not the message of New Testament Christianity, as George Whitefield and these other leaders discovered.

According to the biblical teachings of Jesus and Paul, as understood

now by George Whitefield, human beings simply cannot be good enough
for God, no matter how hard we try (and it would be difficult to imagine
anyone trying any harder than George Whitefield or his Holy Club companions). Human righteousness cannot save us. We need to be reborn. We
need God to make us new.

This was the conversion George Whitefield experienced, and it's what
he preached for the next thirty-five years. In one sermon, he acknowledged
the challenge of preaching about conversion to those who already considered themselves Christians. "Preach conversion to the drunkards," they
would say. But he realized from his own life that people could be blinded
by their own religious actions. "If we are truly converted, we shall not only
be turned and converted from sinful self, but we shall be converted from
righteous self. That is the devil of devils: for righteous self can run and hide
itself in its own doings, which is the reason self-righteous people are so
angry with gospel preachers."[17]

It's evident from George's repudiation of theater (as well as card playing and other diversions) that he had a strict moral code. Yet he made it
clear that such "holy living" was not an attempt to win God's favor, but a
reflection of the ongoing relationship with God that had already begun. A
person reborn lives differently. "There will be new principles, new ways,
new company, new works; there will be a thorough change in the heart and
life; this is conversion," he preached.[18]

George might have learned this principle in that life-changing book by
Henry Scougal, who differentiated between good deeds that are "actuated
only by external motives, driven merely by threatenings, . . . bribed by
promises, [or] constrained by laws" and the behavior of believers who are
"powerfully inclined to that which is good, and delight in the performance
of it." He went on to say:

> The love which a pious man bears to God and goodness, is not so much
> by virtue of a command enjoining him so to do, as by a new nature
> instructing and prompting him to it; nor doth he pay his devotions as an
> unavoidable tribute only to appease the divine justice, or quiet his clam-
> orous conscience; but those religious exercises are the proper emanations

of the divine life, the natural employments of the new-born soul. He prays, and gives thanks, and repents, not only because these things are commanded, but rather because he is sensible of his wants, and of the divine goodness, and of the folly and misery of a sinful life.[19]

Thus, according to Whitefield's newly adopted belief system, reborn Christians are highly motivated to live God-pleasing lives, not because they're afraid of the alternative, but because they are now "new creations."

Compare this approach to personal morality with that of Benjamin Franklin. In some ways, they're similar. Franklin kept embracing the attitudes and actions that led to what we might call "the good life," and he avoided vices that would keep him from living fully, freely, and successfully. For instance, when he worked in a London print shop as a young man, he withdrew from the beer-drinking customs of his coworkers. Not that he didn't enjoy an occasional pint, but he recognized that this would diminish his productivity at work. As he posited, "certain actions might not be bad because they were forbidden . . . [but] forbidden because they were bad for us."[20] He was not cowering in fear of a score-keeping God. He was just choosing the ways that helped to improve his life.

Similarly, Whitefield observed a strict personal morality and preached it widely, and this too was in pursuit of "the good life"—only he would define that as a life full of love for God and a desire to please him. He wasn't cowering, either, but grateful for God's grace and responding with the disciplined behavior of a "new creation."

It might have been refreshing for George to find a friend who cared about living right, yet unbound by legalistic religion. Perhaps he felt that Ben would make a really good Christian if he ever received God's gift of grace. He certainly kept trying to woo Franklin into the kingdom. And Ben kept resisting.

We can't know what transpired in Ben's soul in the later years of his life, but we know he never responded to George's calls to convert. In his autobiography, he wrote that George would sometimes "pray for my conversion, but never had the satisfaction of believing that his prayers were heard."[21]

FOURTEEN

A Better Place

Immigrants were pouring into Philadelphia, thousands each year in the 1730s. The idyllic corner of land that William Penn had bought from the Lenape less than half a century earlier was now teeming with activity, as refugees, runaways, and opportunists tried to make a new life in a new world.

As a leading printer in the colony, and now a newspaper editor, Ben Franklin had a front-row seat. His home and office were within a few blocks of the wharf where the immigrants would disembark. Would he observe them poking through the stalls set up in the middle of Market Street, buying food after their long journey? Would he smile to see them wearing layers of clothing and tucking bread under their arms, as he once did? Or would he worry that the city couldn't hold them all?

Penn's peaceable kingdom was now chaotic. Yes, many of the newcomers moved right on through the city to establish new towns north and west, but the city population was growing rapidly too, and even the outliers were still part of the Pennsylvania colony. The political structures set up in the 1701 charter were becoming obsolete, and the social structures—well, there really were no social structures. Until Ben Franklin got involved.

Nowadays we talk about some people being "joiners." They move into town and quickly sign up for the Rotary, the Town Watch, the Little League, the public library, and so on. Franklin was more than a joiner; he was a "linker." He *created* many of the organizations that other people joined—and that many are still joining today.

For instance, along with other members of the Junto, he formed a lending library. Books were expensive, especially if they had to be shipped from England, so it only made sense for a group that was highly literate but financially challenged to pool their reading material. But Ben went beyond the Junto, selling fifty memberships (subscriptions) at forty shillings each (and then ten shillings a year) to establish a fund from which they could buy new books for lending.

Forty years later, there were many such libraries throughout the colonies. Sounding strangely modern, Ben Franklin boasted in his autobiography, "This was the mother of all the North American subscription libraries now so numerous."[1]

While the Library Company was certainly a convenience to its members, it also revealed a broader vision Ben had for society. *Together,* the colonists could succeed. Many of them were rugged individualists, but they needed each other. Ben was an individualist himself. He had great sympathy for that mind-set, but he knew that teamwork was the only way to tame this new world. Flung across the ocean and landing on this spot of earth, the colonists could struggle separately or thrive collectively.

It's clear that Ben also understood the social value of knowledge. If only rich people could afford books, then the lower classes could never rise up—power would remain in the hands of a few highborn leaders. As a middle-class business owner, Ben had an interest in breaking this class system. A public library was not just an entertainment center—it was "power to the people," an early blow for democracy.

As Franklin wrote triumphantly in 1771, "These libraries have improved the general conversation of the Americans, made the common tradesmen and farmers as intelligent as most gentlemen from other countries, and perhaps have contributed in some degree to the stand so generally made throughout the colonies in defense of their privileges."[2]

Later, Franklin would create a political cartoon of a segmented snake—each segment labeled for one of the colonies. The caption read "Join or Die."

That wasn't a threat, just a political and military reality. Yet, as a young civic leader, Ben saw this as a social reality as well, which was why he kept creating structures in which people could work together for mutual benefit.

Writing under a pseudonym in the *Gazette* in 1733, Ben presented the idea of a volunteer fire company. The steady growth of the city had made it susceptible, and while there were always brave souls who jumped into action, they lacked organization and equipment. The following year, Ben published another piece on the subject, carefully nudging public opinion. The idea eventually took shape, and Franklin himself organized the Union Fire Company in 1736. Members not only kept equipment at the ready (including leather buckets), but they also met socially once a month to discuss "such ideas as occurred to us upon the subject of fires."[3]

Seventy years earlier, the Great Fire of London had nearly obliterated that great city, displacing more than 80 percent of its residents. Philadelphia was still small compared to that metropolis, but it was becoming the largest town in the American colonies, welcoming new people every day. Franklin rightly saw that wise preparation might prevent such a disaster. As he wrote in one of his pseudonymous editorials on the subject: "An ounce of prevention is worth a pound of cure."[4] Ben's idea was so popular that there were too many applicants. Additional fire companies were formed.

More than thirty years later, Ben boasted about Philadelphia's fire protection: "I question whether there is a city in the world better provided with the means of putting a stop to beginning conflagrations; and in fact since these institutions, the city has never lost by fire more than one or two houses at a time, and the flames have often been extinguished before the house in which they began has been half-consumed."[5]

But of course Ben made it more than just a safety issue. It was another opportunity for citizens to gather together to *be citizens*. It was another step in the "Join or Die" strategy. Philadelphia was becoming a world-class city because its people banded together to create a better life for them all. Franklin was in the middle of it, making things happen. He was just thirty years old when he formed the fire company. He had already established the Junto and library. All of these had spawned other similar groups around the region. In addition, Ben was proposing major upgrades of the City

Watch program, suggesting a sort of progressive tax to fund professional constables. He also pushed the legislature to adopt paper currency, which sped up the economy (and gave him a print job). He was working hard to make Philadelphia a better place.

All this time he was also publishing the town's leading newspaper, printing not only reports received from overseas but also local stories and opinion pieces on political issues. He was not only informing citizens, he was also engaging them. Edmund S. Morgan put it, "As a printer and publisher Franklin had his finger on the pulse of life in Philadelphia, and he was continually bringing companies of people together in associations to prove it."[6]

Dream Job

After George Whitefield's tumultuous conversion, his life changed rapidly. While Ben was amassing leather buckets at town meetings in Philadelphia, George was quickly becoming the toast of London. While Franklin was seeking to make the world a better place, starting in Philadelphia, Whitefield began summoning souls to a far better place, an eternity with God.

Back home in Gloucester, with a spiritual peace he had never known before, George struggled with his future direction. He clearly felt called into the ministry, but now he had second thoughts. It was his dream job, quite literally (he'd had dreams about being a preacher). It had been his mother's longing and his own planned method to restore respect to his family. He wrote later about his time at Oxford, "I entertained high thoughts of the importance of the ministerial office."[7] Yet now he was stricken with humility, a keen awareness of his own insufficiency. In fervent prayers, he begged God *not* to send him into the ministry. Friends in Gloucester were urging him to seek ordination, so he wrote to friends in Oxford, asking them to pray for the opposite.

Someone recommended him to the local bishop, who explained that he never ordained anyone so young, but in this case he would make an exception. Finally realizing that holding out any longer would mean fighting against God, George was ordained on June 20, 1736, at just twenty-one years old. He had finally given up his insecurities and yielded to God's call. "Known unto him are all future events and contingencies," he wrote to a friend on that ordination day. "I have thrown myself blindfold, and I trust without reserve, into his almighty hands."[8]

At a certain point in this time, George discovered something important: *he could preach*. He had practiced plenty during his boyhood and between errands at the inn. Now he found he was good at it. When he gathered Christian friends in Gloucester for Bible study, when they visited prisons, and when he returned to Oxford, he would speak about Scripture, and people liked it. All those quirks that had kept him from entirely fitting in at Oxford or even St. Mary's now worked to his advantage—his dramatic style, his penchant for breaking into tears, even his cross-eyed stare. All of these traits made him a delight to listen to. And now he had a message and a passion for it. Cicero was right: you had to believe what you were saying, and you had to care about it. The "passions" that the acting manuals taught about were now springing up in his soul. George Whitefield had now experienced the new birth, and he wanted to share it with everybody.

A week after his ordination, George Whitefield returned to preach at the old church where he had gone to school, St. Mary de Crypt. He spoke on "The Necessity and Benefit of Religious Society," which sounds like a snooze fest until you really get what he was saying. Using the text "Two are better than one" (Ecclesiastes 4:9), he challenged his church mates to spur one another on to greater experiences of faith, to hold one another accountable, to rejoice and weep with one another—in short, to *be* the church. It was a very Methodist message—the "Holy Club" had been a laboratory for just this sort of thing—but we also see a line of thought parallel to that of Ben Franklin, who was calling citizens to *be* citizens. "Let your practice correspond to your profession," Whitefield preached.[9] If you profess to be a Christian in this church—or a citizen in Philadelphia—live like it!

Later, George wrote to an Oxford friend about the experience of returning to his alma mater. "Curiosity, as you may easily guess, drew a large congregation together on the occasion. The sight at first a little awed me; but, I was comforted by a heart-felt sense of the divine presence, and soon found the unspeakable advantage of having been accustomed to public speaking when a boy at school, and of exhorting and teaching the prisoners."[10]

The written text of Whitefield's sermon still exists, and in it we can sense the passion he brought to this crowd. They were Christ's soldiers, he said, charged with resisting the devil's wiles. They were in danger of being Judas, who isolated himself and turned traitor.[11] In the place where he had learned drama, George now dramatized the call of God, and with great effect.

"As I proceeded I perceived the fire kindled, till at last, though so young, and amid a crowd of those who knew me in my infant, childish days, I trust I was enabled to speak with some degree of gospel authority. Some few mocked, but most, for the present, seemed struck." Even his description in the letter was dramatic. There's a "fire kindled." Hearers are "struck." He even mentioned a report that his preaching drove fifteen people mad. "The worthy prelate, as I am informed, wished that the madness might not be forgotten before next Sunday."[12]

The Big Time

Whitefield's ordination (and a short time in Oxford to finish his degree) gave him credentials to serve in a church, but not a church to serve in. He found that church less than two months later, when an old college friend asked him to fill in as preacher at the prestigious Tower Church of London.

On August 4, 1736, he took a stagecoach there, praying all the way. In his journal, he noted that only a few years earlier he would have paid a lot of money, if he'd had it, to see a play in London. Now people would be seeing him. Once again, he was fighting his long-time battle with pride. It provided some much-needed "ballast," he said, when people would see him walking down the street in his priestly garb and say, "There's a boy parson." In spite of this amazing opportunity, he was still little more than a child. In light of such humbling reminders, young George found some comfort in the apostle's words to the "boy parson" Timothy—"Let no man despise thy youth" (1 Timothy 4:12 KJV).[13]

This young preacher from Gloucester was an instant sensation. "As I went up the [pulpit] stairs almost all seemed to sneer at me on account of my youth," he wrote later, "but as I came down they showed me great tokens of respect."[14] He stayed two months in London, preaching at various venues during the week, meeting with soldiers and prisoners, but packing the Tower Church each Sunday. "His emotion was always fresh," wrote one early biographer, "streaming from his heart as from a perennial fountain; and, unless the hearer could not feel, could not be touched by tenderness or awe, he was sure to find his soul made more sensitive. The hearts of most were melted in the intense heat of the preacher's fervour like silver in a refiner's furnace."[15]

Shortly after this Tower Church experience, George felt called to go as a missionary to the American colony of Georgia. John and Charles Wesley had been serving there, and now they were sending letters to the Oxford Methodists requesting reinforcements. Whitefield felt they were talking to him—or rather, that God was talking to him through them.

Georgia was the newest of the American colonies, chartered just a few years earlier, in 1732. James Oglethorpe, a member of Parliament and social reformer, had envisioned this colony as the capstone of a policy of prison reform. His complaints about the conditions of London's debtors' prisons in the 1720s had led to the release of a substantial number of prisoners, but then these debtors were launched into an urban society with little work available, and many were resorting to crime (remember, this was the era of *The Beggar's Opera*). Oglethorpe's colonial idea was ingenious. Provide "the worthy poor" with new opportunities in the New World, keeping them out of debt, crime, and prison. Let them settle this southernmost terrain—which would then serve as a buffer region between the Carolinas and Spanish-held Florida.

From the early days of the Holy Club, the Wesleys had been visiting prisons as part of their Christian ministry, and George Whitefield eagerly joined them. So it's no surprise that Oglethorpe's grand scheme would find support with these young ministers. Charles Wesley actually served as Oglethorpe's personal secretary during his time in Georgia in 1736. When Charles returned to England that December, he fanned Whitefield's interest in the new colony.

"Georgia was an infant, and likely to be an increasing colony," George journaled, "and the government seemed to have its welfare much at heart.

I had heard many Indians were near it, and thought it a matter of great importance, that serious clergymen should be sent there." It was the perfect combination of need and opportunity, an ideal outgrowth of his prison ministry, virgin territory for the gospel, the involvement of his friends, and a potential outreach to Native Americans. George even thought that Georgia might provide a respite from his increasingly hectic schedule. "Retirement and privacy were what my soul delighted in. A voyage to sea would, in all probability, not do my constitution much hurt; nay, I had heard the sea was sometimes beneficial to weakly people."[16]

What could possibly go wrong?

All Ready but Not Yet

The next year proved to be one of the most fortuitous delays in religious history. Oglethorpe was in London, preparing to return to Georgia soon, but first he wanted to be commissioned by the king as a military officer. With rising tensions between England and Spain, and with Georgia's proximity to Spanish Florida—especially the fort at St. Augustine—Oglethorpe wanted to have the military authority necessary to lead a colonial militia. This took some time. (Eventually he was made a colonel, and in 1739 he jumped into action, leading a siege of that Spanish fort.)

But for most of 1737, George Whitefield was all prayed up with no place to go. Oglethorpe kept rescheduling his departure, and Whitefield kept waiting. As he waited, people asked him to preach, which he gladly did, and his fame grew.

For the first few months of that year he was saying his goodbyes to family and friends in Gloucester and Bristol and dazzling the hometown crowds with his preaching. "During my stay, here, I began to grow a little popular," he wrote about Gloucester. "God gave me honour for a while, even in my own country. I preached twice on the Sabbaths. Congregations were very large, and the power of God attended the Word; and some I have reason to believe were truly converted."[17]

A few weeks later, he was sitting in a church in Bristol when the minister asked him to give a sermon. Soon crowds were flocking to hear him there, and not only on Sundays. "The whole city seems to be alarmed," he wrote to his friend Gabriel Harris. "Churches are as full week days, as they use to be on Sundays, and on Sundays so full, that many, very many are obliged to go away, because they cannot come in. Oh pray, dear Mr. H., that God would always keep me humble, and fully convinced that I am nothing without him, and that all the good which is done upon earth, God doth it himself."[18]

Some offered lucrative positions to keep him in England, but his heart was set on America. As he preached, he collected offerings for the poor in Georgia, something he would continue to do all his life.

George traveled to Oxford to see old friends and then to London seeking official approval for the Georgia mission. Oglethorpe was promising to depart soon, but this dragged on some more. George had time to travel back to Bristol and Gloucester and preach some more. This little "farewell tour" was turning into a full-blown revival.

His letters from that time show a continual amazement at the work God was doing through him, but also a growing frustration with the travel delays. He seemed a bit befuddled by his emerging popularity, but he was glad that it helped him spread the gospel and raise funds for the poor in Georgia. His note of October 25 to Gabriel Harris was typical:

We sail not for Georgia this month. I suppose you have heard of my mighty deeds, falsely so called, by reading the newspapers; for I find some back-friend has published abroad my preaching four times in a day; but I beseech . . . the printer, never to put me into his news upon any such account again, for it is quite contrary to my inclinations and positive orders. GOD still works here. The collections for the charity schools, in all the churches where I preach, are very large. All London is alarmed. Many youths here sincerely love our LORD JESUS CHRIST; and thousands, I hope, are quickened, strengthened, and confirmed by the word preached. I was never in better health, and never composed more freely. O praise the LORD, dear Sir, and pray that I may not be self-sufficient but humble.[19]

Eventually he decided to travel to Georgia not with Oglethorpe, but on a soldiers' ship, which departed London in the last days of December and poked along the Thames and the Channel, waiting for favorable winds. At each port along the way, people would come to see George off. The vessel did not shove off from England until February 2, 1738.

A Fertile Year

Looking back over that year of delay and revival, we find at least four major developments in George's ministry.

First, he developed multidenominational appeal. As he wrote to a friend, "Quakers, Baptists, Presbyterians, etc. all come to hear the word preached."[20] Though ordained an Anglican and headed for America as an Anglican missionary, George would never limit his message to denominational matters. He had a simple, biblical challenge to offer: "You must be born again." This resonated with people of many different churches or no church at all. The dissenting movements in England—especially Baptists and Quakers—had long been pushing society to be less churchy and more biblical. The German Pietist movement had found support among these groups. In more recent years the Moravian missionary movement and authors such as William Law (*A Serious Call*) had been reawakening a simple faith among the English. They were ready for George Whitefield.

The Methodists were then still within the Anglican fold and would continue to be for quite some time. The Wesleys did not envision their group as a breakaway movement, but as a renewal and outreach endeavor that would strengthen the Anglican Church. Yet even in this early period, Whitefield began to encounter some opposition from Anglican clergy. Some pointedly opposed his doctrine of the new birth. Others feared that his popularity decreased attendance at their own services. Some objected to the offerings he was collecting for Georgia. Surely some were jealous. When George appealed to the bishop to see if there was any official reprimand in order, he got what amounted to a shrug. There was no problem, the bishop said, because George would be leaving the country soon.

Throughout his ministry in America and Britain, Whitefield would face opposition from churches, and often from Anglicans. He actually turned this to his advantage, flaunting his independence from any ecclesiastical organization. His message was bigger than any one church, and his crowds could not be contained in any structure.

Second, he learned to use the press. As that year of delay dragged on, George discovered the value of advertising, though he opposed it at first. "About the middle of September, my name was first put into the public newspapers," he wrote. He saw the notice while having breakfast in London. It described the offering received by this "young gentleman going volunteer to Georgia" and gave details of his next preaching gig. "This advertisement chagrined me. I immediately sent to the printer, desiring he would put me in his paper no more."[21]

Apparently someone had placed the ad in the paper and paid for it. The printer denied George's request, saying "he would not lose two shillings for anybody." Always fearful of his own pride, and also of the danger of *seeming* proud, George naturally had a bad feeling about self-puffery. But this was out of his hands, and so he could step back and examine the results. He noted that, through advertising, "people's curiosity was stirred up more and more." The event mentioned in the ad "was crowded exceedingly. . . . Henceforward, for near three months successively, there was no end of the people flocking to hear the Word of God."[22]

These were not the first sermons to be advertised in newspapers, but we can safely say that, as time went on, Whitefield would use advertising more effectively than any preacher before him and most preachers since. He was helped by William Seward, a London stockbroker who became sort of a business manager for Whitefield. (It was Seward who placed that ad George saw over breakfast.) "Typical ecclesiastical entries in the [London] *Daily Advertiser* announced sermons by presenting the bare essentials: who was to preach, for what charity, in which church, and at what time. . . . By contrast, Seward 'sold' Whitefield to the readers, complete with advertising 'puffs,' appealing details designed to pique interest."[23]

If you view advertising as proud and/or deceptive, you'll have a problem with this—as George did at first. But clearly he began to see the advantage of getting the word out to the public, so he could get the Word out to the public, and he became a pioneer in these methods. In America, Ben Franklin and his *Pennsylvania Gazette* would help him do that.

Third, he became a published author. As George's fame grew during this year, he received many requests for printed copies of his sermons. While, again, he was wary of self-promotion, he saw that this created much more of an audience for his message. London publisher James Hutton printed an early collection of George's texts. This was a role Ben Franklin would assume in America—despite the fact that he thought George would have been better off without a printed record of his sermons. "His writing and printing from time to time gave great advantage to his enemies. Unguarded expressions and even erroneous opinions delivered in preaching might have been afterwards explained, or qualified . . . or . . . denied." But the written record remained, giving George's critics plenty of ammunition. "I am of opinion," Ben wrote, "if he had never written anything he would have left behind him a much more numerous and important sect."[24]

It's a fascinating observation, offered long after the fact by a man who made lots of money publishing those very sermons. Though Ben was no theologian, he recognized that George was not a careful scholar, as other respected clergymen were (such as their contemporary Jonathan Edwards). George's power came not from the brilliance of his thinking but from the compelling manner of his delivery—and perhaps from the simplicity of his message. That in itself might reveal a big difference between Ben and George. While Ben coveted (and received) the acclaim of the intelligentsia in various fields, George unapologetically stuck to his simple message of rebirth. Printing his messages would certainly fuel the critics who wanted more cerebral substance, but it would also spread that simple message to thousands who couldn't hear him in person. Ben was probably right. Today, George lacks the respect given to, say, Jonathan Edwards, whose writings are much weightier. He left behind no Whitefieldist sect. And yet, it's no stretch to say George is a spiritual forefather of just about everyone in the English-speaking world who claims to be "born again" in Jesus.

Fourth, he discovered the power of extemporaneous preaching. He had previously learned to craft a sermon, to write it out, and to read it dramatically. This is how good preaching was done in Anglican churches of the time. But John Wesley had accidentally discovered extemporaneous preaching one day in 1735 when he forgot his notes, and he had been using that method well. For George, the discovery occurred December 29, 1737. So often was he invited to speak that he usually carried notes with him. On this occasion, however, in the little town of Deptford, near London, he had forgotten. Still, he agreed to preach, fearfully at first, but then "without the least hesitation."[25] This style of preaching unleashed his power as a communicator, allowing him full use of his theatrical mannerisms. This in turn made him the most popular preacher of his generation.

FIFTEEN

Doppelgängers

When Ben Franklin began running the Philadelphia print shop of Samuel Keimer in the late 1720s, one of the workers was a young man named George, at eighteen only a few years younger than Ben. Like many others in colonial America, this George had recently come from England. He held the job of compositor, placing the letters properly in the printing frame.

It was an "odd thing," Ben noted, that George was both an Oxford scholar and an indentured servant.[1] He would expect an Oxford education to lead to a comfortable life, but this was not the case with the young print shop laborer, George Webb.

The commonalities between this George and the other George—Whitefield, whom Ben would befriend more than a decade later—are startling.

Webb had grown up in Gloucester and attended a grammar school there. We're dependent on Ben's memory here—he wrote about Webb in his autobiography—and he didn't offer the name of the school, but if it was St. Mary de Crypt, Webb would have been there about five years before Whitefield.

In addition, Webb "had been distinguished among the scholars for some apparent superiority in performing his part when they exhibited plays." We know that Whitefield was instructed by a theater teacher who even wrote new dramatic pieces for his students. This suggests that St. Mary's had an exceptional theater program, something that George Webb might have benefited from.

In another detail that's more Franklinesque, George Webb was also a gifted writer, belonging to the "Witty Club" at school and writing some verses for the Gloucester newspapers.

Webb then attended Oxford for a year, but he longed for the actor's life in the big city. He walked away from school—literally—stashing his scholar's gown in a bush and footing it to London. But the acting career never materialized. Webb "fell in with bad company, soon spent his guineas . . . pawned his clothes and wanted bread." Roaming the streets in this condition, he saw a handbill offering "immediate entertainment and encouragement" to those who would "bind themselves to serve in America." Desperate, he signed his life away—or at least several years of it—as an indentured servant. After the ship landed in Philadelphia, the printer Samuel Keimer bought Webb's four-year contract and put him to work.

This was the way business was done. Ben's written account shows no criticism of the system of indentured servitude. He himself had been indentured to his brother and had escaped that servitude. The skills he learned as an indentured apprentice had helped him rise to a leadership position and would soon lead to an ownership position. Maybe the same would happen to Webb.

Webb's story, as remembered by Franklin, was a cautionary tale. In many ways, it was the reverse of Ben's own story—not rags to riches, but riches to rags. Webb had made some bad decisions and was paying the price—namely, a price of four years. Ben described Webb as "lively, witty, good-natured and a pleasant companion, but idle, thoughtless, and imprudent to the last degree." We can see here a shadow of Ben's old friend James Ralph, who also failed to launch an acting career, who was also both witty and imprudent, and who might also have fallen into ruin in London if it weren't for Ben's support.

Ben appears drawn to thoughtless thinkers: to lively, witty, good-natured, and pleasant companions who also turn out to be imprudent. Ben suffered much from these relationships, but by the time he wrote about Webb he might have begun to learn caution.

When Ben pulled together the Junto, he included George Webb among a few other print shop workers. Networking for professional advancement, the Junto was a great group for an intelligent young compositor trying to make a new start—all the more so when a friend bought out Webb's contract, releasing him from servitude. Maybe the riches-to-rags story could have a third act, back to riches.

After Ben started his own business, Webb came looking for a job. There was nothing available at the time, Ben said, but he confided in his old colleague that he might be starting a newspaper soon, and then there would be more work available. It sounds as if Ben even shared some elements of his business plan with Webb, in strict confidence, of course.

That trust was broken when Webb shared those plans with their old boss, Samuel Keimer, who rushed into print with his own poorly published periodical, employing Webb in the task. This in turn launched an intricate strategy of revenge on Franklin's part, driving Keimer's paper out of business and then resurrecting it himself.

Franklin said he "resented" Webb's betrayal. It's not clear whether Webb was trying to hurt Ben (for not hiring him) or just scrambling to find work for himself (and acting imprudently to do so). Perhaps Webb saw it as "just business." That might explain Ben's business-like response: not verbal vitriol but calculated actions driving Keimer—and his new hire—to ruin.[2]

Apparently Webb landed on his feet. In the following years there was a George Webb working as a printer in Virginia and South Carolina, and there's evidence he might have returned to England later.[3]

Ben refused to hold a grudge. In 1731, he printed a poem by George Webb in pamphlet form. "Batchelor's Hall" celebrated the building of a new meeting place in north Philadelphia near the Delaware River. "But chiefly that proud Dome on Del'ware's stream," Webb wrote. "Of this my humble song, the nobler theme."[4] By all accounts, Franklin's artistic design of the pamphlet exceeded the poetic value of Webb's verse. Some think that Webb was part of a new Junto-like group that met at Batchelor's Hall—along with Franklin. So was the printing of this poem a peace offering, a way of supporting an old colleague again after a spat? Perhaps it was a fond fare-well gift, as Webb left for a new job in South Carolina. Or maybe, with his excessive efforts in printing this mediocre poem, Ben was launching a final passive-aggressive cannon shot at a fickle former friend. *Look what I could have done for you, if you had just remained loyal.*

This is not to suggest that Ben carried over any animosity or regret from Webb to Whitefield. Yet it's reasonable to think that he made a con-nection between the two Georges—at least growing up in the same town, possibly going to the same school, and studying drama there. Whitefield had made very different decisions, and he came to Franklin in 1739 at a very different point in life. He didn't need a mentor or patron, as Webb did, but a teammate in an already successful enterprise.

Still, we must recognize that Ben had been dazzled before by glib-talking would-be actors—and hurt by them. James Ralph, George Webb, and now—would George Whitefield be any different? Business was one thing. Ben had shown that he could do business with anybody. But would he ever let this new George W. be his friend? That might be a challenge.

The Hemphill Affair

Five years before George Whitefield came to town, another preacher showed up in Philadelphia and captured Ben Franklin's interest.

Ben had married into a family of loyal Anglicans, and thus the Franklins were members of Christ Church on Second Street. But as we've seen, Ben was a maverick in religious matters. In Ben's amalgamated faith, there was still a deep appreciation for the moral discipline of the Puritans he had grown up with. Presbyterians were now the main guardians of Puritan teaching, and so Ben connected with the First Presbyterian Church at Bank and Market, even donating money there. Jedediah Andrews, the long-time senior minister there, sometimes visited Ben and invited him to services. In his autobiography, Ben boasted that he did, in fact, hear Andrews preach occasionally—at one point, even five Sundays in a row! "Had he been, in my opinion, a good preacher, perhaps I might have continued." These sermons seemed "very dry, uninteresting, and unedifying, since not a single moral principle was inculcated or enforced." Ben concluded that the aim of this service was to make people Presbyterians rather than "good citizens."[5]

This in itself provides fascinating insight into Ben's personal beliefs. The proper "aim" of a church, as he saw it, was to help people become better citizens, providing moral instruction and encouragement to do so.

Then a new assistant arrived from Ireland and began to preach at First Presbyterian. Samuel Hemphill "delivered with a good voice, and apparently extempore, most excellent discourses," Franklin wrote. His preaching attracted people of many different denominations, since it was not "the dogmatical kind, but inculcated strongly the practice of virtue."[6]

Of course Franklin loved it. It was the best of Ben's Puritan background without any of that disagreeable theology. But others in the church opposed Hemphill, including the senior minister. In a letter to a colleague, Jedediah Andrews complained about Hemphill's broad popularity: "free thinkers, Deists, and nothings, getting a scent of him, flocked to him."[7]

Ultimately the opponents hauled Hemphill before a church synod, accusing him of heresy. There were numerous problems with this Irish assistant and his teachings. Most prevalent was the fear that he was squeezing out of Christianity everything that made it, well, Christian. Pursuing some modern rationality, Hemphill seemed to deny the power of the blood of Christ, the Spirit of God, and the Lord's Supper. According to him, Jesus was a model of sacrificial behavior, a teacher of morals. Hemphill's preaching was popular, the critics charged, because it was the spirit of the age. It just wasn't biblical. It certainly wasn't Presbyterian.

The trial began on April 17, 1735, and lasted ten days without a ruling. The synod met again that September to consider the case some more. In the midst of the controversy, Ben Franklin entered the fray. Considering Hemphill a better speaker than writer, Franklin penned several pieces on his behalf, including a mock dialogue he published in the *Gazette* between two unnamed Presbyterians on opposite sides of the Hemphill affair. This dialogue was classic Franklin—winsome, smart but accessible, and seemingly fair-minded while making a strong case on one side. And anonymous.

The pro-Hemphill character in this imaginary conversation

acknowledges that Scripture calls for faith, but only "as a means of producing morality." It was moral behavior that would produce salvation. "Our Saviour was a teacher of morality or virtue," he said, adding that people needed to "*believe* in him as an able and faithful teacher." The idea that salvation could result from faith alone "appears to me to be neither a Christian doctrine nor a reasonable one."[8]

Franklin's affable style made this exchange very persuasive. But he was still dead wrong. It is certainly a "Christian doctrine" that we are saved by faith alone and not by our deeds. A major theme of the apostle Paul in the epistles to the Romans and Galatians (and elsewhere), salvation by faith alone was a rallying cry of the Protestant Reformation. You can surely debate how "reasonable" this doctrine is—Saint Paul himself acknowledged that the gospel seemed like foolishness to the world (1 Corinthians 1:23)—but it is eminently "Christian." And Presbyterians, grounded in the Reformation theology of Luther and especially Calvin, had good reason to stand up for the principle of *sola fide*—faith alone.

Ben overreached here, inserting himself in an ecclesiastical struggle where he had no business. His writings on the Hemphill affair show an impressive knowledge of the Bible, as well as a facility with philosophy and a sweet Socratic style, but this was a case where diehard Presbyterians had to decide what it meant to be Presbyterian.

Ben might argue that he had every right to enter this debate because he attended and supported Hemphill's church, but his interest in the case was actually much broader. Nowadays we assume that religion and society in general are completely separate spheres of life. *Keep improving society, Ben, but since you're not really a church guy, it's best to stay out of church business.* Yet there was no such division recognized in that time. In the Puritan Boston where Ben grew up, the church *was* the society. Yes, the church had steadily eased its grip on society, but there was still a powerful connection, and Ben understood this. In his ongoing efforts to create a good society, it made perfect sense to fight for the right of a Presbyterian preacher to flout church rules and promote social morality.

And there was a greater passion at work in Ben Franklin. Remember that he was always inventing things. He kept tinkering with religion, trying to create a belief system that really worked. At the time of the Hemphill affair, he hadn't even turned thirty yet, but he had already written philosophical treatises, created lists of virtues, and committed himself to self-improvement. Puritanism was present in all those inventions—he was either fighting against it or trying to improve it or both. In general, he loved its work ethic but hated its rigid theology.[9] If only he could combine the free thinking of, say, the deists with a Puritan sense of personal responsibility, that might be the perfect faith.

That's pretty much what Samuel Hemphill was preaching.

So this wasn't just a social issue for Ben Franklin. It was his Holy Grail. If he could sway some readers, change the tone, and help the Presbyterians step into the eighteenth century, he might just have the religion he had always been looking for.

It didn't work. In September 1735, the synod stripped Samuel Hemphill of his duties, finding him "unqualified for any future exercise of his ministry."[10] He returned quietly to Ireland.

About two years later, in the London papers he regularly drew from, Ben Franklin would begin reading about another newfangled preacher, George Whitefield. In another year, he would start including news items about Whitefield in the *Gazette*. A year after that, he would meet George and begin publishing his work. He would also fill his newspaper with letters and articles about this hot new preacher, expressing opinions for and against. Controversy always sold papers.

But was there anything in the Hemphill affair that paved the way for the relationship Ben had with George Whitefield?

There were similarities. Ben describes them both with good voices, speaking extemporaneously and engagingly. It appears that Ben liked them both personally. Both preachers found an audience among those who didn't usually go to church—the "nothings," as Jedediah Andrews described them. Both cared little for denominational traditions and openly challenged expectations. As a result, both faced strong opposition from the church establishment. Ben thought both of them should stick to preaching and avoid writing, so as not to provide easy ammunition to the enemy. (Ben might have learned this from Hemphill and applied it to Whitefield.)

Yet the two preachers stand opposite each other in what might be the most important factor—the content of their preaching. For Hemphill, morality was the goal and Jesus was a teacher of virtue. Whitefield urged his hearers to respond to God's call in faith; good works would be the by-product of a new life in Christ. This was no fine point of distinction. It was the very essence of the message delivered by each of them.

Ben must have recognized this difference eventually. But it's possible that, in those early reports and interactions with Whitefield, he saw a hint of his old pal Hemphill.

SIXTEEN

Georgia on My Mind

George Whitefield finally found his ride to Georgia. One might say he was also finding himself. This first journey to America was another stage in a significant gestational process for him. We can see the five-year period of 1735 to 1739—from just before his conversion experience to his arrival in Philadelphia—forging his adult identity.

This was the boy who was steered toward the Anglican priesthood before he had much idea of what that meant. Young George carried the weight of his family's fortunes—as a minister, he would restore their good name. He grew up as prodigy and prankster, overindulged in religious asceticism, and was now preaching to enthusiastic crowds, but who was he really? Struggler, servant, speaker, saint? At this point, he was prepared to find his life's meaning as a missionary.

On board the ship, George volunteered his services as a chaplain. The captain, crew, and a large group of soldiers were now his congregation. Determined to convert them to Christ, he held daily services for prayer and preaching.

On this trip, Whitefield began keeping his journal, with daily reports of his meetings and preachings. Some entries are dry, others wonderfully detailed. He reported how he preached against swearing or drunkenness, or how he traded some books for someone's playing cards, which he promptly threw overboard. Then he said he was "delighted with seeing the porpoises roll about the great deep," and he quoted a nature psalm.[1]

In other entries, he described the storms or calms encountered on the way:

> The waves broke in like a great river on many of the poor soldiers, who lay near the main hatchway. . . . I arose and called upon God for myself and those who sailed with me, absent friends, and all mankind. . . . the waves rose mountain high. . . . Then creeping on my knees (for I knew not how to go otherwise), I followed my friend H[abersham] between decks, and sang Psalms and comforted the poor wet people. After this, I read prayers in the great cabin. . . . Though things were tumbling, the ship rocking, and persons falling down unable to stand, and sick about me, I never was more cheerful in my life.[2]

Some of this prose recalls the shipwreck story of the apostle Paul in Acts 27, and this might have been intentional. George was living out an apostolic adventure, and he knew it. Like the journals of John and Charles Wesley, these entries were sent to friends in England, who had them published. They sold well.

But there's another key feature of these journal entries. Amid the adventures and the preaching, George routinely visited the sick—and there were many who fell sick aboard this vessel, including Whitefield himself, for a time. It's likely that this was the activity that won the hearts of the soldiers and sailors. We could imagine that these hard-living souls wouldn't take kindly to a fancy preacher who chided them for their salty language, but when he came to their sickbeds, bringing food and water, cleaning up after them, and offering comfort—that might have made a difference. This sense of service set a tone for George's whole Georgia mission. And there is some irony in the thought that perhaps his best preparation for this mission was not the Oxford degree or the Holy Club or even the practice preaching, but his work as servitor for ungrateful rich kids, or just helping out at his mother's inn.

On May 17, 1738, with the ship anchored at Savannah, Georgia,

Whitefield preached a farewell sermon to his fellow travelers. It was gracious, humble, and heartfelt. He had seen "some marks of partial transformation" among them. "Swearing, I hope, is in a great measure abated with you."[3]

But George wasn't just concerned with their outward behavior. He called them to a new awareness of God that would affect every aspect of their lives. Acknowledging that it was "uncommon" to see a "devout sailor," he wondered why that would be so—especially when sailors live on the brink of death. "Remember the resolutions you made when you thought God was about to take away your souls," he challenged them, "and see that, according to your promises, you show forth your thankfulness, not only with your lips, but in your lives."[4]

Cleaning Up

Georgia was a mess. Much of it was swampland. Travel was often along creeks, by boat. And there were alligators.

The good-hearted experiment of James Oglethorpe had plenty of challenges: offering a new life in a new world to those who couldn't pay their debts in the old world; dropping a colony in tribal territory with Spanish troops at the doorstep; trying to create a functioning economy with little connection to the rest of the American colonies. That's not to say it was a failure. It was just difficult. Whitefield kept calling Georgia an "infant," and it was indeed going through growing pains.[5] Remember: it had been a scant six years since this colony had begun. Now new adventurers were showing up all the time—not just from the debtors' prisons of London but also from Scotland, Ireland, Germany, and France. They stirred together a rich gumbo of cultures, languages, and religions.

The Wesleys had done more harm than good for the Methodist cause in Georgia. As Oglethorpe's secretary, Charles had just seemed to be overwhelmed by the conditions in the backwoods colony. He was a poet, not a pioneer. He had left Georgia in late 1736.

John had stayed longer, making a number of enemies along the way. His rigid insistence on his own Methodist ways of worship did not succeed in the variegated religious landscape of the new colony. He also fell madly in love with the wrong woman, a much younger daughter of a leading citizen. She was not so interested in him. His unwise wooing resulted in charges brought against him—and the colonial kangaroo court tacked on a number of complaints about how he pastored the parish. After trying to respond to the charges, John ultimately fled prosecution, literally hiking through the swamps before dawn to evade constables and get to the coast to catch a boat to England.

This was the situation George Whitefield entered. Welcome to Georgia.

As we chart George's learning curve, we can add a few more bits of wisdom that would affect his ministry in the years to come. First, *any successful work in America would have to recognize a much broader religious background.* England had its Anglicans and a few groups of Dissenters, and the Methodist movement was sort of bridging that gap, but America had a larger menu of faith traditions. How could someone effectively minister to all of them? Eventually George would proclaim a message that could be embraced by those in many different denominations. This strategy might have begun in the Georgian gumbo.

A second bit of wisdom came from *John Wesley's sad infatuation.* We have no indication that George was smitten with anyone yet, but this would happen later, and George would be extremely cautious about it. As he experienced the fallout of Wesley's bad romantic decisions in Georgia, he might have determined never to let courtship derail a ministry.

A third point of growth for Whitefield in this time would be his *growing independence from John Wesley.* Remember that John was a mentor, more than a decade older, a "big brother" not only to Charles but to the whole Holy Club. But John was already in America when George had experienced his emotional conversion. George had processed that mostly on his own, without John's guidance. In the Wesleys' absence, George had taken a leading role among the Oxford Methodists, and he had attained a level of fame far beyond John's. Yet he was now beginning a ministry in Georgia largely because John had asked him to come there. There is no doubt that he highly respected John and valued his wisdom—which makes this next story all the more remarkable.

When John Wesley fled Georgia, he took a ship that landed him in England, putting in at the seaport town of Deal in the early days of February 1738. By chance (if anything is "by chance"), Whitefield's ship was still docked there, waiting for favorable weather to begin its ocean journey. Wesley sent a quick message to his old friend, saying that Whitefield should not proceed to Georgia. John had sought the Lord's guidance on this matter, and this was the answer he got.

Of course George was stunned. As he explained it later, "Here was a good man telling me . . . that God would have me return to London. On the other hand, I knew that my call was to Georgia."[6] He prayed with a friend about this, and they read a strange story in 1 Kings 13, in which God tells a prophet, "You shall not . . . return by going the way you came" (v. 17). This was the confirmation George needed. He would not return to London but sail on to America.

Then imagine how George must have felt when he reached Savannah and learned of the mess that John had left there. This did not ruin the relationship between these two men (though it would be broken later), yet it might have reminded George that he was not a disciple of John Wesley, but of Jesus. He would not be trying to do the will of John Wesley in Savannah, but the will of God. And even the so-called Methodist doctrine that he was developing would not need to be vetted by John Wesley. It was the Lord's message, and George Whitefield would speak as the Lord instructed.

Cords of Love

After the huge delay in getting there, Whitefield spent only three months in Georgia in 1738. The tone of his ministry there was very different from John Wesley's. Perhaps he learned to avoid the mistakes of his predecessor—though his journal praised Wesley and complimented his work. George spent much of his time visiting the people of the Savannah area, listening to them, overcoming barriers of language and culture to show them compassion.

"I have endeavoured to let my gentleness be known amongst them," he journaled, "because they consist of different nations and opinions; and I have striven to draw them by the cords of love, because the obedience resulting from that principle I take to be most genuine and lasting."[7] George saw people trying to build a society in a wilderness, and his heart went out to them. He recognized that it would do little good to try shaming them out of their unholy behavior. The only "genuine and lasting" obedience to the call of God would come from a response of love to a God who loved them, as demonstrated by a loving minister. Yes, he warned a young Native American about the dangers of drinking, but he also sat quietly with that boy's ailing uncle, who knew no English. With the money he had raised in England, George provided food and medicine to the neediest people in the colony. He also set up schools.

This emphasis on love represents a sea change in Methodist ministry. This is not to say that the Holy Club was unloving. They were known for charitable deeds in their community—visiting the sick and prisoners, for example—but by their own accounts, they were lacking a certain spiritual passion. They were striving for holiness and obedience and urging others to follow, but there was a crucial motivational component lacking. It's not an oversimplification to call this component *love*—the love of God that woos human souls, the love for God that compels his ministers, and the loving response of their hearers.

John Wesley had served in Georgia before the conversion experience that changed his life. He had urged the locals to get serious about following God, and he chided them for their failure to live God's way. Whatever obedience Wesley could muster from them was apparently not "genuine and lasting," in George's analysis.

When Whitefield arrived in the second shift of Methodist ministry in Georgia, he had already had his conversion. The love of God had awakened his soul, bringing meaning and power to his search for holiness. He had been preaching about the new birth, but it seems he was still figuring out how that worked. In his year of preaching in England, he had continued to rail against the various vices that were keeping so-called Christians from communing with God. He knew that giving up card playing and theater going would not win entry into God's kingdom, yet this was the fruit of repentance. Holy living went along with the new birth. Without worldly distractions, a person could hear and respond to God's call.

Yet Georgia had a whole new audience. George could not assume that they had any Christian background. In fact, he encountered a number of different religious traditions. This had tripped Wesley up. How can you scold people for not being serious about their faith when you don't know what their faith is? When all your assumptions are shattered, where do you start? You start, Whitefield decided, with love.

This transformed George's ministry—and his attitude. In a report quite different than those John Wesley had sent back, George wrote to a friend in England, "All things have happened better than expectation. America is not so horrid a place as it is represented to be. The heat of the weather, lying on the ground, etc. are mere painted lions in the way, and to a soul filled with divine love not worth mentioning."[8]

Note that, in these same weeks that George Whitefield was learning to practice the principle of love in his ministry, John and Charles Wesley were both back in England, opening up to God's love. It was May 24, 1738 when John Wesley stepped into a London meetinghouse and felt his heart "strangely warmed." Charles had experienced something similar a few days earlier. The ministries of George, John, Charles, and their associates would be forever changed by this principle of love. They would never give up their commitment to holiness, but their service would be propelled by love.

For the Children

About two weeks into his stay in Georgia, George began focusing on an idea that would dominate the rest of his life. As he visited the people of Georgia, he "also enquired into the state of their children, and found there were many who might prove useful members of the colony, if there was a proper place provided for their maintenance and education. Nothing can effect this but an Orphan House, which might easily be erected at Savannah." Here, in the genesis of the idea, there's not only a sense of charity, but of empowerment. This would not just be a poorhouse, getting undesirables off the streets, but a place of education, preparing children to be "useful members of the colony." Even then he recognized that it would require contributions from "some of those who are rich in this world's good."[9]

George had already proven himself as a successful fund-raiser. In less than a year of preaching throughout England, he had used his oratorical gifts to gather thirteen hundred pounds for the vague cause of "Georgia's poor."[10] Imagine how people would respond to a specific project such as an orphan house! In a way, such an endeavor would provide legitimacy to George's preaching. That's not to say there was anything illegitimate about evangelism. George knew he was doing God's work, calling souls into the kingdom, but an orphanage would be a tangible outcome of this ministry. If God could use George's speaking skill to melt the hearts of those who were "rich in this world's good" enough to part with some of those goods and help some children, that would be a lasting testimony.

Ben Franklin testified about George's unique ability to tug at heartstrings and elicit contributions. Once, as George brought his preaching tour through Philadelphia, Ben attended one of his meetings. Knowing that George would finish by taking up a collection, Ben said, "I silently resolved he should get nothing from me." In his pockets, Ben had "a handful of copper money, three or four silver dollars, and five pistoles in gold." You can probably guess what happened next.

"As he proceeded I began to soften, and concluded to give the coppers. Another stroke of his oratory made me ashamed of that, and determined me to give the silver; and he finished so admirably, that I emptied my pocket wholly into the collector's dish, gold and all."[11]

At that time George was, of course, raising funds for this Savannah orphanage project. And while this story could be one of Ben's fabrications, it might also be a delightful retelling of actual events in April 1740, when Ben reported in the *Pennsylvania Gazette*: "On Sunday last the Reverend Mr. Whitefield preached two sermons on Society Hill, and collected for the orphans in Georgia . . . about £150 Sterling, besides sundry benefactions sent in since."[12]

Clearly George had a persuasive gift, which he had been using both to win souls and to inspire charity. He would continue to do both. Over the years, as thousands responded to Whitefield's preaching and received new birth in Christ, there would always be naysayers. Some would claim the preacher was just whipping up a temporary emotional fervor and that people would just settle back into their old lives. But the orphanage would stand as a very tangible result of God's work through him.

"Pure and undefiled religion before God and the Father is this," the Bible says, "to visit orphans and widows in their trouble, and to keep oneself unspotted from the world" (James 1:27). Jesus urged his people to care for "the least of these" (Matthew 25:40). The neediest members of society and orphans would certainly fit that category. The Methodists' spiritual forebears, the German Pietists, had already established an orphanage in Halle. They realized they couldn't just talk about communing with God; they had to act in accordance with God's desires. So they set up an orphanage, with a school, in 1695, and it became a centerpiece of their spiritual movement. Perhaps a similar thing could happen in Savannah.

As George left Georgia in late August 1738, the orphanage was still just a dream, but he was committed to make it a reality. "What I have most at heart," he wrote to a friend, "is the building of an orphan-house, which I trust will be effected at my return to England."[13]

Field Day

Back in England in December 1738, George picked up his preaching ministry where he left off, visiting various churches and consistently drawing crowds. But something had changed. Opposition to his work had grown, especially among the clergy.

While he'd been away, the early installments of his journals had been published and distributed in England. As a result, all sorts of feelings for him and against him had intensified, even in his absence, and he had no opportunity to mollify his critics or rein in his fans. He now returned to a highly charged environment. Pamphlets ripped his preaching style as too dramatic and exposed the so-called errors in his theology. His fame had increased, so he was drawing even greater crowds, but more and more churches were being closed to him.

George's main task now was to get approval and funding for the orphan house in Savannah. To that end, he needed another level of ordination. He had already been ordained a deacon of the Church of England, and that equipped him for certain ministries. But now he needed to be fully recognized as an Anglican priest. That would allow him to preach in any Anglican church in support of his new charity. That was the plan, anyway. In order to receive this ordination, he needed a "living"—that is, a church in which to serve, or perhaps an appointment as a missionary.

As it turned out, the trustees of the Georgia colony approved Whitefield's orphanage idea. This, then, became his living, with the somewhat grudging approval of the archbishop of Canterbury and the bishop of London. (According to one early biographer, they received him "civilly" but "coldly."[14]) George was fully ordained by his old friend, the bishop of Bristol. "And now my prayer is answered," he wrote to a friend.[15]

Yet controversy continued to swirl around him. Though he was officially permitted to speak in any church about his orphanage, many church leaders opposed him, and others were pressured to turn him away. Some of this opposition was based on misunderstandings and slander, but much of it just came from a basic disagreement with Whitefield's message. The idea of a "new birth" rankled many church leaders. Was George really saying that all their loyal church members needed some sort of personal spiritual experience? They were already good people. Why would they need to become "new creatures"? That might be necessary for those of other cultures, or those who had wasted their lives in debauchery, but church people were just fine. How dare this preacher suggest they were missing something! A message like Whitefield's could tear a church apart.

As more and more churches denied him access, George turned this to his advantage. About a year earlier, he had struck up a correspondence with a Welsh preacher named Howell Harris. A maverick himself, Harris had specialized in holding outdoor services, in the countryside of Wales. Whitefield began to think that this option would work for him.

He began to preach in the open. His brother let him use a field near the old Bell Inn. People in one community gathered on the town's bowling green to hear him. There, he stood on a table in his ministerial gown. Some of his critics sneered that this was "unconsecrated ground," but George didn't care. The more resistance he faced, the clearer his message became.

In one journal entry, he mentioned a sermon he preached on the parable of the Pharisee and the publican (Luke 18:9–14). As Jesus' story went, the religious leader and the smarmy tax collector both offered their prayers in the temple. The Pharisee was full of self-congratulation and disdain for the sinner beside him. The publican knew he was a sinner and begged God for mercy. This could have been a portrait of English society. "I was very earnest in endeavouring to convince the self-righteous Pharisees of this generation," George journaled, "and offering Jesus Christ freely to all, who, with the humble publican, feelingly and experimentally could cry out, 'God be merciful to me a sinner.'"[16]

Venturing outside church walls, he was finding more and more "publicans" to preach to—those who were sinners and knew it, who had long since given up any hope of impressing God with their behavior. In the familiar area of Bristol, George found such people in the coal mines. "The colliers [miners], he had heard, were very rude, and very numerous; so uncultivated, that nobody cared to go among them; neither had they any place of worship; and often, when provoked, they were a terror to the whole city of Bristol." So wrote John Gillies, George's friend and early biographer. Considering it "a matter of great importance" to bring them "to the profession and practice of Christianity," George stood on a hill near the mines and began preaching about being "poor in spirit." About a hundred miners came to hear him, then more, and eventually an estimated twenty thousand. Gillies exulted in more than just numbers: "But with what gladness and eagerness many of these despised outcasts, who had never been in a church in their lives, received the word, is above description."

The biographer quoted Whitefield himself: "Having . . . no righteousness of their own to renounce, they were glad to hear of a Jesus who was a friend to publicans, and came not to call the righteous, but sinners, to repentance." George said he knew he was getting through when he saw "the white gutters made by their tears, which plentifully fell down their black cheeks, as they came out of their coal pits. Hundreds and hundreds of them were soon brought under deep convictions, which . . . happily ended in a sound and thorough conversion."[17]

George had a message of redemption for everyone, and if the churches didn't want it, he would find those who did. He continued this strategy as he preached in America. In August 1739, it was time to leave England once more. He was headed for Georgia again, but first he would check in at the heart of the American colonies, Philadelphia.

SEVENTEEN

Face to Face

"The Reverend Mr. Whitefield preached to about 10,000 people, at Kensington Common. This day he is to preach at Wapping Chapel for the benefit of the Orphan House in Georgia."[1]

So wrote Ben Franklin in the *Pennsylvania Gazette* a year before he met this preacher. Clearly he was aware, at least vaguely, of Whitefield's ministry and his growing fame. Ben scanned the London papers for news from the old country and printed what seemed interesting to his readers. Like any good newsman, he would have kept an eye out for "Man Bites Dog" stories—tales of the unexpected and twists on familiar themes. Ben might have been bemused by the thought of a preacher drawing crowds not in churches, but in open fields. Or maybe he just needed to fill three lines on page one.

On November 8, 1739, Ben printed this news item: "Last week the Rev. Mr. Whitefield landed from London at Lewes-Town in Sussex County, where he preached, and arrived in this city on Friday night, on Sunday, and every day since he has preached in the church. And on Monday he designs (God willing) to set out for New York, and return hither the week after, and then proceed by land through Maryland, Virginia and Carolina to Georgia."[2]

Ben's dates agreed with George's journal. He arrived in Philadelphia on Friday, November 3, and quickly rented a room downtown, within a block or two of Ben Franklin's printing office. He had in fact preached at Christ Church, as Ben reported, in the days since his arrival. It was the evening of Thursday, November 8 (the day the paper came out), when he began preaching from the Courthouse steps, drawing larger crowds than ever. This continued on Friday and Saturday nights.

That same November 8 issue of the *Pennsylvania Gazette* carried a for-sale ad:

> To be sold, at the house of the Rev. Mr. Whitefield, in Second-Street (the same in which Capt. Blair, lately dwelt) the following goods: being the benefactions of charitable people In England, towards building an orphan-house in Georgia:
>
> Brass Candlesticks, Snuffers and snuff-Dishes, four, six, eight, ten and twenty-penny Nails, Pidgeon, Duck and Goose Shot, bar Lead, Pistol Powder in quarter and half Barrels, English Duck Numb. 1, 2, 3, and 4, English Cordage, Ratling, Worming, Marline and Spun-yarn, Ruggs and Blankets, Duffills strip'd, Drills for Bed-sacking, seven eighths and three quarter Garlix, white Roles, white Hessins, Russia Hempen Ditto; narrow Lawns, Scotch Cloth, cotton Romalls, Seirsuckers, white Dimities, Carradaries, Cherconees, long Romalls, colour'd Ginghams with Trimings, Gorgoroons black, black Persian Taffities, strip'd Linseys, Swanskin Bays, broad Cloth, Shalloons, long Ells, Buttons, Buckrams, and sewing-Silk.[3]

Ingeniously, George was mixing charity and commerce. Using money donated for the orphanage, he had bought these goods in England and transported them to Philadelphia for the express purpose of selling them at a profit. In this way he leveraged the donations, creating even more of a bankroll for the Savannah orphan house. We can only imagine what his rented room must have looked like, or what the landlord thought as he saw the merchandise carted in. But we might guess that Ben Franklin admired the business acumen George displayed.

As planned, George set off on Monday for parts north—Burlington and Trenton in New Jersey and eventually New York City. The following week's *Gazette* reported more on George's whirlwind trip to Philadelphia:

> On Thursday last, the Rev. Mr. Whitefield began to preach from the Court-House-Gallery in this city, about six at night, to near 6000 People before him in the street, who stood in an awful silence to hear him; and this continued every night, till Sunday. On Monday he set out for New York, and was to preach at Burlington in his waygoing, and in Bucks County coming back. Before he returns to England he designs (God willing) to preach the Gospel in every province in America, belonging to the English. On Monday the 26th he intends to set out for Annapolis.[4]

Whitefield returned to Philadelphia in two weeks, but then just to settle some business matters and say some goodbyes. Apparently his garage sale worked well; he wrote that he gained "considerably by the goods that were sold for the poor."[5] Among the other matters he attended to in these days was the publishing of his sermons and journals. And that would require a meeting with the printer Benjamin Franklin.

We have no definite record of the first encounter between Ben and George. This is surprising, since both of them wrote so fully and freely about their lives. George kept a journal that listed numerous personal meetings. For instance, he described a visit on November 10 from William Tennent, a leading Presbyterian minister in the Philadelphia area. Why wouldn't he make a note of an interview with the city's leading publisher—especially if they were talking about publishing this very journal?

Ben wrote his autobiography years later, and he devoted several pages to his remembrances of George Whitefield. You might expect him to describe his first impressions of the man who stopped into the print shop between prayer meetings—or something like that. But we get nothing of the kind.

Of course the news that Ben printed about Whitefield's preaching schedule and the sale of goods had to come from Whitefield's camp, but it's likely that George's business manager, William Seward, provided this information, as he had previously done in London. It's possible that George was too busy to meet personally with Ben during his first sweep through Philadelphia, November 3–11. He was preaching once or twice a day, receiving visitors, and counseling spiritual seekers. Seward could certainly deal with the printer.

For his part, it's hard to imagine Ben staying away from the biggest event his town had experienced for some time. He probably attended several of Whitefield's sermons that week, maybe all of them. (This is probably when Ben paced out the distance and made his estimate of how many people could be reached by George's voice.) And he might have ambled down to George's rented room to check on the estate sale. Maybe he met George face to face on an occasion like that. But Ben had enough outward humility (or inward pride) to avoid barging in on a busy man. He saw George thronged by people begging for a bit of his spiritual power. Maybe Ben decided to do his haggling with Seward and leave the preacher alone.

The craze had subsided slightly by the time George returned from his New York jaunt on November 23. He preached at Christ Church again, but he got embroiled in a theological debate. He spoke at a Quaker meeting and traveled to suburban Germantown, where he preached from a balcony. But he was also planning the future of his ministry and making necessary arrangements.

In his journal entry for November 28, he included a helpful detail. "One of the printers has told me he has taken above two hundred subscriptions for printing my sermons and journals. Another printer told me he might have sold a thousand sermons if he had them; I therefore gave two extempore discourses to be published. Lord, give them Thy blessing."[6]

The first printer he referred to was certainly Benjamin Franklin, who had perfected subscription sales as a way of funding his publishing ventures. The second printer is probably Andrew Bradford, Ben's main competitor. George was giving them both material to print. This note tells us that there had been a face-to-face meeting between George and Ben at some point on or before November 28—and apparently it was all business. Ben's name wasn't important enough to jot down. This also tells us that, in 1739, George was far more famous than Ben was. *Poor Richard's Almanac* may have been a hit in the colonies, but this British preacher had no clue that Ben was a best-selling author. He was just "one of the printers."

A likely date of the first meeting between these two titans, then, would be the morning of November 28. Whitefield's journal indicated his schedule eased up a bit on that day—he finally had time to write some letters. He was heading out of town on the twenty-ninth, so this would have been a good time to finalize the printing arrangements. It also makes sense that he would have recorded the meeting in his journal while it was still fresh in his mind. Franklin's news—two hundred presold subscriptions!—was a great encouragement to Whitefield, who sorely needed it now that he was beginning to see the same sort of opposition in Philadelphia that he had faced in England. "An opposer told me I had unhinged many *good sort of people*," he wrote on November 28 (italics his).[7] Complaints like this would plague him for years to come. Rebirth was fine for the "sinners" of society, but the good, churchgoing sort of people resented Whitefield's call to conversion. The idea that hundreds of people, and ultimately thousands, would continue to read this message, even after George had left town, was quite welcome.

The meeting likely occurred in the house George had rented on Second Street. It was much-needed downtime for George, and Ben wouldn't have minded walking the few blocks. It's likely that Seward was also present, since he had certainly been negotiating the deals with Franklin and Bradford before then.

What did Ben think of George at that time? This powerful orator was certainly a curiosity. Ben saw George's effect on the city, especially his positive impact on the behavior of Philadelphians. As a man of science, Ben was intrigued by this social phenomenon—not only the physics of a voice being heard by a huge crowd, but the psychology of people who flocked to hear a preacher tell them what terrible sinners they were. Ben recognized the opposition rising from the church establishment, and this would make him appreciate George all the more. All of these reactions would develop over the course of their friendship, but in 1739 this was still just a business connection. Ben was "one of the printers" helping to get George's story out. George was the celebrity who would make Ben a boatload of money.

Defending the Faith

Whitefield left Philadelphia on November 29, heading for Georgia, preaching often along the way—Wilmington, Annapolis, Williamsburg, Charleston, and many stops in between. He traveled with seven others, a group he often called his "family." (He was not yet married, so this was a metaphorical term.) Thousands would flock to hear him. Journaling about one Maryland appearance, he acknowledged that there was little advance notice, and so there were "not above fifteen hundred people" in attendance.[8] Besides the congregations, there were often local preachers and town dignitaries seeking private meetings with him. And, as always, he was staying with an assortment of gracious hosts along the way. Everywhere he talked with people about his favorite subject: being born again.

The entourage reached Savannah on January 10, 1740, and immediately visited a property that would become the site of the orphan house. Two weeks later it was purchased, and before month's end, three orphans were welcomed in. Soon there would be twenty more, then another twenty. George also met with a builder to go over plans for a new structure on that land. He named it Bethesda, a biblical name meaning "house of mercy."

James Habersham, who had accompanied Whitefield on his 1738 trip to Georgia, was still there, running schools they had set up. He would manage operations for the orphanage, but George would be a very hands-on executive whenever he was in the area.

Meanwhile, back in Philadelphia, local churches were coping with the fallout of Whitefield's ministry. Thousands had heard his sermons, and hundreds had experienced the new birth. A few preachers, such as Gilbert Tennent, tried to carry on a Whitefield-like ministry, with moderate success. Yet leaders of some established churches had to deal with a sudden discontent on the part of their parishioners. *Why haven't you taught us about the new birth?* In an effort to calm everyone down, to return the religious climate to normal, some opponents published pamphlets and wrote letters against Whitefield.

One of George's strongest defenders in this time was Benjamin Franklin. In the pages of the *Pennsylvania Gazette*, Ben published a few negative letters, but he regularly responded with glowing praise for Whitefield. And, using one of his favorite tactics, Ben published letters he wrote himself, using fake names, to answer the criticisms. His support was so strong that critics accused him of conspiring with Whitefield to create good publicity.

They might have been right. As publisher of some of George's sermons and journals, Ben had good reason to uphold George's reputation while also stirring the controversy. It was good for business. But the content of Franklin's defense shows that he might not have been entirely mercenary here. Ben noticed that this religious experience George was hawking had a highly beneficial effect on society. As he wrote later, "It was wonderful to see the change soon made in the manner of our inhabitants."[9] This was close to Ben's heart. He always wanted Philadelphians to become better citizens. So as he monitored the human results of George's preaching—the improved courtesy, charity, and self-discipline of the responders—he saw that his own agenda wasn't all that different from George's.

Whitefield returned to Philadelphia on April 14, "and my soul was much rejoiced, in hearing how mightily the Word of God had prevailed since I was at Pennsylvania last."[10] He picked up where he left off, holding meetings in the city and suburbs. Balconies became his pulpits as he adapted field preaching to an urban setting.

During this time, he probably met with Ben Franklin again, filling him in on the orphanage project—the acquisition of land, the start of construction. This was important information for the newspaper editor to have and to transmit, but Ben had a problem with it. "I did not disapprove of the design," he wrote later, "but as Georgia was then destitute of materials and workmen, . . . I thought it would be better to have built the house here [in Philadelphia] and brought the children to it. This I advised, but he was resolute in his first project, and rejected my counsel, and I thereupon refused to contribute."[11]

This, then, was the occasion when the tightfisted Franklin was moved by Whitefield's persuasive preaching to give not only his copper coins, but his silver and gold as well. After telling that story in his autobiography, he added another about his good friend Thomas Hopkinson, a fellow Junto member, who was listening to the same sermon. Hopkinson agreed with

Franklin about the orphanage, and he was similarly determined not to give, so he intentionally emptied his pockets before attending Whitefield's service. Well, the preacher got to him, too, and when he saw a neighbor standing nearby, he asked to borrow some money to put in the collection plate. The neighbor, who was apparently a Quaker, replied, "At any other time, Friend Hopkinson, I would lend to thee freely; but not now; for thee seems to be out of thy right senses."[12]

After holding meetings in and around Philadelphia for about a week, George headed northeast, through New Jersey to New York, and back again, preaching at several stops along the way. This hectic travel schedule occasionally affected his health. In his journal, George exulted whenever he could get a good night's sleep, which was rare. Still he was grateful for the hospitality he found. "How differently am I treated from my Master! He taught the people by day, and abode all night upon the Mount of Olives. He had not where to lay his head; but go where I will, I find people receiving me into their houses with great gladness."[13]

In early May, he was preaching in Ben Franklin's city once more. "I believe God has much people in the city of Philadelphia," he wrote. "The congregations are very large and serious, and I have scarce preached this time amongst them without seeing a stirring amongst the dry bones."[14]

There's one brief section of his journal, dated May 7–8, 1740, that reveals an important aspect of Whitefield's work. First he commended a Baptist minister, "who preached the truth as it is in Jesus," going on to observe that "the poor people are much refreshed by him." The next day's entry began with an account of a trader who had "just come from the Indian nation, where he has been praying with and exhorting all he met." Then another encounter: "I conversed also with a poor negro woman, who has been visited in a very remarkable manner. God was pleased to convert her by my Preaching last autumn." Though her public outbursts of praise to God caused some to call her mad, George wrote, "the account she gave me was rational and solid."[15]

The poor, the Indians, a "negro woman"—Whitefield was actively reaching out to the outcasts of society and encouraging others to do the same. As he had preached to coal miners in English fields, now he was connecting with all classes of society in American cities. And this was part of the controversy he sparked. Established churches, most notably the Church of England, but also some of the more comfortable Quakers and Presbyterians, had crafted a Christianity of privilege. Discipleship had given way to manners. Propriety took the place of devotion. As a result, the church was now dominated by the "better sort" of people—gentlemen, the wealthy, the landed.

Whitefield's revival threatened all that. Not only did he dare to suggest that good manners might not be enough to win entry into the kingdom of heaven, he was actively inviting those of the lower classes to respond to God. It was "the Pharisee and the publican" all over again. Prostitutes and swindlers—and miners and tradesmen and Indians and slaves—were entering the kingdom of heaven before the "better sort." The common folk knew they needed a new birth, and they were grabbing it. Uppity church folk resisted.

Ben Franklin knew all about social classes. He had been dealing with uppity gentlemen his whole life. A tradesman himself, he had worked his way up to a position of leadership and respectability. He was almost a gentleman, but occasionally he still ran into stark prejudice on the part of those who were higher born than he. Surely this played a part in Ben's early support of George's ministry. This revival was not only challenging the religious power of the elites, but it was also inspiring the oft-undisciplined lower classes to live better. For Franklin, that was win-win.

We see some of this in a series of letters Ben wrote and printed that May. As he had often done before, he adopted alter egos. "Obadiah Plainman," a plain man of the working class, rose to Whitefield's defense after critics posted "incoherent stories" and "invectives" against the preacher and his associates. This was Franklin, of course, stirring the pot, but he included a rather telling observation. "We take notice, that you have ranked yourself under the denomination of the BETTER SORT of People, which is an expression always made use of in contradistinction to the *meaner sort*, i.e. the mob, or the rabble. Though *we* are not displeased with such appellations when bestowed on *us* by our friends, yet *we* have ever regarded them as terms of outrageous reproach, when applied to *us*

by our enemies." In the fake outrage of a commoner, Ben was taking issue
with the snobbery of the upper class.[16]

The next week there was a reply from "Tom Trueman," to which
Plainman replied the next week. They were "arguing" over Whitefield,
but Franklin was addressing other social issues in the process. By printing a mock debate between high-class and working-class correspondents,
he was modeling democracy. Long before there was any thought—even
in Franklin's mind—of breaking away from England, Ben understood
that a successful American society would need meaningful involvement
from all classes. His newspaper informed and motivated a broad swath of
Philadelphia's citizens. And he saw Whitefield's message giving common-
ers the spiritual confidence to own their own destinies.

Reasonableness

After little more than a weekend back in Philadelphia, George was off
again May 12. He headed south again to Savannah, this time by boat. That
September he sailed north to Rhode Island and took a grand tour of New
England, working his way south to New York and then Philadelphia again
along a now-familiar route. It's likely that he met with Ben during that stay
(November 8–17, 1740), at least to discuss their publishing ventures. We
have no specific record of this meeting, but a follow-up letter gives us some
clues—and they must have talked about more than just business.

Whitefield was still splitting his print work between Franklin and
Bradford, but Ben would get more and more of it as time went on. George
(and business manager Seward) possibly saw Ben as a superior businessman, and perhaps the subscription approach worked out better for everyone.
Maybe Ben was selling far more of Whitefield's work than Bradford was.
Ben had proven himself with a year's worth of positive treatment in the
Gazette. Without compromising his editorial integrity, Franklin had stood
up for Whitefield in print. Surely George appreciated this, and he might
have rewarded Ben with more business.

Yet it's also possible that Ben just charmed George, as he did with many others throughout his life. The old Franklin wit, combined with his basic humility, made people like him. Remember also that George was just twenty-five years old for most of 1740, and Ben was thirty-four. Perhaps there was a "big brother" quality in the wise Ben Franklin that made George want to work with him. But there's one other possibility we shouldn't overlook. Maybe the preacher saw a spiritual need in this printer, and he wanted every chance he could get to address it.

On November 26, 1740, a week and a half after he left Philadelphia, George sent Ben a letter. He was on Reedy Island in the Delaware Bay, waiting for a fair wind to carry his sloop south to Savannah. He paused to catalog this latest leg of his American tour. "I think I have been on shore 73 days"— he was just counting from his September arrival in Rhode Island—"and have been enabled to travel upwards of 800 miles, and to preach 170 times, besides very frequent exhortations at private houses. I have collected, in goods and money, upwards of £700 sterling, for the Orphan-house; blessed be God!" It was the kind of detail that a newspaperman would love.

The letter was mostly business, but for the first time we see a concern for Ben's soul. After granting permission to publish his autobiography and promising to edit two batches of sermons that Ben could publish, George wrote, "I shall embark for England, God willing, about February. I desire I may hear from you there also, as often as possible." Then more business. And then: "Dear Sir, Adieu. I do not despair of your seeing the reasonableness of Christianity. Apply to God; be willing to do the divine will, and you shall know it."[17]

This appears to be in reference to a prior conversation. It's clear to George that Ben did *not* "see the reasonableness of Christianity" at this time. One might assume that this didn't come up at their initial meeting in 1739 when Ben was drumming up business and George was confirming a deal Seward had arranged. If they'd gone through Franklin's résumé, they would have seen he was a member of Christ Church (Anglican) and a supporter of First Presbyterian, raised Congregationalist, and a personal friend of Cotton Mather. Ben could quote Scripture readily, so George likely assumed initially that Ben was a convinced Christian.

Until November 1740.

Somehow the friendship went to a deeper level. Perhaps George pressed the point about the new birth. As an Anglican, Presbyterian, or Congregationalist, Ben would still need to be born again. George frequently had such conversations with people he met on his travels. Regardless of Ben's connection to respected Puritans, he needed to be a personal friend of *Jesus*.

Ben would balk at this, though to his credit, he was always honest with George about his misgivings. He must have realized he could lose George's business, but he still confessed his doubts about George's gospel. He believed in God, in an afterlife, and in virtue. He just had trouble believing that Jesus was divine or that Jesus' blood was some sort of payment for human sin.

As George saw it, those were essential truths of Christianity. Someone as smart as Ben Franklin would surely see that eventually—especially when these truths were being played out every day in the lives of converts.

We might also guess that, in their conversation of November 1740, Ben displayed his characteristic humility. Perhaps he said something like, "Who can really know the truth about God? I don't want to be presumptuous about the fine points of any particular theology." This was his beef with the Puritans. He loved their self-discipline, but he opposed the rigidity of their theology. It violated his sense of intellectual freedom to boot someone out of the community for honestly believing something different. The Puritans had a history of that, and Ben saw it again in the Hemphill affair. Ironically, he was seeing it yet again as church leaders opposed Whitefield's theology of rebirth, and that made him stand up for George's right to express his views. He just didn't want to get locked into that theology.

So it might be in answer to this that George wrote, "Apply to God; be willing to do the divine will, and you shall know it." He trusted that, if Ben came to God as a sincere seeker of truth, God would show it to him.

EIGHTEEN

Cooling Off

Can there be too much righteousness?

The answer depends on the definition. One person's pastime is another one's vice. When Whitefield's revival came sweeping through town—any town—it demonized many behaviors that were previously considered quite innocent. We've already seen how George's adolescent piety ruled out card playing and theater going. At minimum, these were diversions, mindless entertainments that kept people from seriously focusing on the things of God.

"Oh that the divine spark may again kindle in the heart till it become a flame of fire!" George wrote from Philadelphia to a clergyman friend back in England. "When with you last, I thought you spoke too favourable of horse-races, and such things. But what diversion ought a Christian or a clergyman to know or speak of, but that of doing good?"[1]

This was the method of the Methodists, devoting so much time to prayer, praise, Bible study, and good deeds that there was little left for anything else. This was the life a convert was reborn into—as George described it in that same letter, "a life exactly conformable to the holy JESUS."[2]

Wherever George went, he saw so-called Christians who had lost their ardor for true holiness. Instead, they were spending their time and energy in worldly pursuits, such as card playing, drinking, dancing, or horse racing. This was evidence that they had not been reborn into the righteousness God wanted for them. George wasn't just telling people to avoid these "sinful" actions; he was summoning them into a new Christlike life in which those diversions would not belong. People responded emotionally to his emotional message and then confirmed their emotional response by rejecting these unholy behaviors.

As a result, the purveyors of such distractions found George Whitefield bad for business. This proved true later for the London theaters, as Whitefield preached outdoors in their neighborhood, and it proved true in 1739 for a dancing hall in Philadelphia.

A notice appeared in the *Gazette* the week after George's second sweep through Philadelphia: "Since Mr. Whitefield's preaching here the Dancing School Assembly and Concert Room have been shut up, as inconsistent with the doctrine of the Gospel: And though the gentlemen concerned caused the door to be broke open again, we are informed that no company came to the last Assembly night."[3]

This anonymous news item, accepted by Franklin for inclusion in his paper, was apparently a victory cry from Whitefield's supporters. *Look how thoroughly the gospel has taken hold of this city. Even the dancing school has shut down!*

One problem: it wasn't entirely true. Some of those who ran the dance hall demanded that Franklin print a retraction, which he did in the next issue, declaring, "I have often said, that if any person thinks himself injured in a public newspaper, he has a right to have his vindication made as public as the aspersion." And then he printed a lengthy message from the aggrieved parties, stating that "William Seward, who came into this place as an attendant and intimate companion of Mr. Whitefield's, . . . took upon him to invade other men's property; and contrary to law and justice, on the 16th of April, shut up the door of the Concert Room, without any previous application to, or consent had of any of the members."[4] It was true that there was no one attending the next night, but that was because the season was over, and there were no more dance nights scheduled for a while. The dance hall would be back in business, thank you very much. Those overrighteous zealots had not won a victory here.

The letter went further, charging Franklin and other newspaper editors with puffery in regard to Whitefield. "Nor is this the only instance of misrepresentation in favour of Mr. Whitefield's success; for in all those articles of news, which give an account of the vast crowds who compose his audience, their numbers are always exaggerated, being often doubled and sometimes trebled."[5]

To his credit, Franklin printed the entire complaint. Because many elite Philadelphians attended concerts at the dance hall, this incident was taken seriously. And Franklin now had to answer charges of twisting the facts to favor Whitefield. This was a turning point for the printer. He began to put some distance between himself and Whitefield. While his early treatment of the preacher was 90 percent positive, he now began to even it out, printing more critical letters.

Early in his newspaper-publishing career, Ben had printed an "Apology for Printers," in which he set forth some principles of fair play. "When men differ in opinion, both sides ought equally to have the advantage of being heard by the public; and that when truth and error have fair play, the former is always an overmatch for the latter."[6]

Some of these principles seemed to anticipate future criticisms: "It is unreasonable to imagine printers approve of everything they print, and to censure them on any particular thing accordingly; since in the way of their business they print such great variety of things opposite and contradictory."

He further noted, "If all Printers were determined not to print anything till they were sure it would offend nobody, there would be very little printed."[7]

These were the principles he touted once again. From this new, more evenhanded position, Ben benefited from the controversy as much as the craze. The dance-hall debate was the underlying subject of that ersatz exchange between "Obadiah Plainman" and "Tom Trueman." The elite Trueman was highly offended that an unruly mob of Whitefield supporters would close down a refined place of entertainment where the "better sort" gathered. Plainman was offended that the working class was considered a "mob."

William Seward seemed unrepentant, but he met with Franklin and the dance-hall owners to work things out. "Call'd at Mr. Franklin's the printer's,"

Seward recorded in his journal, "and met Mr. P—and several other gentle-men of the [Dancing School] Assembly, who accosted me very roughly, concerning a paragraph I had put in the papers, alleging it to be false."

Seward claimed that he acted with "great sweetness and calmness of temper," but his account of this meeting seems rather belligerent. After explaining that he was once as fond of dancing as they were, he added, "I prayed the Lord to convince them of their error, as he had done me of mine." He told Mr. P that "if he could prove that Jesus Christ, or his Apostles, or the primitive Christians, approved of these diversions, I would yield up the point; but as they could not pretend to do that, I did insist they were as odious in the sight of God, and did as effectually promote the Kingdom of Satan, as any of the heathen idolatries."[8]

So much for sweetness and calmness of temper.

In modern times, we might call this a culture war. Here's a born-again Christian trying to change society in what he thinks is a positive way—by shutting down the dance hall. And here are some members of that society who don't want to be changed. And there, literally in the middle of that discussion, is Benjamin Franklin. While he promoted and prac-ticed a life of self-discipline, he would have had no problem taking an occasional quaff of ale or a spin around the dance floor. From his youth, he was familiar with the strictures of Puritan life, but he seemed to have sorted through those to arrive at a general policy of moderation: work hard, play well, and get a good night's sleep. Was this paragon of practi-cality now to be linked with the methodical overrighteousness of George Whitefield? Would Methodist zealots squeeze all fun out of public life? Granted, Seward might not have handled this dispute the way Whitefield would have, but his aversion to diversions lined up with George's. One can imagine Ben sinking lower in his chair as he heard Seward rail on about the "Kingdom of Satan."

Or maybe he enjoyed watching the dance-hall snobs sweat. As we see in the ensuing Plainman-Trueman dialogue, Ben understood this not only as a culture war but also as a class war. If the dance hall was where the "better sort" went to get away from the rabble, then maybe it *was* a "heathen idolatry," or something like that. If the working class wanted to let out their frustrations at people who never did a lick of work, and if they used religion to do it, why not give them the power of the press?

Always the pragmatist, Ben found a way to make this work. As a newspaper editor, he would reposition himself at the center of this debate. He would consider all sides and give everyone a hearing. Yet, as a publisher, he would continue to put out Whitefield's best-selling books. He would be Whitefield's printer, but not his lackey.

The dance-hall debacle did not destroy Franklin's relationship with Whitefield, but it might have raised a red flag. If Ben felt an initial attraction to George's energy, his passion, or his nonconformity, it was now balanced by the realization that George's vision of a perfect world was much different from Ben's. George was calling people to be fully Christian even if they thought they were Christian before. Righteousness meant more than good citizenship; it involved a radical change of priorities, a complete immersion in the things of God. As he learned more about George's vision, Ben might have found it less inspiring and more alarming.

As Franklin biographer Walter Isaacson put it, "By the fall of 1740, Franklin showed signs of cooling slightly toward Whitefield, though not toward the profits that came from publishing him. The preacher's efforts to make him a 'new born' believer in Calvinist orthodoxy wore thin, and valuable patrons among the Philadelphia gentry began to denounce the *Gazette*'s ardent flackery."[9]

Ups and Downs

By the time George Whitefield delivered a farewell sermon in Charleston, South Carolina, in late August 1740, his second American tour had already been remarkable. He had been in the colonies nearly a year, visiting Philadelphia four times, Savannah twice, and New York twice, with many sermons delivered in between. An orphanage was now being built for him in Georgia and a meeting hall for him in Philadelphia. Thanks largely to Ben Franklin, his publishing efforts extended his message to those who couldn't hear him personally or those who just wanted to take in more of his message. From New York City southward, people were talking about Jesus. They were excited about their new relationship with God. Lives were being changed.

Yet 1740 was turning out to be difficult for George on several fronts. The trip had taken a toll on George's already sketchy health. "Several times I was so weak before I began to preach, that I thought it almost impossible for me to get through half the discourse; but the Lord quickened, enlightened, and supported me above measure. Out of weakness, I became strong."[10]

George had also faced more opposition on his second time through the area. In the fall of 1739, he was a curiosity, a celebrity, a burst of energy in a humdrum world. Supporters thronged, and opponents were awed. But when he returned to these same towns in the spring of 1740, his enemies were ready for him. More churches were closing their doors. Preachers were warning against him. There were even some critical letters appearing in the newspapers. George's victory parade had become a march into battle.

As with the dancing hall, the Whitefield camp itself sparked some of this opposition. Seward's news reports, reprinted fully by many editors (including Franklin), were effusive in their praise of Whitefield, and this invited mockery. Whitefield did not shrink from criticizing errors of theology or practice wherever he saw them—especially among the religious elite. In particular, he had written a lengthy diatribe against the writings of Archbishop Tillotson, a well-respected liberal churchman who had dominated Anglican thought in the previous half century and had died in 1694. Years earlier, Franklin himself had written in praise of Tillotson's clear writing style—and still he published Whitefield's scathing critique, in which George famously charged that the archbishop "knew no more about true Christianity than Mahomet [Muhammed]."[11]

Papers throughout the colonies and back in England picked up the quote. Churchmen who had been weaned on Tillotson's writings cried foul. As a result, many more Anglican churches were closed to Whitefield's services, their leaders specifically referring to this piece about Tillotson.

This, then, was the context of Franklin's new distancing policy. Ben was declaring his independence, in a way. He would keep Whitefield in the news, but he would not be George's pet publisher. Controversy sold papers, and Ben would play both sides. That was just good business.

And it was *very* good business. One scholar reported, "From 1739 to 1741, Franklin published 110 titles—as many as he printed during the previous seven years. Almost all the increase came from Whitefield." In certain cities Whitefield's works were more profitable for Ben than his own bestselling *Poor Richard's Almanac.* In 1740 alone, "Whitefield wrote or inspired thirty-nine titles, or 30 percent of all works published in America."[12] Other printers throughout the colonies were publishing volumes by and about Whitefield, but Franklin remained the most active. George kept giving Ben sermons and journals to publish. Apparently he was willing to accept the new reality: Ben would not always avoid printing critical pieces.

Heartstrings

There were also some major relationship issues tugging at George's heart in the summer of 1740—a failed romance with a woman back in England and an even more painful rift with his old mentor, John Wesley, who was preaching and writing about God's grace in a way that George disagreed with. Put in its most basic terms, Whitefield had become a Calvinist and Wesley had not. Whitefield believed that God called (elected) certain people into salvation and that an emotional response to the gospel was evidence of God's calling. Wesley held that salvation was available to all. One other sticking point between the two preachers was perfectionism. Wesley believed that God's sanctifying work could and should make a believer effectively perfect. Whitefield insisted that earthly perfection was unattainable.

The differences came to light in 1740 with publications by the two men and letters between them. "Why then should we dispute, when there is no probability of convincing?" George asked in a March 26 letter to John. "Will it not in the end destroy brotherly love, and insensibly take from us that cordial union and sweetness of soul, which I pray GOD may always subsist between us? . . . How glad would the enemies of the Lord be to see us divided? How many would rejoice, should I join and make a party against you? And in one word, how would the cause of our common Master every way suffer by our raging disputes about particular points of doctrines?"[13]

There were many more "Dear John" letters as the year unfolded, always with the same call for peace—although George was not compromising his convictions. On May 24 he wrote: "I write not this, honoured Sir, from heat of spirit, but out of love. At present, I think you are entirely inconsistent with yourself, and therefore do not blame me, if I do not approve of all that you say."[14]

On June 25 it was "For Christ's sake, let us not be divided amongst ourselves."[15] On August 25: "I cannot bear the thoughts of opposing you: but how can I avoid it, if you go about (as your brother Charles once said) to drive John Calvin out of Bristol?"[16] A month later: "I am sorry, honoured Sir, to hear by many letters, that you seem to own a sinless perfection in this life attainable."[17]

There were letters received from other friends in England, reporting on Wesley's preaching. George longed to hear from John directly. Part of the problem, of course, was the ocean that separated the two men. On November 9 Whitefield wrote that he had just received John's letter dated March 11. It's hard to carry on a civil debate with an eight-month lag. George could only reiterate his own position and ask for understanding. "Oh that we were of one mind: for I am yet persuaded you greatly err."[18]

The emotional agony of this situation is evident in the correspondence. "Honoured Sir" was not just eyewash—Whitefield truly honored John Wesley as a trusted advisor and role model. No one, with the possible exception of Charles Wesley, had meant more to the early development of George's faith. Yet now they were on opposite sides of a theological argument that both felt was crucial to a proper understanding of the gospel. "My dear brother," George wrote on November 24, "for Christ's sake avoid all disputation. Do not oblige me to preach against you; I had rather die."[19]

As if the emotional ups and downs of 1740 weren't yet enough, at some point that fall George got a letter from Charles Wesley. It was a welcome document for several reasons. For one thing, Charles had been seriously ill, and some newspapers in England had even reported his death. Here he was announcing his recovery. The letter was also a sort of olive branch, acknowledging the division between Whitefield and the Wesleys and seeking peace between them. "Be assured, my dearest brother, our heart is as your heart."

But Charles had bad news to pass on as well. Concerned about the spiritual welfare of his mother and his sister, George had asked Charles to look after them. Reluctantly, Charles reported, "Your mother continues dead in sin. . . . Your sister (God help her! God convert her!) is far, very far, from the kingdom of heaven."[20] In America George Whitefield was welcoming crowds into the kingdom, but his loved ones back in England were still on the outside.

The Next Step

Why didn't Whitefield just head back to England in August 1740? After a year of constant travel, frequent preaching, health issues, and emotional turmoil, he could have packed it in, declaring this mission accomplished and heading home victorious. He had taken Philadelphia by storm. He had conquered the middle colonies with the power of the gospel. He had returned in triumph to Savannah. But there was one more challenge he chose to tackle.

New England.

The ship he took from Charleston landed not in the old ports of old England, but in Newport, Rhode Island, arriving September 14. From there he visited Boston and the surrounding towns for several weeks, then worked his way west through Massachusetts and south through Connecticut to New York, Philadelphia, and back to the orphanage. It was an ambitious addendum to an already grueling trip.

Avoiding John Wesley might have been one reason he extended his American tour. In his May 24 letter he told Wesley, "I dread coming to England. . . . I dread your coming over to America, because the work of God is carried on here (and that in a most glorious manner) by doctrines quite opposite to those you hold."[21] Maybe God was marking out different turfs for the two preachers. Wesley was carrying on a very successful ministry in England, picking up where Whitefield had left off, especially with outdoor meetings among the coal miners and other common folk. Though George was refusing to budge on his theology, he didn't want to cause division among the new believers who had come to faith through this international revival. "Sometimes I think it best to stay here, where we all think and speak the same thing: The work goes on without divisions, and with more success, because all employed in it are of one mind."[22]

While George was evading *internal* controversy in the Methodist cause, he knew there would be plenty of *external* controversy. There always was—but New England would bring even greater challenges, and this might be why George had not ventured there before this time.

Boston was, of course, home to the Puritans. While George's Calvinism would be welcome there, his dramatic, emotional methods would not. Harvard College was there, and George had all sorts of issues with the way it overintellectualized the faith. And in Northampton, Massachusetts, was a famous minister named Jonathan Edwards—a man George Whitefield highly respected and possibly feared. Would George be able to get through this gauntlet?

The common folk of New England were quite ready for Whitefield. They had been reading about him for a year now, as Franklin's colonial printing network shared stories about his work in the other colonies. When he disembarked in Newport, Rhode Island, George was welcomed with the usual mixture of acclaim and curiosity.

Franklin's *Gazette* printed a news item from a Newport correspondent: "Last Lord's Day arrived here the Rev. Mr. George Whitefield from South Carolina, who preached two excellent sermons on Monday in the Church of England. . . . Great numbers of people flocked from all quarters both in town and country to hear his sermons and exhortations, and many of them could not refrain shedding tears."[23]

The final stage of Whitefield's phenomenal preaching tour had begun.

NINETEEN

The Awakeners

As George went traipsing through New England, Ben kept providing coverage in the *Pennsylvania Gazette*. Readers couldn't get enough of this fascinating orator, and the savvy Philadelphia printer was happy to address that need. Even if the relationship was "just business" at this point, it was good business for any printer. As one historian put it, "Franklin was a newspaperman and Whitefield was news."[1]

The *Gazette* reported on a "sorrowful accident" that occurred when Whitefield spoke at a Boston church in September 1740. As usual, "vast numbers of people crowded in there before the time of service," and suddenly there was a noise from the gallery ("some persons breaking a board to make a seat"), but "some imprudent person" said the gallery was giving way, causing a panic. "Some jumped out of the galleries into the seats below, others out of the windows, and those below pressing hastily to get out, several were thrown down and trod upon, whereby many were much bruised, and some had their bones broke." There were five fatalities.

Yet even such a tragedy couldn't stop the Whitefield mania. The same *Gazette* article reported that George was preaching twice a day, traveling to Cambridge, Roxbury, and Charlestown, and speaking Saturday night on the Boston Common. We might wonder if Ben had a pang of nostalgia when he printed that "Rev. Mr. Whitefield preach'd at the Old South Meeting House" on Sunday and collected a huge offering for the orphanage. That was Ben's boyhood church.[2]

The visit to Cambridge was especially significant, since that was the home of Harvard College. The school had only about a hundred students at the time, but it was the most prominent institution of higher learning in the American colonies. This was where the young men of New England received training for the ministry. Going back to his own time at Oxford, George had difficulty with the direction of theological training. The Enlightenment was rewriting the rules. Scholars were scrapping the traditional faith for the sophistry of deism and a general skepticism toward received tradition. On this visit, George wrote in his journal that Harvard was "not far superior to our [English] universities in piety. Discipline is at a low ebb. Bad books are become fashionable among the tutors and students."[3]

Despite that critique, Whitefield was received well at Harvard, welcomed by the president and heard by thousands in the courtyard. Later, when this volume of his journal was published, his critical comments about Harvard caused a ruckus. In a later edition, he tried to ease the matter: "I spoke and wrote too rashly of the colleges and ministers of New England, for which . . . I take this opportunity of asking public pardon from the press. It was rash and uncharitable and though well-meant, I fear, did hurt."[4]

Whitefield spent several weeks in the Boston area, eventually moving west to Worcester and Brookfield. On October 17, he arrived in Northampton, a guest of the pastor-scholar Jonathan Edwards.

A Glorious Alteration

When historians discuss the Great Awakening in America, two names are commonly invoked: George Whitefield and Jonathan Edwards. As pastor of the Congregational Church in Northampton, Edwards was an unlikely revivalist. His sermons were long and erudite, and he read them from manuscripts. He was a scholar, steeped in Calvinist theology, but also well acquainted with Enlightenment thinking.

In the 1720s and 1730s there were other glimmers of revival in the American colonies, notably in the preaching of Theodore Frelinghuysen and the Tennent family (William and sons Gilbert, John, and William Jr.). But if you wanted to pin down one event as the beginning of the Great Awakening, it would be the revival in Northampton in 1735. Jonathan Edwards not only pastored this event, but he also studied it. And his careful analysis of this spiritual outpouring provided an important intellectual framework for the ministry of George Whitefield and other revivalists to follow.

Edwards was just thirty-one years old when he began preaching to his central Massachusetts church about justification by faith. Soon afterward he noticed that "the Spirit of God began extraordinarily to set in and wonderfully to work amongst us." The following spring and summer saw a "glorious alteration in the town." Within half a year, Edwards counted "more than 300 souls" who were "savingly brought home in Christ." That would be a significant number in any small town, but it was more than a head count. "There were remarkable tokens of God's presence in almost every house," Edwards wrote. "It was a time of joy in families on account of salvation being brought unto them."[5]

The revival spread through the surrounding communities as well. As Whitefield found later, revival always upsets the status quo. A number of traditional leaders opposed this new emphasis on religious experience. Proponents of the revival became known as "New Lights"; opponents were known as "Old Lights." (Among Presbyterians, the terms *New Side* and *Old Side* were in play.)

There was a fear that people would become overemotional, seeking some passionate experience that had little grounding in good theology. And there were some preachers who went to such extremes, but not Jonathan Edwards. His carefully reasoned account of the Northampton revival, *A Faithful Narrative of the Surprising Work of God*, was well read and well respected.

Key to the Edwards analysis was an understanding of salvation as both a spiritual and experiential event. This observation was anchored not only in Scripture but also in the Enlightenment philosophy of John Locke and others. If humans are sensate creatures, then it makes sense that God would engage with us through our senses. Thus we would not only know

God with our minds but also experience him with our emotions. When many churches were following the Enlightenment into a highly cerebral approach to faith, this was a stunning coup. Edwards cerebrally opened the door to religious experience.

"He that is spiritually enlightened . . . does not merely rationally believe that God is glorious," Edwards preached in 1733, "but he has a sense of the gloriousness of God in his heart. There is not only a rational belief that God is holy, and that holiness is a good thing, but there is a sense of the loveliness of God's holiness."[6]

This was the environment George Whitefield entered as he toured New England in the fall of 1740. The fervor of 1735 had died out somewhat. There were still Old Lights and New Lights throughout the region, as well as a longing for a revival of the earlier revival. In a 1739 letter inviting Whitefield to visit him, Edwards wrote that the people of New England might be "more hardened than most of those places where you have preached." Still, he felt that George had "the blessing of heaven attending you wherever you go, and I have a great desire, if it be the will of God, that such blessing as attends your person and labours may descend on this town."[7]

If Whitefield was daunted by this task, he didn't show it. In his journal he called Edwards "a solid, excellent Christian," adding that he hadn't met anyone like him in New England. Over the weekend of October 17–19, 1740, George preached four times in Jonathan's church and was well received, especially when he talked about their previous revival, five years earlier. "When I came to remind them of their former experiences, and how zealous and lively they were at that time, both minister and people wept much."[8]

There is nothing negative in Whitefield's journal entries about the visit to Northampton, and yet something seems missing. George expressed his respect for Edwards, but he actually had more praise for Sarah Edwards, Jonathan's wife. While the Northampton scholar was apparently moved by the evangelist's oratory ("Preached this morning, and good Mr. Edwards wept during the whole time," George reported[9]), we might guess that he was somewhat reserved in his personal reaction to Whitefield. (However, after that weekend, Edwards made some comments indicating that *Whitefield* seemed reserved, so maybe George was daunted after all.)

A Wife's Perspective

Sarah Edwards was not so reserved. In a letter to her brother, describing the time with Whitefield, she offered both affirmation and analysis. "He is truly a remarkable man, and during his visit has, I think, verified all that we have heard of him. He makes less of the doctrines than our American preachers generally do, and aims more at affecting the heart."

For the Old Lights, "affecting the heart" would be a bad thing, but Sarah had been through the Northampton revival of 1735, where her own heart had been "affected." She worked closely with her husband in evaluating the "religious affections" of that experience.

"It is truly wonderful to see what a spell this preacher often casts over an audience by proclaiming the simplest truths of the Bible," she told her brother about Whitefield.

"I have seen upward of a thousand people hang on his words with breathless silence, broken only by an occasional half-suppressed sob. He impresses the ignorant, and not less the educated and refined."

Here we begin to imagine that Sarah was still carrying on an argument with her husband. Jonathan would agree that George impressed the ignorant, but Sarah might have pointed out that Jonathan himself was crying his eyes out. Maybe the "educated and refined" were affected in a different way.

Sarah's letter went on: "A prejudiced person, I know, might say that this is all theatrical artifice and display; but . . . he is a very devout and godly man, and his only aim seems to be to reach and influence men the best way. He speaks from a heart all aglow with love, and pours out a torrent of eloquence which is almost irresistible. Many, very many persons in Northampton date the beginning of new thoughts, new desires, new purposes, and a new life, from the day on which they heard him preach of Christ and this salvation."

The letter's conclusion confirms our suspicions. Apparently she and Jonathan had been discussing their reactions. "Perhaps I ought to tell you that Mr. Edwards and some others think him in error on a few practical points; but his influence on the whole is so good we ought to bear with little mistakes. I wish him success in his apostolic career."[10]

In November Jonathan Edwards preached to his congregation on Jesus' parable of the sower (Matthew 13:1–30), fearing that they would be like the seed sown on rocky soil, which sprouts up quickly, but withers. Whitefield had sown seed and stirred an excitement that led to rapid growth, but now the new believers needed to get rooted in a deeper understanding of God. "Religion that arises only from superficial impressions," Edwards taught, "is wont to wither away . . . when it comes to be tried by . . . difficulties."[11]

Whitefield might not disagree with that. Just a few months earlier he had written to his other prominent colleague/critic, John Wesley, using another agrarian Bible reference. "My business seems to be chiefly in planting; if God send you to water, I praise his name.—I wish you a thousand-fold increase."[12] George understood his role in a divine process. He was the sower of seed, the planter of an awareness of God—in Sarah's term, *apostolic*. Other people would nurture those tender souls, instructing them, gathering them, and helping them to grow. But God was using George Whitefield to break through to people's hearts, even if they didn't fully understand it.

Titans

While Edwards had some issues with Whitefield's seeming superficiality, his own teaching and writing created an important role for Whitefield-like preaching. If God's Spirit affected the emotions as well as the mind, then God could use powerful oratory to open up people's emotions. Whether he liked it or not, Edwards had paved the way for Whitefield, creating a theoretical framework in which George's gifts could flourish.

It's hard to overstate the importance of Jonathan Edwards to the development of American evangelicalism, and that doesn't take anything away from Whitefield's role. It's tempting to say that Whitefield was the heart of the Great Awakening and Edwards the head, but we really have to see Edwards as much more than that. He was the spinal cord, if you will, connecting the head with the heart and body. Without Whitefield's energy—both the power of his preaching and his ambitious itinerary—the brilliance of Jonathan Edwards might have been confined to a small region, a narrow culture, and a short span of time. Whitefield took this experiential Christianity to the masses.

While Edwards and Whitefield are clearly the two titans of the Great Awakening, Edwards is paired with someone else when scholars talk about the major thinkers of Colonial America—Benjamin Franklin. Both Edwards and Franklin came out of a Puritan background, adapting it to a new era. Both were fans of John Locke's philosophy and used it to craft their own. Both deeply affected the way Americans would think for the next three centuries.

In an insightful essay, "Franklin, Edwards, and the Problem of Human Nature," Daniel Walker Howe drew some fascinating conclusions. "Edwards's message urged people to let God take over their hearts, and all else would follow. Franklin's message was that God helps those who help themselves. There have always been many Christians in America who can't help feeling that both are somehow true."

Howe acknowledged that it's "remarkable" to think that these divergent philosophies would find any point of commonality, but they did: *George Whitefield.* "Edwards and Whitefield had in common the desire to save souls; Franklin and Whitefield had in common a concern with social morality and organized social reform. Franklin welcomed Whitefield's energy, rhetorical power, and organizational skills in humanitarian causes." Over the next century or so, Howe said, American evangelicals "developed along the lines Whitefield pioneered and Franklin approved."[13]

So when George preached in Jonathan's pulpit in the fall of 1740, he completed a strange triangle that would affect the world in ways that neither of them—nor Ben Franklin—would ever dream.

TWENTY

Love, Maybe

Ben Franklin loved the ladies. Everybody knows that. In fact, it's probably one of the top five things that anyone off the street can tell you about this Founding Father.

1. He signed the Declaration of Independence.
2. He helped write the Constitution.
3. He said clever stuff.
4. He flew a kite.
5. He had lots of affairs.

Yet the truth about Ben's romantic life is actually quite elusive. The historical record—including personal correspondence—teases us with several women who were clearly objects of Ben's affection at certain points during his long life. But it's difficult to determine whether they were paramours or just friends.

We know that Ben made a pass at James Ralph's girlfriend, which was rebuffed. A few years later, Ben fathered an illegitimate child, William. Were there other dalliances, in London or Philadelphia? We would be naïve to deny it. He was in his early twenties, a strapping lad, sowing his wild oats.

What's more, in the codes of conduct he carefully constructed through the years, he often omitted sexual matters, or at least underplayed them. He had thrown off the Puritan yoke. While he worked at cultivating virtues like honesty and temperance, he was looser in his attitude toward sexual mores. In the 1730s he developed a "project of arriving at moral perfection," in which he targeted one of twelve virtues each week. (A Quaker friend convinced him to add a thirteenth: humility.) Number twelve on this list was chastity, but see how he defines it: "Rarely use venery [sex] but for health or offspring; never to dullness, weakness, or the injury of your own or another's peace or reputation."[1]

This is an ethic observed by many today: responsible, but not religious. There's no mention of holiness, the body being God's temple, or a sacred bond between marital partners. The concerns are practical. Overattention to sex can dull you, weaken you, or disgrace you. It can also disgrace those you love.

By the time Ben composed this plan he was married to Deborah. From the letters they exchanged, we gather that he truly appreciated and loved her. And while he was certainly attracted to other women, he did not want to "injure" Deborah's "peace." He was also protective of the "reputation" of the women he fancied. As a result, we don't know what really went on between Franklin and those women. He kept it secret.

Take Catherine Ray. She was twenty-five years his junior, sister to the wife of Ben's nephew. Ben met her in Boston in 1754, while staying with his brother John. They hit it off, engaging in lengthy conversations, taking walks in the rain, and eventually trading extremely flirtatious letters. Ben destroyed most of her letters, but those that survived, on both sides, reveal a kind of game between the two of them—hot talk but restrained action. Franklin sometimes gave paternal advice and frequently mentioned his wife in positive ways. One biographer said, "From reading their letters, and reading between the lines, one gets the impression that Franklin made a few playful advances that Caty gently deflected, and he seemed to respect her all the more for it."[2] Eventually she married, apparently with Ben's blessing, and had six kids.

Home Away from Home

Ben traveled a lot. During the 1750s and 1760s, he spent more time in London—away from Deborah—than he did at home. Would he indulge in a sexual affair "for health" without Deborah finding out? His personal ethic would seem to allow that, as long as there was no injurious scandal.

On his stay in London from 1757 to 1762 with his son William, he rented rooms in a house belonging to Margaret Stevenson, a middle-aged widow. Over the years, she would become close to him, but in a pragmatic way—not unlike the relationship he had back home with Deborah. She kept house, fixed meals, and provided companionship. Among their circle of friends in London, Ben and Margaret were treated as a couple, but we don't know if there was any romance or sex involved. Margaret's daughter, known as Polly, was just eighteen when Ben met her, and she became a fast friend. Ben charmed her with his attention and was charmed by her eager mind. After she moved to the country, he wrote often to her, sharing his scientific ideas as well as personal tidbits. He was flirtatious as always, but the circumstances suggest that the relationship was always platonic. She was not so much a stand-in for Catherine Ray as she was for Sally Franklin, Ben's teenage daughter back home.

The rules changed when Franklin went to Paris in late 1776. Deborah had died a few years earlier. Ben was seventy years old, and yet he was greeted in the French court as an example of American primitivism, a "wild man" from the frontier—and he played the part well, even wearing a fur hat to public functions. He quickly learned that the French appreciated good flirtation, so he obliged them, engaging in torrid correspondence with some of the leading ladies of French society. (When one woman complained that he hadn't visited her all summer, he reportedly said he was waiting for the nights to grow longer.) Whether he actually engaged in sexual liaisons with them is beside the point. It's likely that it was all a game, a character he was playing. Any *actual* sex would run the risk of injuring someone's reputation—and, beyond that, hurting the chances of America getting much-needed French aid.

Much of Ben's current reputation as a philanderer comes from that period. It was a character he cultivated, like the dozens of phony characters he adopted in print. John Adams, the prim congressman from Puritan territory, didn't get it. When he visited Paris to check up on Ben, he was appalled. His outrage probably fortified Ben's image as a party animal. In his seventies, Ben probably didn't mind being charged with such virility.

Biographer Walter Isaacson issued a helpful analysis of Ben's relationships with those of both genders. "Franklin only occasionally forged intimate bonds with his male friends, who tended to be either intellectual companions or jovial club colleagues. But he relished being with women, and he formed deep and lasting relationships with many. For him, such relationships were not a sport or trifling amusement, despite how they might appear, but a pleasure to be savored and respected. Throughout his life, Franklin would lose many male friends, but he never lost a female one."[3] He maintained a correspondence with Caty Ray all his life (though it became less flirtatious after her marriage), and Polly Stevenson was at his deathbed.

Curious George

For George Whitefield, it was quite the opposite. He had good relationships with men and some contentious ones, but he seemed clueless about women. Passionate about God's work, he had little desire for anything, or anyone, else.

Until he fell in love.

The Delamotte family was a jewel in the crown of the young Methodist movement. Mr. Delamotte was a local magistrate, living in the town of Blendon with his wife and several grown children. Son William was a Cambridge scholar. Son Charles was assisting John Wesley in Georgia. And one of his daughters was named Elizabeth, a.k.a. Betsy or Betty. In late 1737 and early 1738, Charles Wesley talked at length with various Delamottes about spiritual matters, as he described in his journal. On November 5, 1737, Charles wrote, "I met and turned back with Betty to hear Mr. Whitefield preach, not with the persuasive words of man's wisdom, but with the demonstration of the Spirit and with power. The churches will not contain the multitudes that throng to hear him."[4]

This was the year that George was waiting to leave for Georgia, the year his preaching first catapulted him to fame. The journal entry is notable not only for the positive and prescient things Charles said about his old Oxford pal, but also for the fact that he was accompanied by Elizabeth (Betty) Delamotte, who would later steal George's heart.

A year and a half later, in the spring of 1739, Whitefield was back in England after his own trip to Georgia (where he connected with Charles Delamotte). As he resumed his preaching ministry in England, he spent a great deal of time in Blendon, sometimes speaking to crowds in the Delamottes' backyard, and sometimes just relaxing with that family. In his own journal he referred to it as his "sweet retreat." That fall, from Philadelphia, George sent the Delamotte parents a letter of gratitude, in which he particularly mentioned their happy marriage: "It hath often given me pleasure to see in what harmony you seem to live. . . . Surely, thought I, these are a happy pair. These I trust are help-meets for each other."[5]

Clearly George liked this family, and he found a nourishing Christian fellowship in their home. His journal entries about his times in Blendon were almost giddy with good feeling. He was praising God for all the Delamottes—but perhaps especially for daughter Elizabeth. Historian Harry Stout astutely observed the "enthusiasm and vigor" displayed in Whitefield's journal entries after George stayed with the Delamottes. Though George "never specifically identified these enraptured feelings with Elizabeth," Stout suggested that George was falling in love without recognizing it.[6]

It makes sense. Being "in love" would be an uncomfortable feeling for George, who had dedicated his passion to the Lord alone. He had carefully eliminated distractions from his life—not only extraneous activities like card playing and theater, but sometimes more necessary things like friendship and even food. Feelings of attraction for this recent convert might lead him away from his true calling. His attention to Elizabeth might sap his already flagging energy. She might become an idol to him, a temptation. She might seem like an angel of light at this point, but wasn't that the way temptation worked?

He would have to be very careful about this business of love.

Over the following year George acted like a lovesick schoolboy afraid to admit his true feelings—telling his friends matter-of-factly that it might be time for him to find a wife, writing letters to Elizabeth's parents and brothers that he hoped she'd see, even writing an overly spiritual epistle to her, exhorting her to stand firm in the faith. "There is nothing I dread more than having my heart drawn away by earthly objects," he wrote from Savannah in this letter to her, dated February 1, 1740. Whether she understood or not, *she* was the "earthly object" he was talking about. "For alas, what room can there be for GOD, when a rival hath taken possession of the heart?" It was a generic bit of exhortation, but he was also referring to his own heart, and *she* was the "rival." In closing, he briefly let his emotions be seen. "My heart is now full. Writing quickens me. I could almost drop a tear, and wish myself, for a moment or two, in England. But hush, nature."[7]

If this was a courtship, he was successfully squeezing it dry of any passion. He actually scolded himself for wanting to be with her. The apostle Paul wrote about the struggle between the "natural man" and the spiritual man (1 Corinthians 2:14–15; see also Romans 7). This was the war George was waging as he shushed the longings of his own romantic nature.

About two months later came the oddest proposal you'll ever see. He wrote it April 4, 1740, on shipboard between Georgia and Philadelphia, in the midst of his grand tour of America. First he wrote to her parents: "It hath been therefore much impressed upon my heart, that I should marry, in order to have a help meet for me in the work whereunto our dear Lord Jesus hath called me." He asks "whether you think your daughter, Miss Elizabeth, is a proper person to engage in such an undertaking?"

Even here he tried to strip all emotion from the matter. "If I know anything of my own heart, I am free from that foolish passion, which the world calls LOVE." And yet it's clear he was still wrestling with deep feelings. "After strong crying and tears at the throne of grace for direction, and after unspeakable troubles with my own heart, I write this."[8]

He enclosed a letter for Elizabeth as well, which said, in part:

Do you think you could undergo the fatigues that must necessarily attend being joined to one who is every day liable to be called out to suffer for the sake of Jesus Christ? . . . Can you undertake to help a husband in the charge of a family, consisting perhaps of a hundred persons [the orphanage]? Can you bear the inclemencies of the air both as to cold and heat in a foreign climate? Can you, when you have an husband, be as though you had none, and willingly part with him, even for a long season, when his Lord and master shall call him forth to preach the gospel, and command him to leave you behind?

After these and other challenges, he got to the point: "I have great reason to believe it is the divine will that I should alter my condition, and have often thought you [were] the person appointed for me."

To his credit, George realized this was not a very good love letter. "The passionate expressions which carnal courtiers use, I think, ought to be avoided by those that would marry in the Lord." He realized that Elizabeth might not be ready for the challenge of life with an itinerant preacher, and he invited her to be honest in her response.[9]

These letters were launched toward England in early April. It routinely took two months to get a letter across the ocean and another two months to get a response—sometimes much longer. In a letter dated June 26, George shared with his old colleague William Seward, who was now back in England, some second thoughts about Elizabeth Delamotte. George had received a message indicating that she was "in a seeking state only"—that is, she hadn't fully committed to Christ but was still examining her options. "Surely that will not do," George told his friend. "I would have one that is full of faith and the Holy Ghost. Just now I have been weeping, and much carried out in prayer before the Lord. . . . I want a gracious woman that is dead to everything but Jesus, and is qualified to govern children, and direct persons of her own sex. Such a one would help, and not retard me in my dear Lord's work."

Was he regretting the proposal? Was he afraid that his desire for Elizabeth had run ahead of his desire to serve God, or did he simply fear rejection and guard his heart by undermining her first? In any case, he told

Seward he was still trusting God in this matter and had received assurances "that he will not permit me to fall by the hands of a woman."[10]

George didn't know, or maybe was just beginning to find out, that the Delamotte family was in the process of rejecting Methodism in favor of a Moravian group. Charles Wesley wrote in his journal about a painful visit on June 10, 1740, to these old friends in Blendon. "They could hardly force themselves to be barely civil." When he returned the next day, "Betty" and her mother asked him not to come back.[11]

This situation might have contributed to Elizabeth's "seeking state only" status. It also seems that she was seeking a husband elsewhere. The following March, she married a member of her new religious society.[12]

We're not sure when George received any of this news. It's possible that he got a reply from the Delamottes in August or later, rejecting his proposal. This would coincide with a time of physical sickness that might have been brought on by this emotional jolt. "God has been pleased to bring me low, for some time, by inward weakness, and faintness of spirits," he wrote at the time. "The Lord is purging me, that I may bring forth more fruit."[13]

The Good Wife

These personal events all contributed to George's emotional state when he launched his New England tour in the fall of 1740. Was he depressed about Elizabeth's rejection, or her parents' defection? Was he in denial, still holding out hope that Elizabeth would come back to the Lord, and to him? Was he despairing about ever finding a suitable wife? Whatever his inner feelings, he pushed them aside in order to focus on the work ahead of him. But those feelings crept back into his heart that October, when George stayed with Jonathan and Sarah Edwards in Northampton, Massachusetts.

While we might expect George to rave about the intelligence or piety of the great Jonathan Edwards, it was Sarah who dazzled him. "A sweeter couple I have not yet seen. . . . Mrs. Edwards is adorned with a meek and quiet spirit; she talked solidly of the things of God, and seemed to be such a helpmeet for her husband, that she caused me to renew those prayers, which, for some months, I have put up to God, that He would be pleased to send me a daughter of Abraham to be my wife."[14]

The "daughter of Abraham" he wanted would be one who was justified by faith, as Abraham was (Romans 4:16–22), and as George was. Whitefield also liked the story of God leading Abraham's servant to find a wife for Isaac (Genesis 24). Wouldn't that be nice? Courtship was problematic and full of distractions. Why couldn't he just let someone else find the right woman for him?

Essentially, that's what happened. The following year, as George was back in the British Isles, his friend Howell Harris, the Welsh field preacher, suggested that he consider marrying Elizabeth James, an affluent widow about ten years older than George. If the proposal to Miss Delamotte was odd, this was odder still. It seems that Harris and James were fond of each other, but Harris had the same ambivalence about love that Whitefield had. He feared that romantic passion might distract from his ministry. So Harris handed Elizabeth James over to George. She wasn't happy to be treated this way ("If you were my own father you had no right of disposing me against my will," she complained to Harris[15]), but after a four-day courtship, she agreed to become Mrs. Whitefield. They married November 14, 1741, with Howell Harris giving the bride away. During the following week, staying in Elizabeth's home, George preached twice a day, as usual. Married or not, his ministry would go on, unimpeded.

George got what he wanted: a passionless marriage. He wrote to his American colleague Gilbert Tennent, "About eleven weeks ago I married, in the fear of God, one who was a widow, of about thirty-six years of age, and has been a housekeeper for many years; neither rich in fortune, nor beautiful as to her person, but, I believe, a true child of God, and would not, I think, attempt to hinder me in his work for the world. In that respect, I am just the same as before marriage."[16]

The Birth of Romance

That might trouble some modern readers accustomed to romance, a honeymoon, and wedded bliss. But the world of 1741 was different. The idea of romance in marriage was just beginning to gain traction, but it hadn't arrived yet. Both Whitefield and Franklin came out of cultures where marriages were generally practical in nature, often arranged by parents and/or approved by the community. George was looking for a "helpmeet," in the language of the King James Version, someone who could help him in fitting (meet) ways. He needed a housekeeper, a surrogate mother for orphans, someone who wouldn't distract him from preaching duties. The Franklin marriage wasn't much different. Ben boasted about Deborah's "industry and frugality . . . She assisted me cheerfully in my business, folding and stitching pamphlets, tending shop, purchasing old linen rags for the paper-makers, etc., etc."[17] He was a romantic, to be sure, but he found romance in his flirtatious games with Catherine Ray and others. Apparently he saw little connection between romance and marriage.

The ironic thing about George's lack of marital romance is that he himself was ushering in a sort of Romantic Age for religion. He was promoting a kind of "falling in love" with Jesus. Without that feeling, there was little evidence that anyone really had a relationship with Christ, as he saw it. Generations of churchgoers had been trudging along in their "arranged marriages" with the Lord, without any passion. It was quite revolutionary to suggest that passion was important—in either religion or in marriage.

Though he himself seemed blissfully unaware of this, there was a certain seduction going on when George preached. This was not lost on Boston pastor Charles Chauncy, a strong opponent of both George Whitefield and Jonathan Edwards. Chauncy wrote a scathing condemnation of the 1740 Whitefield revival.

"Wherever he went he generally moved the passions, especially of the younger people, and the females among them; the effect whereof was, a great talk about religion, together with a disposition to be perpetually hearing sermons, to neglect of all other business," Chauncy wrote.[18] It was true: the twenty-five-year-old Whitefield was quite popular among young people. Even Jonathan Edwards noted his effect on the youth in his town. And throughout his ministry critics charged George with using his versatile voice to excite women.

Chauncy went on to describe how "Mr. Whitefield's doctrine of inward feelings" caused such havoc that people "cried out, fell down, swooned away, and, to all appearance, were like persons in fits. . . . Scores in a congregation would be in such circumstances at a time; nay some hundreds in some places. . . . If this has its intended effect upon one or two weak women, the shrieks catch from one to another, till a great part of the congregation is affected."[19]

George Whitefield was Elvis. His dramatic phrasing and movement touched the hearts of his hearers. His preaching was a sensory experience that left women shrieking and swooning. Critics assumed that this was all show, that Whitefield and his copycats manufactured these emotional experiences. Of course George insisted that these were manifestations of the surprising work of God, drawing people to himself.

Still, there's a remarkable contradiction here. This man, who excited passions on two continents, scoured his own soul to remove passion, even from his own marriage. This eighteenth-century rock star, who taught millions to fall in love with Jesus, fought against his own falling in love.

TWENTY-ONE

Fireside Chats

Something happened between Ben and George in the mid-1740s that cemented their relationship. In 1742 and 1743 they were passing acquaintances, both recovering from George's exhausting tour. Savvy businessmen, they used each other for economic gain, but can we call them friends? Hardly. George was too fanatical. Ben was too skeptical. They'll join for profitable publishing enterprises, but don't invite them to the same party.

America itself was recovering from that first tour. Converts were struggling to grow in their newfound commitment. When your faith is forged in a divine lightning strike, what do you do when the fire goes out? In England, John Wesley was using his great organizational skills to form Methodist "societies"—ongoing small groups for Bible study, prayer, and mutual accountability (not unlike the original Holy Club). Whitefield had tried to do the same in America, with limited success. Especially in New England, Christians were divided. Whitefield had criticized the clergy, and they were striking back. Many parishioners were caught in the middle, distrusting the established church but having nothing to replace it. Various revivalists, like the Tennents and over-the-top James Davenport, tried to follow in Whitefield's train—again, with limited success. Opponents who had kept mum at the height of Whitefield-mania now gained the courage to speak out against him, often sending critical letters and articles to newspapers. Newspapers like the *Pennsylvania Gazette.*

Ben printed a number of these attacks—not only in the newspaper, but in books, pamphlets, and broadsides. Ever since the dance-hall flap, he had tried to maintain neutrality. He would print whatever served the public interest, and at this point he apparently felt the public needed to sort things out.

This was good for business, of course. Not only was the anti-Whitefield crowd a previously untapped market, but every attack would generate a response—which would also need to be published. Ben played both sides. He sold the controversy.

Some historians have highlighted Franklin's mercenary qualities in this matter. More than anything, they say, he was a shrewd businessman. That he was, but he was also a public servant who loved a win-win situation, in which he could serve the public and make some money in the process. Ben would have loved the Whitefield controversy—both sides of it—because it got people thinking and talking about religion. It jolted those prissy Anglicans and docile Quakers into action. Ben did all he could to promote good citizenship, and an *active* religion made good citizens. Whitefield's theology could be right or wrong, but he had started a chain reaction among the religious folks of America, and Ben wanted to keep that going.

Would George understand and accept Ben's independence? His journals and letters in this period don't tell us, but published attacks were nothing new to him. He was used to having enemies. The *South Carolina Gazette* ran a continuing pro-con debate throughout much of 1740, and the *Boston Evening Post* printed regular diatribes against him. In England and Scotland he faced angry mobs; his agent, William Seward, was killed by one. So George might not have felt very threatened by mere words on a page printed by B. Franklin.

However, his previous publishing experience had been with a loyal supporter, James Hutton in London, and it would be hard to find a more devoted associate than Seward, who had faithfully managed his press relations. But Seward was now gone, a martyr for the cause. Hutton had shifted his loyalty elsewhere and was now refusing to print Whitefield's work. Perhaps George viewed the attacks Ben printed as another defection.

In any case, it seems the relationship went silent for several years. In his letter of November 26, 1740, presumably just weeks after a personal meeting, George pushed his evangelistic appeal upon Ben one more time: "Apply to God; be willing to do the divine will, and you shall know it." There is no recorded reply. In fact, after that, we have no record of communication between them until 1745.[1] Ben continued to publish some Whitefield sermons, so there might have been some business transactions, but the friendship lay dormant.

Rekindling

Whitefield had ridden his personal fame back to the British Isles and carried his revival to Scotland. He set up a tabernacle in Moorfields, one of his favorite open-air preaching spots, to accommodate even larger congregations. He bought a magazine and used it to promote his meetings. Yet wherever he went, he continued to spark controversy. Opposition came from all corners—the theater crowd, the established church, even Wesleyan Methodists. Unwittingly he got embroiled in Scottish church politics when a radical Calvinist group claimed him as one of their own and reacted badly when he refused to sever ties with the moderates. Wherever he went, crowds were wildly enthusiastic, but there were angry protests too. He took some protesters to court, and won, but he and his supporters still met with violence. We shouldn't be surprised that this preacher who passionately called for passionate faith would arouse a full array of passions in his hearers—negative as well as positive.

Planning a return to America in mid-1744, George had to delay the trip as he recovered from injuries sustained in a confrontation with late-night intruders. (His powerful voice, yelling "Murder!" scared them off and probably saved his life.) He finally set off in the closing months of that year, heading straight for Boston, the most contentious of the American cities he had visited.

"Circumstances from without and within now compelled the boy preacher to grow up," wrote one biographer.[2] And these early months of his third American tour show evidence of a new maturity in George as he turned thirty. He made a point of garnering support from the clergy. He apologized for causing division in the churches. He even tried to reconcile with opponents at Harvard. "I have no intention . . . to stir up people against their pastors," he wrote, and later in the same letter, "I ask public pardon for any rash word I have dropped, or anything I have written or done amiss."[3] This sweeter tone did not quell all opposition, but it greatly improved the situation. From a historical perspective, this reconnection with churches helped make the Great Awakening more than just a passing fancy.

It was probably late summer of 1745 when Ben heard from George again. George was in Boston, coming soon to Philadelphia, but his previous host in the city had moved to Germantown and so he wasn't sure where he would stay. As Ben related this story in his autobiography, it's not clear that George was asking for lodging. Surely he had many other friends in Philadelphia who would offer hospitality. He was probably just saying he'd be in town, but he didn't know where. Surely these two had new business to discuss, so George probably suggested that they meet up.

Ben replied, "You know my house, if you can make shift with its scanty accommodations you will be most heartily welcome."

It was a sweet response to an old colleague. Perhaps Ben felt he had put enough distance between them at this point. Maybe he liked what he was hearing about a kinder, gentler Whitefield who had been mending fences in New England. Maybe he wanted to mend his own fences with his best client. In any case, this kind offer led to a fascinating exchange, as Ben described it: "He replied, that if I made that kind offer for Christ's sake, I should not miss of a reward. And I returned, *Don't let me be mistaken; it was not for Christ's sake, but for your sake.*"

This is a classic Franklin witticism, but it's plump with meaning. Ben himself observed wryly that "knowing it to be the custom of the saints, when they received any favour, to shift the burden of obligation from off their own shoulders, and place it in Heaven, I had contrived to fix it on Earth."[4]

George lived in a world of Christian charity, Christian hospitality, Christian duty. Every kindness was a bit of treasure stored in heaven. God would reward the good deeds of the faithful. While Ben appreciated the good deeds of faithful Christians, he focused more on the earthly effects of those deeds. Hospitality made the world a better place—not because there was some divine payoff ahead, but because it led to hospitality in return. Kindness begat kindness, creating a pleasant society.

A mercenary view of Franklin would see here an expectation of quid pro quo: "I'm being nice to you, George, so you'd better give me more sermons to publish." But with Ben, it's always both/and. Friendship is a great thing in its own right, but there's also an exchange involved. Let's treat each other right—not "for Christ's sake," with some eternal reward, but because we see value in being friends here and now. And might Ben also be saying, in subtext, "Stop trying to convert me all the time, just *friend* me"?

This marked a major step in the restoration and deepening of their friendship. If Whitefield stayed in the Franklin home, he would have had some quality time with Ben—not just a rushed meeting in a print shop, but a relaxed conversation by the fire (or by the new "Pennsylvania stove" that Franklin had recently invented). The differences between them were still great, but now they would be able to understand each other, perhaps to learn from each other. Make no mistake: they were still very busy people. They would not have had a lot of time to lounge, but surely they would have found occasional moments to chat—not working through any particular agenda, but just sharing their lives and thoughts.

Once again, Philadelphia served as a hub for Whitefield's travels in America from 1744 to 1748. This itinerary was not as well documented as that of the previous trip, but we can piece some of it together. It appears that George first stayed with the Franklins in September 1745, but he was also in Philadelphia most of the summer of 1746, and he came through again in May or June of 1747. It's unclear whether he continued to stay with the Franklins every time, but it's reasonable to think he returned there at least occasionally.

Conversation Pieces

So what would they talk about, by the fire, as they unwound from their hectic days?

Family

George's wife, Elizabeth, accompanied him to America, though she didn't join him on every leg of his journey. (She had some health problems along the way, so she might have stayed put at the orphanage or elsewhere as George traveled.) Still, she might have joined in some of these Franklin visits. Even if she wasn't there, Ben would have asked *about* her, and George would have gotten to know Deborah.

We know from later correspondence that Ben's sister, Jane Mecom, living in Boston, had become a fan of Whitefield. This was also true of Ben's brother John, whose wife proudly showed her friends a letter written by Ben about some encounter with George. It's rather amusing that, while Jane and John took their brilliant brother for granted, they seemed very impressed that he knew the great George Whitefield.

The Franklins and Whitefields would also be united in tragedy. George would still be grieving the death of his four-month-old son, John, in 1743. In addition, Elizabeth had suffered several miscarriages. The Franklins had lost a four-year-old son, Franky, to smallpox in 1736. We can't assume that George would open up to Ben about such personal misfortune (especially when we see little about it in his correspondence with other friends), but who knows? This might have been an odd role reversal—the skeptic offering grief counseling to the clergyman. Yet, from his own painful experience, the older Franklin might have been able to offer wisdom to the younger Whitefield. Was it also a bittersweet reminder to see little Sally Franklin toddling around the house? Born in 1743, she was the age the Whitefields' son would have been.

Publishing

Of course the two men would talk shop. But this wasn't just a printer and his best-selling author; these were two publishing moguls. They were enterprising entrepreneurs revolutionizing the industry. Ideas they shared over the course of their partnership benefited both of them.

Franklin had brought his extraordinary wit into the otherwise mundane field of almanac publishing. He had outpaced two competitors to edit the best newspaper in America's biggest city. He had made an art of subscription sales, a goof-proof approach to speculative printing. He had assembled a network of printers throughout the colonies for effective distribution of books and news. And he had established a newspaper as an independent, neutral voice, a "fifth estate" that would serve its society as a free marketplace of ideas.

But let's not overlook Whitefield's contribution to the fields of publishing and publicity. Stockbroker Seward got him started by advertising his preaching gigs, but Whitefield continued this after Seward's death, writing news items for local papers and supplying publishers (Franklin, but also others) with sermons and pamphlets to print. George found great success in serializing the publication of sermons and journals, rolling out a bit at a time to maintain interest and to keep the market wanting more. In this he adapted techniques used by the secular press in England. He also pioneered pricing strategies. In 1748 he would write, "I think practical books cannot be too reasonable. The poor must have them cheap, and the rich will like them the better for it."[5]

Ben had tried his hand at publishing a magazine for about six months in 1741. Now George had recently bought up a magazine in England, the *Weekly History*, and retooled it into a widely accessible revival update, delivered to people's homes at the price of one penny. "And for consumer convenience, the magazine would be made available in pocket size," wrote Frank Lambert in a study of George's business skills, noting that this was "perhaps an innovation Whitefield borrowed from Franklin, who produced a pocket-sized version of his almanac."[6]

Lambert also notes that Whitefield could have gained his merchandising skills from the time he spent working with his brother James, a sea captain and successful trader. Among George's close friends in Gloucester were Gabriel Harris, whose father ran the local bookstore, and Robert Raikes, son of the newspaper editor. Unlike other religious leaders of the time, George saw no conflict between faith and commerce. He was in the marketplace, sometimes literally, competing for attention with sellers of other wares.

In 1745 Whitefield was also assembling an impressive network of letter writers who could quickly disseminate news of his revivals to supporters throughout the colonies. This was another innovation in communication, an independent news stream that presaged the Twitterverse of modern times. Two decades later, George would use this network to save the reputation of his friend Ben.

The War with France

The conflict known in America as the French and Indian War did not begin until 1754, part of a worldwide Seven Years' War between England and France, but tensions had already erupted in North America. England was always at war with France and, despite truces and treaties, would continue to be for quite some time.

As Ben and George sipped tea on Market Street in 1745, one of them had already been swept into the conflict, and the other would get heavily involved later.

The French had built a fortress at Louisbourg at Nova Scotia, from which they harassed some of the sea travel, shipping, and fishing around New England. It was rumored that the French would launch a full-scale attack from there on the British colonies. The colonists decided on a pre-emptive strike. The commanding officer, Colonel Pepperell, was a devout Christian and a friend of George Whitefield. In early 1745, shortly after George arrived in New England, the officer asked the evangelist for help in rallying the troops. Whitefield turned out to be an excellent recruiter, and it should come as no surprise that he gave an effective pep talk to the largest expeditionary force yet assembled in the British colonies. (Ben's brother John was part of this army.) The powerful preacher likened the walls of Louisbourg to those of the biblical Jericho, formidable but ready to fall before the people of God. (The conflict between England and France was regularly viewed as Protestant vs. Catholic. While Whitefield was notably interdenominational in his revival ministry, that acceptance did not extend beyond Protestants.)

Coming at a time when George was restoring relations in America, this involvement in the war effort helped him greatly. For his role in energizing these troops, he was viewed as an American patriot—especially when the expedition succeeded. On June 17, after an effective siege, the French forces at Louisbourg surrendered. (Three years later, the British gave the fortress back to France in exchange for some Belgian border towns—only to reconquer it in the Seven Years' War.)

Fundraising for the Orphan House

George and Ben shared an interest in money. Neither could be described as greedy. Both lived rather frugally, considering the vast sums they were responsible for, and yet both seemed fascinated by how money worked. Ben invested in property, business, and various social improvements. George's project was, of course, the Bethesda Orphan House. He raised a great deal of money in England and America, but the charity swallowed that up. It was a major undertaking—buying land, constructing buildings, hiring staff, and providing food and clothing for the orphans. In a colony with great economic needs, George found it hard to say no to anyone. "We have a house that will hold 100 and hearts that will hold 10,000," he wrote.[7]

He kept running the numbers, tweaking the business model, trying to make it work. Could Bethesda grow its own food? Could it employ the residents in making products that could be shipped and sold elsewhere? Later George thought of creating a college on the premises. And how many offerings would he have to collect—and how many sermons would he have to give—to keep this operation solvent?

We must not underestimate the importance of the orphan house to Ben Franklin. As we've seen, Ben had his problems with George's theology of rebirth, and he didn't share George's rigorous commitment to abstain from worldly pleasures. The one thing he really loved about George's ministry was the orphanage. In a letter sometimes connected with Whitefield, Franklin wrote:

> The Faith you mention has doubtless its use in the world. . . . But I wish it were more productive of good works than I have generally seen it: I mean real good works, works of kindness, charity, mercy, and public spirit; not holiday-keeping, sermon-reading or hearing, performing church ceremonies, or making long prayers. . . . Your great Master thought much less of these outward appearances and professions than many of his modern

disciples. He preferred the doers of the Word to the mere hearers . . . and those who gave food to the hungry, drink to the thirsty, raiment to the naked, entertainment to the stranger, and relief to the sick."[8]

Ben could easily write off George Whitefield as another puritanical preacher—if it weren't for the orphan house. This ambitious attempt to help the needy validated everything else George said and did. From his own accounts, Ben donated a substantial sum to Bethesda, and he also came up with a great idea. Subscriptions.

Together, they had used this concept for book sales—why not donations? Ben suggested that they publish a general appeal in the newspapers, asking people to commit a regular sum to the orphanage each month. He even wrote an introduction for that appeal, but George rejected the idea. "I thank you heartily for your kind preamble to the subscription," he wrote to Ben on June 23, 1747. "I only object against its being made public so as to engage persons in America and Great Britain." He was afraid it would show a lack of confidence in God's provision. "I think a private subscription among my friends here and *elsewhere* would raise as much as I want."[9]

A number of people did sign up for such a subscription, but the unreliability of the mail kept it from working as well as it should have.

Education

As early as 1743, Ben had discussed with the Junto his dream of starting a college in Philadelphia. His thoughts continued to percolate through that decade, and in 1749 he published a proposal in pamphlet form. He sent this to George, who responded early in 1750 with some thoughts of his own. As you might expect, the two men had different visions of what that college should look like.

While Ben had laid out a broad curriculum of mental, social, and physical education, covering the arts and sciences as well as training in particular professions, George wanted more of Christ in it. He urged Ben to find "proper masters that are acquainted with the world, with themselves, and with God," and (unsurprisingly) he suggested that a "Christian orator" be employed to help the students with public speaking. His own involvement, he admitted "would be of very little service."[10]

As it turned out, George got involved in a roundabout way. Back in 1740, his Philadelphia supporters had put up a building for him to preach in, and he had used it that fall before it even had a roof (in fact, he got snowed out one night) and on his next visits in 1745, 1746, and 1747. It had been intended as a place for Whitefield's converts to continue meeting even when he wasn't there, but it had never really caught on in this way. As a result, the association that owned the building (of which Franklin was a board member) was having trouble paying the bills. Now Ben was raising money for a college and looking for a building in Philadelphia to house it. He was able to negotiate a win-win (his specialty): the college would use the building but reserve part of it as a hall for visiting preachers. The school would open in 1751, and it later became the University of Pennsylvania—which now honors both Benjamin Franklin and George Whitefield as founders.

This conversation and correspondence about higher education might have planted a desire in George Whitefield that he developed later—the addition of a college to the Bethesda project.

Retirement

During George's visits in 1747, Ben might have mentioned the next step he planned to take in his career: retirement. His printing business was making a great deal of money. He could live comfortably on half of it—and that's exactly what he did the following year. Foreman David Hall took over the business after signing an agreement giving Franklin half the profits for the next eighteen years.

The Franklins moved to a larger home at Second and Sassafras (now Race), allowing Hall to move into the house on Market adjoining the shop. Now Ben would have time to pursue new interests—science, inventions, civic leadership, and more. He had been doing all these things already, but now he'd have the time to focus on them. "I am in a fair way of having no other tasks than such as I like to give myself," he wrote to a friend in 1748, "and of enjoying what I look upon as a great happiness, leisure to read, study, make experiments, and converse at large with such ingenious and worthy men as are pleased to honour me with their friendship or acquaintance, on such points as may produce something for the common benefit of mankind, uninterrupted by the little cares and fatigues of business."[11] What's more, he was now a man of leisure. He had always portrayed himself as a common tradesman, and he continued to do so when it suited him, but now—with his wealth and free time—he could almost be considered a gentleman. He had a portrait painted. He learned European languages. And, while he kept writing his almanac, now with the title *Poor Richard Improved*, it now had a more patronizing tone.

Social status might have been a significant point of connection for these two men, especially now that Franklin was on the verge of stepping up. While both were genuinely humble in character, they shared a sense of upward mobility. Yes, they saw themselves as servants—of God or of the common good—and they worked extremely hard, but both chafed at the haughtiness of certain higher-class "gentlemen" they encountered. Opposition to Whitefield's ministry was not just theological, but also social. He was bypassing the normal leadership of society and taking his message directly to the people. Clearly this populist spirit was one reason Franklin supported him. In Ben's case, the aristocrat Thomas Penn, absentee governor of Pennsylvania, was a common object of ire. Ben had already done a thousand times more for the colony; why should Penn have all the power?

In the following years, as George returned to England he would also do some stepping up, largely through the patronage of Lady Selina Hastings. This upper-class widow was a Methodist convert who took a special interest in Whitefield and introduced him to her high-society friends. He dazzled them, just as he had dazzled the coal miners. When Ben heard about this, he sent a letter commending George for the new direction of his ministry. "I am glad to hear that you have frequent opportunities of preaching among the great. If you can gain them to a good and exemplary life, wonderful changes will follow in the manners of the lower ranks." The upper classes set the style for the general public, Ben observed. There are many who "perhaps fear less the being in Hell, than out of the fashion."[12] This letter might say more about where Ben was, or wanted to be, in the early stages of his retirement than about George's mission.

Back in 1747, as George kicked off his shoes at Ben's place, he was thinking of a different kind of retirement. He was exhausted. Doctors soon began urging him to take a break. Surprisingly, he did so, spending a few months of 1748 in Bermuda. Of course he preached there too, but not as often.

Faith

It is inconceivable that George would spend significant time with Ben and not talk about faith in Jesus. This was a frequent part of their correspondence; it would surely get into their conversation. But, given the fact that these two remained friends for several decades without Ben's conversion, we must assume that they figured out a way to disagree without alienating each other.

Ben discussed theology with a number of his correspondents. Some of these letters give the impression that he was continuing a debate he began with Whitefield—even if he was writing to someone else. In some letters he mentioned George specifically: in one he complained about Whitefield equating deists with atheists. This rankled him, because he thoroughly believed in God—something he had to keep telling his worried sister.[13] He just didn't buy the whole born-again thing.

This conversation would continue for the next twenty years.

TWENTY-TWO

The Arc of Friendship

If there had been a cooling-off period between 1740 and 1745, Ben's hospitality and the resulting conversations certainly warmed things up. In addition, through the *Gazette*, Ben helped George restore his reputation.

Whispers continued about the orphanage funds. It seemed that Whitefield was always asking for money, and where was it really going? Had anyone actually seen this so-called orphanage, all the way down in Georgia, where no one could get to it? There were even reports in the press from some traveler who had poked around Savannah without finding any such orphanage.

George decided to hit this skepticism head on (and we may wonder if Ben advised him in this matter). While in Georgia in April 1746, George and the orphanage manager, James Habersham, went to court and opened their accounts for a public audit. They swore affidavits saying that Whitefield had "not converted or applied any part [of the donations] to his own private use and property, neither hath charged the [Orphan] House with any of his traveling, or any other private expenses whatsoever." Court officials also examined the accounts and approved. This official document was sent to Ben Franklin, who reprinted it in the *Gazette*.[1]

But Franklin extended even more support in a remarkable editorial a few months later. Perhaps, with George staying at his home, Ben got a close-up look at the rigors of his ministry and the daily toll it took on his fragile body. The piece, entitled "Appreciation of George Whitefield," had an emotional undercurrent that seemed out of character for the playful editor.

After offering the basic news item—that Whitefield, though "indisposed," had preached twice the previous Sunday to crowds at the New Building and left the next day for New York—Franklin got a bit weepy:

> When we seriously consider how incessantly this faithful servant (not yet 32 years old) has, for about 10 years past, laboured in his great Master's vineyard, with an alacrity and fervent zeal, which an infirm constitution, still daily declining, cannot abate; and which have triumphed over the most vigorous opposition from whole armies of invidious preachers and pamphleteers; under whose performances, the pulpits and presses, of *Great-Britain* and *America*, have groaned; We may reasonably think with the learned Dr. Watts, "That he is a man raised up by Providence in an uncommon way, to awaken a stupid and ungodly world, to a sense of the important affairs of religion and eternity."[2]

The lines were from Isaac Watts, a renowned English hymn writer. Franklin added some lofty poetry from Charles Wesley before concluding:

> His sermons here this summer have given general satisfaction, and plainly proved the great ability of the preacher. His rich fancy, sound and ripening judgment, and extensive acquaintance with men and books of useful literature, have been acknowledged by every unprejudiced person. Purity of language, perspicuity of method, a ready elocution, an engaging address, and an apt gesture, peculiar to this accomplished Orator, considered with his unspotted character in private life, have added force to the plain strong arguments, and pathetic [dramatic] expostulations, wherewith his discourses abounded. And, it cannot be doubted, that many have been awakened to a sense of the importance of religion, and others have been built up in their most holy Christian faith under his ministry.[3]

Was this impassioned praise simply damage control, a calculated attempt to rebuild the career of Ben's biggest author? It doesn't seem so. Ben was still selling plenty of books. This appears to be the heartfelt prose of a man genuinely convinced that his friend was changing the world for the better. As biographer Stout put it, "Franklin had no reason to applaud Whitefield's character unless he sincerely believed it."[4]

Ben also seemed genuinely concerned about George's health. These concerns would continue. About a year later, after an early summer stay in Philadelphia, George headed north again. Apparently Ben got a letter from his brother John with news of the preacher's arrival in Boston. Ben wrote back: "I am glad to hear that Mr. Whitefield is safe arrived, and recovered his health. He is a good man and I love him."[5]

This personal regard between Ben and George set the tone for the remaining years of their friendship. They certainly had their differences and disagreements, but there was a genuine love within this friendship. And with Ben soon retiring, the business nature of their relationship gave way to more personal interaction. Their letters show them exchanging ideas, books, good wishes, and greetings to other friends. They talked about getting together when they could, and apparently they did manage to fit this into their busy schedules. And every so often, George challenged his friend to get right with Jesus.

Science Guy

Ben Franklin always had an inventive mind. He sought to understand forces of nature and to use them in practical ways. As a boy, he flew a kite while swimming, allowing the wind to pull him across the water. On the ocean voyage back from his adolescent trip to London, he studied crabs and currents. Back in Philadelphia, he talked science with the Junto. With them, he established that dark-colored fabric gets hotter than light-colored fabric, conducting a simple experiment involving the melting of snow. He made observations about weather patterns long before weather prediction was a science. He invented a stove that could warm a house more efficiently.

But it was electricity that made him a scientist.

At some point in the 1740s, he saw a carnival act that used static electricity for various stunts. Of course Ben was fascinated. This combined his interest in natural forces with his love of practical jokes. How did this work? Could electrical force be controlled?

Franklin was not the first person to think about electricity. Though he was not scientifically trained, this may have turned out to be an advantage. Unfettered by previous doctrine, he was free to observe electricity on his own—and he had a knack for creating cool experiments. He also wrote about these experiments very clearly.

After his retirement from printing, Ben had more time to devote to scientific pursuits, particularly experiments in electricity. His curiosity was relentless. Which materials carry electricity and which don't? Can it be stored? How does it act? On his own time, he had the luxury of trial and error. In the process, he essentially created electrical science: positive and negative charges, batteries, and conducting. He not only discovered these features, he also named them. He learned that certain materials and certain shapes actually drew electricity to them. One key question that nagged at him: Is lightning electricity? The similarities were strong, but how could it be proved?

He wrote up some ideas for experiments involving church steeples and sent them to a scientist friend in London, Peter Collinson, who shared them within the European scientific community. Franklin was pleased to see those scientists accept his ideas and actually conduct those experiments, especially in France, which had led the way in electrical theory. "The electrical experiments have something very surprising in them," Collinson wrote to Franklin. Later he added, "Thou has set the French to work."[6]

Of course, France had plenty of high cathedral steeples to work with. Philadelphia didn't. Ben had to wait for Christ Church to build a steeple high enough for him to perform his own lightning experiment. (In a classic win-win strategy, Franklin was on the fundraising committee for the steeple project, but the progress was slow.) Then he wondered if, instead of a steeple, he could use his old childhood plaything—a kite.

The rest is history.

On a stormy day in June 1752, with a key on a kitestring, assisted by his son, Benjamin Franklin "completely demonstrated" the "sameness of the electric matter with that of lightning."[7] This was a scientific breakthrough, confirmed with the French experiments (which had actually happened earlier, though Ben didn't know it). It propelled Franklin into the scientific community. He was granted honorary degrees from Harvard and Yale and received a medal from London's Royal Society. But Ben did something even more important with this knowledge: he used it.

Having established that a pointed metal stick attracts electricity, the crafty inventor created the lightning rod. Before he even publicized the results of his experiment, he was putting lightning rods on public buildings in Philadelphia.

In the midst of all this, Franklin received a letter from George Whitefield, who was back in England after a quick trip to Georgia from 1751 to 1752:

> I find that you grow more and more famous in the learned world. As you have made a pretty considerable progress in the mysteries of electricity, I would now humbly recommend to your diligent unprejudiced pursuit and study the mystery of the new-birth. It is a most important, interesting study, and when mastered, will richly answer and repay you for all your pains. One at whose bar we are shortly to appear, hath solemnly declared, that without it, "we cannot enter the kingdom of heaven." You will excuse this freedom. I must have *aliquid Christi* [something of Christ] in all my letters.[8]

This is a remarkable communication from a master of communication. George had learned how to talk with Ben. It's not scolding or preaching. In fact, it has the same sort of wit and self-deprecation we might expect from Ben Franklin. George is honoring his friend, congratulating him on his spreading fame, but he's also challenging him to apply his brilliant mind to an eternally valuable subject.

Traveling Men

On his fifth American voyage George landed in South Carolina on May 26, 1754, sailed to New York in July, and spent much of August in Philadelphia.

He was still preaching wherever he went, though sickness sometimes forced him to cut back to *one* sermon a day. "Congregations rather increase than decrease," he wrote to a friend back home, seeming surprised by his continuing popularity.[9] "Here's a glorious range in the American woods," he wrote to another English friend, urging him to cross the ocean and join this evangelistic effort. "It is pleasant hunting for sinners. Thousands flock daily to hear the word preached."[10] He did, by the way, preach in the Academy—Franklin's new college, which used the old New Building that Whitefield had preached in many times. Apparently the space now reserved for preaching was not as large as George was used to. In a letter, he noted merely that it was not as "commodious" as the new Presbyterian church.[11]

That fall, George traveled to New England, stopping in late September to receive an honorary master's degree from the brand-new College of New Jersey (precursor to Princeton University). Then he revisited old territory, from New Hampshire to Rhode Island. It had been seven years since his last trip there, and his fame had not diminished. At a meetinghouse in Boston with a capacity of four thousand, the overflow crowd was already being turned away at 7 a.m., and George had to enter through a window. With renewed health, he was now preaching two or three times a day.

Then, just like old times, he undertook an ambitious overland journey to Georgia. During this trip, he turned forty, and he was not generally in good health. Still he poked through the American colonies, village by village, church by church, preaching nearly every day or night. He came through Philadelphia, but stayed only a few days, preaching seven times. In February 1755, George reached Georgia, where his old orphanage manager, James Habersham, was now colonial secretary. After checking up on Bethesda, Whitefield sailed back to England in March.

Ben was doing some traveling of his own in 1754. In his "retirement" from the printing trade, he now had three jobs—scientist, diplomat, and postmaster (and of course he was still writing the almanac and overseeing the newspaper). As a diplomat, he was sent to Albany, New York, along with other colonial representatives, to negotiate peace with the Iroquois and to discuss a united response to the French threat. (A young officer named George Washington had been leading a British-American force in unsuccessful raids against French forts.)

Franklin had long been impressed with the ability of the Iroquois to unite their several nations for a common cause and depressed by the inability of the British colonies to do the same. He began tinkering with concepts of unity among the colonies. How would it work? Elected representatives in a common council, with a Crown-appointed president? Ben drew up his ideas in a paper he called "Short Hints towards a Scheme for Uniting the Northern Colonies" and brought it to the Albany Conference in June 1754. His plan was tweaked but generally approved by the conferees in Albany, yet it failed to gain support from the colonial assemblies or the British. Years later, Ben speculated that the Albany Plan, if implemented, would have prevented the American Revolution.

When the Albany Conference adjourned in July, Ben returned to Philadelphia for a month or so before going back on the road. He would have been able to host George Whitefield during that August stay. It's likely that, during this time, Deborah Franklin wrote to Ben's brother John some story about having the famous preacher in her home. She also alerted John that Ben would soon be coming to see him in Boston. (John responded to this letter, saying how proud his wife was to read the Whitefield story to her friends.)

In Ben's role as postmaster for the American colonies, he wanted to tour various regions to see how their delivery systems worked. So, about the time Whitefield went north to New York and Boston, so did Franklin. (It's tempting to imagine them traveling together, but the dates don't match.) They might have connected in either of those cities, but of course both were very busy doing other things. On one of his last days in Boston, November 11, George preached again at the Old South Church, Ben's boyhood haunt. We might expect that other Franklin siblings—at least Jane and John—were there, and one wonders whether Ben might have joined them.

This was the time when Ben met and romanced Catherine Ray. So while George began his southward jaunt, preaching his way through Connecticut, Ben was accompanying Caty home to Newport, Rhode Island. The postmaster continued his postal inspections and arrived home in January, apparently missing the evangelist's breeze-through.

But a few weeks later, still traveling, George wrote, "My dear Mr. Franklin, I hope that this will find you safely arrived at Philadelphia, from your northward expedition, and ready to come further southwards. This leaves me in my last Virginia stage, near the borders of North-Carolina." As a frequent recipient of Franklin's hospitality, he now invited Ben to visit the orphanage. "Glad shall I be to wait on you." That didn't happen. Ben stayed put in Philadelphia for a while.

This was the letter in which George mentioned the epitaph that a young Ben Franklin had written for himself, cleverly comparing his body to an old book. After mentioning his own fatigue, George quoted a few lines of a religious poem: "His presence doth my pains beguile / And makes the wilderness to smile." Remember that he was on the last leg of a grueling journey, often through wilderness, at age forty and in poor health. The Lord, he believed, made all the weariness worthwhile.

Then he shared this eternity-conscious reverie with his worldly wise friend. "Lovely delusion this! Living, dying, and after death I hope to be possessed of it. I have seen your *Epitaph*. Believe on Jesus, and get a feeling possession of God in your heart, and you cannot possibly be disappointed of your expected second edition finely corrected, and infinitely amended. *Verbum sapienti sat est.* I could say more, but time is short."[12]

The Latin quotation means, "A word to the wise is sufficient." Yes, George could say more, and he did so every night to enthusiastic crowds. Ben had heard him many times, in public and in private, talking about this feeling of having God in one's heart. This "word to the wise" seems like a concession on George's part. He might have bent Ben's ear before, preaching to him, haranguing him, abusing the friendship, but now he would merely throw something of Christ into the conversation and then let it rest. Ben was wise enough to respond when he was ready.

Wagon Train

Just as George Washington became a hero of the war with France before it officially started, rallying a colonial army against a French fortress in Nova

Scotia, so Ben got involved a decade later, as General Braddock came from England with a plan to sweep French forces out of the Ohio Valley. The plan lacked some logistical forethought, notably a way to transport troop supplies on the long trek. Ben jumped into action, urging Pennsylvania farmers to lend their wagons to the cause. That expedition turned out badly for Braddock, his army, the wagons, and Franklin, who had put up bond for the wagons' safe return.

A few months later, Ben was back in action as the head of a militia, building stockades in western Pennsylvania. Once again, his leadership was more logistical than military. He probably boasted to George about one of his accomplishments there. When the militia's chaplain complained that the men were skipping Sunday worship, Ben improved attendance by doling out the weekly ration of rum after the service.

These events provide some background for an interesting letter Ben wrote George on July 2, 1756, just a few months after his stockade-building experience: "You mention your frequent wish that you were a chaplain to an American army. I sometimes wish that you and I were jointly employed by the Crown to settle a colony on the Ohio."

At first it sounds like one of Ben's jokes, but as the letter continues, it becomes clear that Ben put some thought into it—though he knew it would never happen. "What a glorious thing it would be, to settle in that fine country a large strong body of religious and industrious people!" Society building had always excited Ben. Here he was imagining how they could build a society from scratch. George's religion and Ben's industry would be an unbeatable combination. He even pandered to George's missionary spirit by suggesting that this would help the spread of "pure religion" among the "Heathen" (he meant the Native American tribes). At age fifty, Ben felt he was in the "last act" of his life, and he was looking "for something fit to end with."[13]

He had no way of knowing that there would be several more acts to his life story—Science, Revolution, Statecraft—and that the younger evangelist would end his earthly drama first.

TWENTY-THREE

Death and Taxes

Overseas travel was more dangerous than usual during the Seven Years' War between England and France, so when George Whitefield came home from his fifth American voyage in 1755, he stayed for a while.

It was a different story for Ben Franklin, who went from wagon wrangling and stockade building to a different kind of public service. He got himself appointed as a representative of the Pennsylvania Assembly, sent to London to petition the colony's proprietors and the British government to give the assembly more power. So Ben crossed the dangerous ocean with his son, William, in mid-1757.

They got a four-room apartment on Craven Street, renting from Margaret Stevenson. With this as his home base, Ben would spend the next six years interacting with the London intelligentsia, exploring his own family heritage, touring other parts of the British Isles and Europe, flirting with Margaret and her daughter, and of course carrying on his official state business.

It was quite different from his first London trip some thirty years earlier. Ben was already rich and now somewhat famous for his scientific experiments. He had a ready entrée with leading scholars, who were eager to meet him. He was in heaven. An early letter he sent home to his wife (who hated ocean travel) revealed his joy, acknowledged his duty, and protested a bit too much about being away from home. "The agreeable conversation I meet with among men of learning, and the notice taken of me by persons of distinction, are the principal things that soothe me for the present under this painful absence from my family and friends; yet those would not detain me here another week, if I had not other inducements, duty to my country and hopes of being able to do it service."[1]

Missed Connections

We have no record of letters between George and Ben during this time that they both were based in London, though this doesn't mean they didn't see each other. Why send a letter if you're having lunch together next Thursday? Yet both traveled much during this period. George found an exciting new mission field in Scotland, and he took extensive preaching tours there nearly every year. Ben got into the habit of taking summer vacations with his son, William. They journeyed through the area north of London, studying the roots of the Franklin clan. They also visited Scotland, where Ben met a number of well-known scholars. They even ventured to Holland and Belgium.

Comparing the schedules of Ben and George, we find few times when they were both in London—maybe September 1757, the winter and spring of 1758, and a longer period in 1760 through 1761. Ben and William rushed back from Holland to attend the coronation of King George III on September 22, 1761. George was probably in London at that time, but he was recovering from a serious illness, and he made no mention of the coronation in his letters.

The most intriguing confluence of their schedules comes in 1759, when they were both in Edinburgh, Scotland. Even then, they just missed each other. George left Scotland in August; Ben arrived in September. It's also interesting that, during this time, Ben was making the acquaintance of philosopher David Hume—someone George already knew, thanks to Lady Huntingdon's high-society connections. After hearing a talk by Whitefield,

Hume said, "This address was accompanied with such animated, yet natural, action, that it surpassed anything I ever saw or heard in any other preacher."[2] He was just as complimentary about Franklin. After Ben announced his intention in 1762 to return to America, Hume wrote back, "I am very sorry, that you intend soon to leave our Hemisphere. America has sent us many good things, gold, silver, sugar, tobacco, indigo etc.: But you are the first philosopher, and indeed the first Great Man of Letters for whom we are beholden to her."[3]

It would be truly delightful if we could find David Hume, Ben Franklin, and George Whitefield in a room together, perhaps sipping tea in a Scottish castle, discussing the nature of reality. Hume's empirical philosophy, Franklin's moral pragmatism, and Whitefield's experiential spirituality actually shared common roots in the Enlightenment philosopher John Locke. Sadly, that party never happened.

In fact, as we look at the letters of both Ben and George, we begin to think they never connected during the period between 1757 and 1763, even if they were just a few miles apart. Ben wrote regularly to his wife back in Philadelphia and his sister in Boston, both of whom knew George Whitefield. Yet, while he passed along greetings from various others, he didn't mention George as far as we know. Neither did George mention Ben in his letters of the period. This might signal another distancing in their relationship.

As he implied in that letter to Deborah, it was very important to Ben to be accepted by London's elite—not only for his own sense of pride, but for the good of Pennsylvania. Back in Philadelphia, he was a very big fish in a small pond. Britain, however, was a huge pond, and Ben could easily be written off as an American hick. And while George was famous in England, he too could be written off by the elite as a populist oddity. Lady Huntingdon provided some inroads to the well-born set, but many would consider Whitefield merely a fad.

In 1760, a play was produced in London lampooning Whitefield in shocking, bawdy ways. This led to a public war of words in pamphlets and newspapers between his supporters and detractors. George himself seemed unfazed, writing to a friend, "Satan is angry. I am now mimicked and burlesqued upon the public stage. All hail such contempt! God forbid that I should glory, save in the cross of Jesus Christ."[4]

George knew there's no such thing as bad publicity, especially when your personal reputation is irrelevant, but that wasn't the case for Ben Franklin. His mission was all about reputation. It was crucial that the officials he lobbied would see him as respectable, important, someone to be reckoned with. He had no newspaper here with which he could manage public opinion. Perhaps an association with Whitefield would prove counterproductive to the image Franklin needed to convey. So maybe Ben was avoiding his old preacher friend.

Or maybe they were just busy.

The factors that had brought them together in Philadelphia weren't there anymore. They had no publishing business to discuss. George didn't need a place to stay. In order to get together, they would have to make a point to do so. It seems that there were more good reasons not to. For now.

As the war drew to a close, both men made their way back to America— Ben in late 1762 and George in the summer of 1763. Whitefield had the feeling it was his last visit to the colonies. He was wrong about this, as it turned out, but this trip had the feel of a farewell tour. His letters show him even more eternity-minded than usual. He had gained weight. He had lost energy. He could preach only about three or four times a week. And still he embarked on the same kind of continent-crossing voyage he had taken before: Virginia, Philadelphia, New York, Boston, and then south again to Georgia. Everywhere crowds attended, with the thought that this might be their final chance to hear him. Gone was the bitter opposition. As one Boston friend told him, "Your enemies are very few, and even they seem to be almost at peace with you."[5] Newspapers reported each stop along the way, with regular reference to his failing health. This added to his heroism. He was already an American treasure, and each weary step across this land confirmed it.

Franklin was traveling too, on a postal inspection tour from Virginia to New Hampshire. Once again, the old friends missed connections. Whitefield was in Philadelphia in November 1763, when Franklin returned home from New England, but they didn't get together. Ben was sorry about that. He had received a package for George and was planning to hand-deliver it when the preacher got back from a quick trip to Princeton, but then he learned that Whitefield was already moving on to New York. Ben wrote that it "mortifies me not a little, that I should so long omit waiting on you here, as to be at length finally deprived of the pleasure of seeing you."[6]

Franklin wrote again the following June. This letter seems to be a reasoned response to Whitefield's evangelistic efforts. In the early lines, he mentioned something George had sent him, and that he was enclosing something in return. But George had probably added a message in his previous post, one last impassioned plea to the brilliant man who hadn't yet seen the value of rebirth. It inspired Ben to respond in kind. This was Franklin's credo. "Your frequently repeated wishes and prayers for my eternal as well as temporal happiness are very obliging. I can only thank you for them, and offer you mine in return. I have myself no doubts that I shall enjoy as much of both as is proper for me."[7]

Let's pause here to note that he's talking about "both" eternal and temporal happiness. Prayers are offered for well-being now and heavenly bliss in the future. While George was, no doubt, worried about Ben's eternal destiny, Ben had no such fears. Whatever was "proper," he would receive.

Ben went on: "That Being who gave me existence, and through almost threescore years has been continually showering his favours upon me, whose very chastisements have been blessings to me, can I doubt that he loves me? And if he loves me, can I doubt that he will go on to take care of me not only here but hereafter? This to some may seem presumption; to me it appears the best grounded hope; hope of the future; built on experience of the past."[8]

There is much that a Christian might like about Ben's statement of faith—a humble belief in the grace of a caring God and a future hope built on gratitude for the past. Just a week later, Ben wrote to his friend William Strahan, a London bookseller, along the same lines. "God has been very good to you, from whence I think you may be assured that he loves you, and that he will take at least as good care of your future happiness as he has done of your present."[9]

This was theism, not really deism. Ben's God was not a disinterested clockmaker, but a very interested bestower of blessing. Yet George would notice something missing: Jesus. His New Testament gospel was built on the sacrificial death of Christ, the justification of believers at the cross, and the resurrection of believers to new life. As beautiful as Ben's sentiments were, they still didn't amount to a Christian conversion, as far as George was concerned.

Ben closed his letter to George with joy in improved health, greetings from Deborah, and a plea to visit Philadelphia again. We have every reason to think that they did get together a few months later, as George spent about a month in Philadelphia before another southward swing.

Stamp Rejector

Both men were back in England in 1765. Oddly, both these celebrities seemed more "at home" away from home. George had hoped that his American voyage would be good for his health. Life had grown so stressful in England that he considered it soothing to go stomping through the colonial wilderness. Yet it wasn't the cure-all he had hoped for.

On the other hand, Ben had difficulty back home in Pennsylvania. Life in Philadelphia had gone on just fine without him. He briefly became speaker of the assembly but then was ousted from the assembly in a failed reelection bid. He found, to his surprise, that he had enemies. As he prepared to go back to London, he wrote a grim letter to his daughter, Sally, warning her that this "enmity will extend in some degree to you, so that your slightest indiscretions will be magnified into crimes, in order . . . to wound and afflict me." He urged her to "Go constantly to church, whoever preaches."[10]

He thought it would be a quick trip to London this time. At least that's what he told his wife. He had just a few loose ends to tie up. Ben was still trying to get Pennsylvania out of the grip of its proprietors—Thomas Penn and his board. He wanted to hang on to the job of American postmaster. And then there was the Stamp Act.

The war with France was expensive. British debt had nearly doubled.

So in March 1765, Parliament passed the Stamp Act, imposing a tax in American colonies on court documents, printed matter, and even playing cards. It all had to bear the stamp of the British government, and that would cost extra. Americans were, of course, incensed.

Ben Franklin played the politics of this situation badly at first. He was just too reasonable. He understood that governments needed to tax citizens to raise money for public projects—like wars. And while he opposed the Stamp Act, he encouraged people to try to live with it. He even set up a friend of his as tax collector for Pennsylvania, assuming that Americans would resist for a short while and then get used to the idea.

He was very wrong about this, and his enemies back home made the most of it. It was easy to see Franklin building his own fortune and reputation at the expense of the American people. Mobs formed throughout the colonies, protesting the new tax. One mob destroyed the home of the Massachusetts governor. In Philadelphia, a similar mob threatened the Franklin home, but Deborah stood her ground, with shotguns at the ready. The British stamp was "the mark of the beast." Preachers—Old Lights and New Lights—railed against it. Throughout America, patriots like Patrick Henry and John Adams raised their voices against the mother country. Delegates from nine colonies gathered in New York to issue a declaration of protest. This was a dry run for the Revolution.

Throughout his life, Ben Franklin had seen the American colonies as a glorious extension of a great empire. He loved England, and while he often bristled at the way the British treated the colonists, he generally believed that a win-win solution could be found. He had long urged the British to include colonial representatives in Parliament, but no one paid much attention. The concept of taxation without representation was fundamentally immoral, he felt, and that's precisely what this Stamp Act was doing. Americans would tolerate tariffs on *external* trade, Ben suggested, but this tax on the *internal* business of the colonies was just wrong.

Soon Ben began lobbying for the repeal of the Stamp Act. There were some like-minded Whigs in the British government who helped him get a hearing. And so Ben found himself testifying before Parliament on February 13, 1766, as the resident expert on America. By some reports he was accompanied by George Whitefield, who observed the proceedings. Ben's parliamentary allies did much of the questioning, but there were occasional challenges from others. What did Americans want, and what would they accept? Franklin spoke forcefully, direly, and prophetically. While he did not question the right of Parliament to tax the colonies (a concession that would get Ben in trouble back home), this levy on internal business was wrong and dangerous.

Deeply divided, Parliament voted to repeal the Stamp Act eight days after Ben's testimony, but only after passing the Declaratory Act, which affirmed its right to tax the colonies whenever it wanted. After the king approved the repeal, George wrote in his diary, "March 6, 1766, Stamp Act repealed—*Gloria Deo.*"[11]

In America, the reaction was mixed. When news of the repeal arrived, there was dancing in the streets. Their protests had smashed the deplorable Stamp Act! But then some began reading the fine print: Parliament had retained its taxing authority. How could Franklin let that happen?

Joseph Galloway, a mutual friend, suggested that George help Ben by writing a letter of support, and he gladly did so, distributing it through his broad letter-writing network in the colonies. "Dr. Franklin has gained immortal honour by his behaviour at the bar of the House. His answer was always found equal to the questioner. He stood unappalled, gave pleasure to his friends, and did honour to his country."[12]

And so, nearly two decades after Franklin had used the *Pennsylvania Gazette* to shore up Whitefield's reputation against unfounded attacks, George used his own worldwide web to return the favor. This seems to have been a step forward in their relationship. If Ben had been dodging George during his earlier stay in England, he wasn't doing so anymore.

Like Family

Two weeks after Ben's testimony, he wrote a rather innocuous note to his wife that includes this, in passing: "Mr. Whitfield [sic] called today and tells me a surprising piece of news."[13] The news was trivial—about someone they knew who was now in England. The point is that George was *dropping by* Franklin's place. Over the next few years there were several more letters between them, some referring to conversations they'd had. They were friends again.

William Franklin wrote from his post as governor of New Jersey to tell Ben how effective Whitefield's support was after the Stamp Act testimony. In a letter to sister Jane, Ben mentioned a story he'd heard from George. (Seeing boys in the distance throwing rocks at a tree, George said he didn't know what kind of tree it was, but he assumed it had fruit. So, with all the slander thrown at Ben, it had to mean he was fruitful.)[14] "Your daughter I find is beginning the world," George wrote after learning of Sally's marriage. "I wish you joy from the bottom of my heart."[15] There was a new closeness here. It's like George was part of the family.

Meanwhile Whitefield had a new project: seeking a charter for a new college at Bethesda. He had alienated so many of the officials whose approval he needed, it was slow going. Franklin, who had started a college already, seems to have served as a valuable advisor in this matter. "When will it suit you to have another interview? The college affair lies dormant," wrote George, before complaining again about his health. "For above a week I have been dethroned by a violent cold and hoarseness."

Everything, even a medical report, provided opportunity for George to share his faith. Ben was probably used to it by now. "Through rich grace I can sing 'O Death where is thy sting'—but only through Jesus of Nazareth." After the death of his wife from a fever a few months earlier, George was vividly aware of his own impending death, and the temporary quality of all earthly life. Sally might be beginning the world, but "you and I shall soon go out of it—Ere long we shall see it burnt—Angels shall summon us to attend on the funeral of Time—And (Oh transporting thought!) we shall see Eternity rising out of its ashes. That you and I may be in the happy number of those who in the midst of the tremendous final blaze shall cry Amen—Hallelujah—is [my] hearty prayer."[16]

George had won his way into Ben's heart. This is how he could get away with preaching him the Book of Revelation. He was like family. As Ben said in his next letter, he held George in "greatest esteem and sincerest affection."[17]

One More Time

George felt he had another American voyage in him. He longed to see his orphanage one more time. "Bethesda lies upon my heart night and day," he wrote a friend.[18] A few months later: "I am every day, every hour, almost every moment, thinking of and preparing for America."[19]

He still struggled with illness from time to time, but he kept preparing for this trip. John Wesley, who had reconciled with George a few years earlier and now met with him regularly, was concerned about his old friend. "His soul appeared to be vigorous still, but his body was sinking apace; and unless God interposes with His mighty hand, he must soon finish his labours."[20]

George's health rallied enough for him to continue preparations. He launched into a final circuit of preaching appearances in England, a long goodbye to his homeland.

Sometime during that year, he received a letter from Benjamin Franklin, who was concerned for a different reason. Violence was brewing in America, especially New England. The British government had used its taxing authority to levy tariffs on all sorts of goods, and the colonists weren't happy about it. Extra troops had been deployed to keep order.

"I am under continued apprehensions that we may have bad news from America," Ben wrote. "The sending soldiers to Boston always appeared to me a dangerous step; they could do no good, they might occasion mischief. When I consider the warm resentment of a people who think themselves injured and oppressed, and the common insolence of the soldiery, who are taught to consider that people as in rebellion, I cannot but fear the consequences of bringing them together. It seems like setting up a smith's forge in a magazine of gunpowder."[21]

These thoughts were prophetic. Early the next year, a Boston mob would incite some British soldiers to shoot, killing five and wounding six in what became known as the Boston Massacre.

In this final letter to George, Ben seemed to continue a political/religious conversation of theirs. "I see with you that our affairs are not well managed by our rulers here below; I wish I could believe with you, that they are well attended to by those above; I rather suspect, from certain circumstances, that though the general government of the universe is well administered, our particular little affairs are perhaps below notice, and left to take the chance of human prudence or imprudence, as either may happen to be uppermost. It is, however, an uncomfortable thought, and I leave it."[22]

He was leaning back into classic deism, with its disinterested clock-maker God. Why should our Creator care about little old us? This struck a nerve with Whitefield. In the margins of the original letter are comments scrawled by George: "*Uncomfortable* indeed, and blessed be God, *unscriptural.*"[23]

Perhaps he intended to send Ben a reply based on that idea. As far as we know, he never did. Sailing for Charleston late in 1769, George visited the Bethesda Orphan House for the last time. After four months, he sailed for Philadelphia and then worked his way up to New York, upstate New York, and Boston. He preached nearly every day in New England towns, dragging himself from place to place, losing energy along the way. He complained of asthma, and fatigue might have brought on additional maladies. His last sermon, in Exeter, lasted two hours. He died at the manse in Newburyport, Massachusetts, on a Sunday morning, September 30, 1770.

There was an outpouring of grief for this amazing minister. Charles Wesley, a prolific hymn writer, composed a eulogy for his old friend. Phillis Wheatley, a seventeen-year-old slave in Boston, published a lengthy poem mourning his passing: "Thou didst, in strains of eloquence refin'd, / Inflame the soul, and captivate the mind."[24] Newspapers throughout the English-speaking world lauded him. The *Pennsylvania Gazette*, now independent of Franklin, said of Whitefield:

[He] astonished the world as a prodigy of eloquence and devotion! . . . With what divine pathos did he not plead with, and persuade, by the most engaging incitements, the impenitent sinner to the practice of piety and virtue? Filled with the spirit of grace, he spoke from the heart; and with a fervency of zeal, perhaps unequaled since the days of the Apostles, ornamented the celestial animations of the preacher, with the graceful and most enticing charms of rhetoric and oratory.[25]

Ben Franklin wrote a simpler remembrance to a friend in the Georgia legislature: "I knew him intimately upwards of 30 years: His integrity, disinterestedness, and indefatigable zeal in prosecuting every good work, I have never seen equaled, I shall never see exceeded."[26]

TWENTY-FOUR

Special Effects

George Whitefield was never Ben Franklin's constant companion. When Ben was living in London and he wanted to while away an afternoon playing chess, he did so with John Pringle, an eminent physician. He met at coffee houses with friends from his scientific circles. He played brainteaser games with young Polly Stevenson. George didn't really believe in "whiling away" anything anyway.

Yet George was one of Ben's longest-lasting friends. It was more than thirty years from their first meeting in Philadelphia to George's last breath in Massachusetts. While there were surely ups and downs between them, there were no clear breaks. Ben kept outgrowing other friendships, and friends kept turning away. But there was George Whitefield, sticking with him, growing alongside him, learning to be a better friend with each new letter. Somewhere along the line, they both stopped using each other and constructed a genuine relationship that was, as Ben put it years later, "sincere on both sides."[1]

There were many other friends in Whitefield's world as well. With most of these he could pray, worship, and share good Christian fellowship. Ben was a special case, consistently refusing George's sales pitch about Jesus, though supporting his push for moral improvement. There was really no one else outside of the evangelical camp with whom the preacher maintained such an enduring friendship.

"Franklin became Whitefield's best American friend," wrote Stout, "and, reciprocally, Whitefield was Franklin's only evangelical friend."[2] Each filled an important niche in the other's life. How did they affect each other?

The practical effects are indisputable. While both were very gifted men in very different fields, they helped each other to enormous success. Without Franklin's printing network, Whitefield would still have been a dynamic preacher, but he wouldn't have captivated America to the same degree. Franklin would have found other ways to make money, no doubt, but without the windfall of Whitefield's contracts, he might have had to wait another decade to retire from the printing business, and then his scientific and diplomatic pursuits would have been delayed. They supported each other in tough times as well. In 1746, Franklin's editorial support helped Whitefield shore up his crumbling relationship with America. And how important was Whitefield's letter-writing network in support of Franklin's Stamp Act testimony? Ben would never have become the diplomatic hero of the new nation if the folks back home suspected he had sold them out.

Yet, apart from the practical matters, how did the friendship itself affect these two men?

This would be easy to answer if their letters told us. It would be great to read, "Thank you for teaching me compassion." Or, "Because of you, I have a brighter outlook on life." But the only inspirational hint we get from their letters is the comment from Franklin after Whitefield's death, praising his "integrity, disinterestedness, and indefatigable zeal."[3] (In that era, a "disinterested" person was fair and selfless, lacking self-serving motives.) Ben also applied these qualities to George in his autobiography. Clearly the preacher modeled these traits for the printer. Ben had a cynical side that must have been challenged by the very existence of this preacher with impeccable integrity, who had the world at his fingertips but still gave everything to serve God.

And George must have grown through his repeated interactions with a man outside his evangelical orbit, a friend who offered rational objections to George's ideas without personal attacks. Despite his fame on two continents, George's world was rather small. He zeroed in on the task at hand, traveling to the next site and preaching the gospel there. Nothing would deter him—not the lure of money, not the love of women, not even his own failing health. He had tunnel vision, focused fully on his calling. Ben, on the other hand, was a man of the world, with a curiosity that could not be contained. Philosophy, science, human behavior, and even religion—it all fascinated him. We see this seeping through in some of his letters to George—dreams of a colony in Ohio, plans for a school of higher learning—so it must have been part of their personal conversations as well. George's vision would have been broadened every time they talked.

Inventing America

Whitefield and Franklin were not just the two most famous people in America in their time—they were also the most significant. The effects of their lives and their work are still being felt today.

After George's death, Ben had two more decades in which he exerted enormous influence on the American nation that came to be. With the Continental Congress, Ben got to see a variation on his Albany Plan at work. He was a force behind, and a signer of, the Declaration of Independence. His shrewd diplomacy in France during the American Revolution probably turned the tide. Washington won the battles, but the French bought the guns, and their fleet scared the British into laying down their swords. That was largely a result of Franklin's careful wooing in the French court. Then, back in America, there was Franklin again, helping to craft the Constitution, doing what he always did best—creating society. He died in 1790, after dominating a century of mind-boggling change.

But let's not overlook the impact of his early years as a printer, especially as he partnered with Whitefield. Ben was perhaps the first media mogul. His *Pennsylvania Gazette* wasn't the first newspaper in the colonies, but with his writing it was surely the best. With his printing network, his yearly almanacs, and his later work as postmaster, he managed the conduits of communication in this developing nation.

Whitefield gave him material to work with. Before George showed up, the *Gazette* ran lost-and-found notices, the daily schedule of ships pulling up to the Market Street wharf, and whatever clever editorials Ben could think up. But suddenly there were people screaming and fainting in church! There were meetings in fields and sermons from balconies. The newspaper had *news*. Ben had more content than he knew what to do with—except he knew exactly what to do with it. Books, pamphlets, newspapers—he fueled his mass-media enterprise with the doings of his friend Whitefield. In the process, he changed the field of communications forever.

The philosopher David Hume once criticized Franklin for making up new words, such as *colonize*. But that's what Franklin did—he created new forms of communication. And that's what the colonies needed—new ways of talking about a new kind of life. They weren't just going to be England West. Ben understood that. There were uniquely American attitudes and cadences in Poor Richard's homespun language. The practical wisdom, the self-deprecation, and the wry humor all became part of the American personality. Maybe he wasn't trying to set a tone for a new nation; he just made sure every colonist had access to his writing. And nearly everyone did.

The media empire was just one of the building blocks of society that Ben hoisted into place, along with the library, the fire company, the militia, the hospital, and the college. These social organizations weren't always the first of their kind, but Ben custom-made them for Philadelphia—and in some cases they became models for other cities to follow. Long before he ever met with Congress or signed a Declaration, he was making America ready to become a nation.

Whitefield was having a similar effect on the religious side of colonial life. His approach was decidedly personal, not ecclesiastical. You, yourself, needed a relationship with God. You needed to feel his presence within you. It was irrelevant which church you attended.

In this way, though he was an Anglican minister, George broke the power of the Anglican Church in America. Or any church authority, really. No church could determine one's spiritual status. You had to take ownership of that, and then give it up to God.

Powerful churches in England and America recognized this threat and denied access to Whitefield, forcing him out to the markets and fields. Yet that made the Whitefield revival all the more independent of church power. These were democratic spaces, with no reserved pews, no privileged positions, no price of admission, just a preacher with a message and all the people who wanted to hear it. Harry Stout referred to Whitefield challenging the "old history—the history of a traditional, aristocratic, and hierarchical culture. A new religious history, fit for a new consumer age, would have to be voluntary, and this meant popular and entertaining. Whitefield's revivals were just that. In them, churches were not supplanted so much as sidestepped to create larger, trans-local associations."[4]

Some historians have suggested that the Methodist revival helped England avoid a violent rebellion such as France had in 1789, since it gave the common folk some spiritual satisfaction. It didn't quite work out that way in America, though. The Great Awakening, driven largely by Whitefield, empowered Americans to break free of their old "traditional, aristocratic, and hierarchical" history. They were already "independent" at a deeply personal level, long before they took up arms against Britain. John Adams looked back in 1818 and said, "The Revolution was effected before the war commenced. The Revolution was in the minds and hearts of the people; and change in their religious sentiments of their duties and obligations."[5]

Just as Franklin knit the colonies together through his communications network, Whitefield did the same through his constant travel. "Religious evangelism was the first continental force," wrote historian Paul Johnson, "an all-American phenomenon which transcended colonial differences, introduced national figures and made state boundaries seem unimportant. Whitefield was the first 'American' public figure to be known from New Hampshire to Georgia."[6]

Not only did George cross state lines, but he also challenged denominational borders. The colonial hodgepodge already included Anglicans, Congregationalists, Presbyterians, Quakers, and Baptists. Whitefield welcomed all and challenged all. Not that theology was unimportant to him, but the most crucial question was not a matter of church polity but *have you received new birth in Jesus?* The rebirth issue cut across all church groups, and George found allies from a variety of church backgrounds.

The same situation has been seen in the centuries since, as evangelists such as Finney, Moody, McPherson, Sunday, and Graham have carried on transdenominational ministries. The "evangelical movement" has had different characteristics in different eras, but it has never been confined to one church organization. We can trace this breadth back to Whitefield, another effect of his extraordinary work.

For all the political and societal ramifications of George's work, we must not miss the most obvious one, and the most important. Because of this Great Awakening, a huge number of Americans were, well, awakened. They were jolted out of the religious same-old and into an authentic relationship with God through Jesus. Some would have been merely curiosity seekers, looking for some ecstatic experience before going back to the way things were. But that's where George's longevity—and his itinerary— became important. Over thirty years, he kept coming back, to Philadelphia, New York, Charleston, Boston, and many points in between. He was no one-hit wonder, and he would not let the call of God be heard and forgotten. If "awakened" Americans hit the snooze button, he would just sound the alarm again. (By the way, one of George's favorite terms for the excited response to his sermons was *alarm*.)

If America was born as a Christian nation, it's because many of its people were genuinely, powerfully Christians. It had less to do with the language in any founding documents and more to do with the fact that George Whitefield had been tromping from town to town, inviting people to hear the call of God. It had even less to do with church membership. God was grabbing lives. People's hearts were flying open. No one was imposing Christianity on society. The power came from within. As Ben Franklin reported, shortly after George had left town:

> The alteration in the face of religion here is altogether surprising. Never did the people show so great a willingness to attend sermons, nor the preachers greater zeal and diligence in performing the duties of their function. Religion is become the subject of most conversations. No books are in request but those of piety and devotion; and instead of idle songs and ballads, the people are everywhere entertaining themselves with

Psalms, hymns and spiritual songs. All which, under God, is owing to the successful labours of the Reverend Mr. *Whitefield*.[7]

This report could be repeated for hundreds of towns and cities in America over the next thirty years.

Forefathers of Our Country

Ben Franklin is duly recognized as one of the Founding Fathers of the United States, thanks to his work with the Declaration and the Constitution. But if we examine the previous three or four decades, before Washington, Adams, or Jefferson staked their claims, there are just a few candidates for the role of *fore*father of the nation. The list quickly narrows to two men: George and Ben.

If these are our fathers, we carry their DNA.

Like George, we are, as a nation, very religious. Like Ben, we like to make up our own beliefs. About half of Americans call themselves evangelical, children of the Great Awakening. Many even use George's favorite term: *born again*. But others do not share this faith. Many, like Ben, are scientific in their outlook. They take an "enlightened" approach to life, focusing on the natural world, not the supernatural.

We are George and Ben.

Thanks to Ben and others, we have religious liberty carved into our Constitution. We have freedom to be religious or not to be. We can be Methodist, Calvinist, Catholic, deist, Pietist, or all of the above. No authority can coerce us to believe anything or force us to say we do. Spiritual life is a personal matter, a transaction between us and God. George and Ben both taught us this.

We're still figuring out how religious freedom works. As a nation, we seem to vacillate between Ben and George, skeptic and zealot, the right to doubt and the right to believe. The question in our deeply divided country is how to preserve the freedom to live out a vibrant Christian faith as well as the freedom to choose something different. The relationship between these two forefathers points to an answer.

Through the decades, George and Ben kept *talking and listening*. The pair didn't just coexist; they were friends. George kept urging Ben to trust in Jesus, and, amazingly, Ben kept writing back, sometimes even thanking George for his concern. Why didn't Ben just walk away? Apparently George was more than just an evangelistic spiel. He had integrity, a selfless spirit, and a driving passion. Ben appreciated these qualities in his friend. As they continued to trade letters, they spoke honestly about their beliefs and civilly about their disagreements.

Character was a key issue for both George and Ben. Qualities such as diligence, discipline, trustworthiness, and humility were upheld in George's sermons and in Ben's more secular writings. Perhaps the religious and non-religious of today can find common cause in promoting such character qualities.

Ben and George also had a commitment to *creativity*. Ben's fertile mind was always seeking new ways to get things done, and George was also a trailblazer in his communication methods. Neither seemed satisfied with the status quo. Both were pushing forward into more effective systems. It's appropriate that they're considered cofounders of one of America's leading educational institutions, the University of Pennsylvania. Both men sought to train new generations to face the challenges ahead with intelligence and creativity. This devotion to creative pursuits resulted in an openness of mind that sought engagement with new ideas, even ones with which they disagreed.

Finally, these forefathers believed in the importance of *loving actions*. Ben was impressed that George's religious commitment involved far more than just church activities—he worked hard to help the poor, the orphans, and the outcasts. Even when Ben rejected the gospel of Christ, he loved the love of Christ.

Shortly before his own death, Ben Franklin was asked to clarify his religious beliefs. He reiterated the theistic ideas he had always shared with George, that the Creator was benevolent and just, worthy of worship. "As for Jesus of Nazareth . . . ," Ben wrote, "I think the system of morals and his religion, as he left them to us, the best the world ever saw or is likely to see." Still, he admitted "some doubts as to his divinity, though it is a question I do not dogmatize upon." There he goes, creating new words again. Though he harbored doubts, he would not make his skepticism a matter of dogma. Maybe he still had George's voice in his head: "Apply to God; be willing to do the divine will, and you shall know it." As Ben approached his death, he noted that he would soon have an "opportunity of knowing the truth."[8]

George built his career on Jesus' teaching that "unless one is born again, he cannot see the kingdom of God" (John 3:3). He kept inviting his ultra-creative friend to experience that recreative power of God. Yet there's another New Testament verse that might apply more closely to Ben's religious journey. "But without faith it is impossible to please [God]; for he who comes to God must believe that He is, and that He is a rewarder of those who diligently seek him" (Hebrews 11:6).

ACKNOWLEDGMENTS

Immense thanks to Joel Kneedler, my agent, who gave me the idea for this book and coached me along the way. I also got crucial answers from my friends Shawn Kairschner (dramaturgy) and Tom Whiteman (psychology). I have always felt that librarians are a special breed of helpful people, and this was confirmed in my interactions at Eastern, Villanova, Temple, and Rowan Universities, as well as Wheaton and Camden County Colleges and the Wesley Center at Northwest Nazarene University. Digby James provided a trove of informational treasure on Whitefield from Quinta Press. In an array of important sources, Harry Stout's Whitefield biography, *The Divine Dramatist*, stands out, providing tremendous insights that I used and developed. Thanks also to the history buffs at Philadelphia's Christ Church and Franklin Museum. My sister and father, Kathryn and Bill Petersen, were helpful goads and counselors. Finally, I have treasured the love and intellectual curiosity of Hope United Methodist Church, urging me on.

Before They Met

Timeline for Ben Franklin and George Whitefield

1706–1739

1706

Franklin:

> Born in Boston January 6 (OS), youngest son of Josiah and Abiah (Folger) Franklin.

1714

Franklin:

> Turns eight. Begins to attend school.

Whitefield:

> Born in Gloucester, England, December 16 (OS), into an innkeeper's family.

World:

Fahrenheit invents scaled thermometer.

Queen Anne dies. George I is king.

1715

Franklin:

In his final formal year of schooling, at George Brownell's English school.

Hears Increase Mather preach.

World:

Isaac Watts publishes *Divine Songs for Children*.

Louis XIV of France dies.

Musical comedies ("vaudevilles") appear in Paris.

1716

Franklin:

Drops out of school when father can no longer afford it.

Whitefield:

Thomas Whitefield, George's father, dies.

1717

Franklin:

Begins reading Plutarch, Defoe, and Cotton Mather.

Invents a pair of swim fins for his hands.

Briefly apprentices as a cutler.

1718

Franklin:

Is apprenticed to his brother James, a printer.

World:

    Blackbeard the pirate is captured (Franklin writes a ballad on the
        occasion).

    William Penn dies.

1721

Franklin:

    James Franklin, Ben's brother, starts publishing the *New-England
        Courant*.

    Smallpox epidemic in Boston; controversy over vaccination.

    Ben briefly becomes "a thorough deist."

World:

    Bach writes Brandenburg Concertos.

    Postal service is established between London and New England.

1722

Franklin:

    Writes Silence Dogood letters.

World:

    Moravians start religious community at Herrnhut.

    Steele's play *The Conscious Lovers* opens in London.

1723

Franklin:

    Takes over the publishing of the *Courant* after James is jailed on
        contempt charges.

    Runs away from apprenticeship, goes to New York and then to
        Philadelphia.

    Arrives in Philadelphia on October 6, where he gains employment
        as a printer.

Takes lodging with John Read, whose daughter Deborah will later
become his wife.

1724

Franklin:

Returns to Boston to get money from his father to start print shop
but is denied.

Returns to Philadelphia and courts Deborah Read.

Travels to London to buy printing equipment.

Stranded in London; works at Samuel Palmer's print shop.

Whitefield:

Elizabeth Whitefield, George's mother, marries Capel Longden, an
ironmonger.

World:

Jack Sheppard, highwayman, is executed in England.

1725

Franklin:

Publishes pamphlet: "A Dissertation upon Liberty and Necessity,
Pleasure and Pain."

Leaves Palmer the printer for the larger shop of John Watts.

Attends theater, reads voraciously, and hangs out at coffee houses.

Back in Pennsylvania, Deborah Read marries someone else.

1726

Franklin:

Returns to Philadelphia, keeping a journal of the ship's passage.

Outlines his personal "Plan of Conduct."

Works for Thomas Denham, a merchant who had lent him the
money to return home.

Whitefield:

   Enrolls at St. Mary de Crypt grammar school, where he enjoys
      reading plays and acting.

1727

Franklin:

   Suffers first pleurisy attack, nearly dies.
   Leaves job with Denham and is rehired by printer Keimer.
   Helps to establish the Junto for "self-improvement, study, mutual
      aid, and conviviality."

World:

   In England, George I dies and is succeeded by George II.
   England is at war with Spain (Gibraltar).

1728

Franklin:

   Establishes a Philadelphia printing partnership with Hugh Meredith.
   Deborah Read's husband, John Rogers, steals a slave and absconds
      from Philadelphia.

Whitefield:

   George's mother leaves her husband.

World:

   William Law publishes *A Serious Call to a Devout and Holy Life*.
   The Beggar's Opera opens in London.

1729

Franklin:

   Writes "Busy-Body" essays.

Purchases the *Pennsylvania Gazette* from Samuel Keimer.

About this time, son William is born, the result of an affair.

Whitefield:

Drops out of school. Works at the Bell Inn.

World:

Jonathan Edwards becomes pastor in Northampton, Massachusetts.

Bach writes *St Matthew Passion*.

Stephen Gray experiments in electricity.

1730

Franklin:

Elected the official printer for Pennsylvania.

Begins common-law marriage with Deborah Read Rogers.

Buys out his printing partner, Hugh Meredith.

After fire destroys southern Philadelphia, starts promoting fire
protection programs.

1731

Franklin:

Joins the St. John's Freemasons Lodge.

Draws up the Library Company's articles of association.

Sponsors his journeyman Thomas Whitmarsh as a printing partner
in South Carolina.

Whitefield:

Family conflicts cause George to leave the Bell Inn and live with
brother in Bristol.

Returns to studies at St. Mary's.

On Christmas, receives Communion for the first time; has new
spiritual commitment.

World:

The London Merchant opens in London.

1732

Franklin:

Son is born: Francis Folger Franklin.

Publishes the first edition of *Poor Richard's Almanack* on December 28.

Whitefield:

Enrolls at Pembroke College, Oxford University, working as a
servitor to pay his way.

Begins praying three times a day and fasting weekly.

World:

Ninepins played in New York.

London theaters attract fourteen thousand customers a week.

1733

Franklin:

Son Francis is baptized at Christ Church.

Conceives of his "bold and arduous Project of arriving at moral
perfection."

Whitefield:

Invited to breakfast by Charles Wesley and introduced to the
Holy Club.

Reads *The Life of God in the Soul of Man* by Henry Scougal.

World:

Georgia, last of thirteen colonies, is settled.

1734

<u>Franklin:</u>

Is elected grand master of Masonic lodge.

Buys property on Philadelphia's Market Street.

Bribes post riders to carry his *Pennsylvania Gazette.*

<u>Whitefield:</u>

Seeks salvation through severe discipline and good works, which causes a breakdown of his health from which he never fully recovers.

<u>World:</u>

Revival takes place in Northampton, Massachusetts, under Jonathan Edwards.

1735

<u>Franklin:</u>

Brother James Franklin dies; Benjamin sends his widow five hundred copies of *Poor Richard's Almanac* for free so she can make money by selling them.

Gets involved in controversy over Presbyterian minister Samuel Hemphill.

<u>Whitefield:</u>

Becomes first of the Oxford Methodists to have a conversion experience.

<u>World:</u>

John Adams and Paul Revere are born.

Sale of spirits is prohibited in Georgia (lasted until 1742).

1736

Franklin:

Named clerk of the Pennsylvania Assembly.

Prints currency for New Jersey.

Son Francis dies of smallpox at age four.

Organizes the Union Fire Company.

Regularly attends meetings of Masonic lodge, Junto, and fire company.

Whitefield:

Completes his degree at Oxford.

Is ordained a deacon in the Church of England.

Preaches at his old grammar school.

Fills in as preacher in London.

World:

Wesleys are missionaries in Georgia.

1737

Franklin:

Appointed postmaster of Philadelphia.

Whitefield:

Voyage to Georgia is delayed.

Preaching draws crowds in Gloucester, Bristol, and London.

Uses press and publishing.

Discovers extemporaneous preaching December 28.

World:

Licensing Act restricts theater in London.

1738

Franklin:

Weathers a scandal over mock Masonic initiation ritual.

Whitefield:

(February) Sails for America, serves in Georgia.

Begins plans for orphanage.

(September) Returns to England.

(December) Resumes preaching in London.

World:

John and Charles Wesley have conversion experiences.

Voltaire introduces French to Newton's ideas.

1739

Franklin:

Franklin's house is robbed.

Leads an environmental protest against slaughterhouses.

Meets George Whitefield.

Whitefield:

(January) Is ordained a priest in Church of England but finds many
    pulpits are now closed to him. Begins preaching outdoors.

Countess of Huntingdon begins supporting him.

(October) Arrives in Philadelphia for the first time.

Meets Ben Franklin.

World:

David Hume publishes *A Treatise on Human Nature*.

Tensions rise between England and Spain, erupting in the War of
    Jenkins' Ear.

George Whitefield's Amazing American Tour

1739–41

In about fourteen months, George Whitefield preached in every American colony, cutting a coastal swath within reach of all colonists. Obviously, Savannah (with nearby Charleston) and Philadelphia (with nearby New York) were significant hubs for this ministry and had repeated visits. But Whitefield also visited scores of other towns. At each of the sites listed on this itinerary (and some omitted), the evangelist spoke to groups numbering in the hundreds and often the thousands, drawing from not only those towns but also the entire region. The Whitefield Experience was a unifying factor in the life of this young nation-to-be—not that everyone agreed with George, but everyone knew him. It's likely that a majority of Americans got to hear Whitefield in person, and nearly everyone heard *about* him.

1739

August 14: Sails from England on second journey to America.
October 30: Lands in Lewes, Pennsylvania (now Delaware).

November 2: Rides into Philadelphia for first time.

November 8–10: Preaches from courthouse steps each evening to thousands.

Meets William Tennent.

November 12–14: Heads through New Jersey to New York City. Preaches at Bordentown.

Meets Gilbert Tennent in Brunswick.

November 14–18: Preaches at several churches (and fields) in New York.

November 19–22: Returns to Philadelphia via Elizabeth, New Brunswick, and Trenton.

Meets Theodore Frelinghuysen, early Dutch Reformed revivalist.

Stays at Tennents' Log College in Neshaminy, Pennsylvania.

November 23–28: Abington and Philadelphia; side trip to Germantown.

November 28: *Possible first meeting with Ben Franklin.*

November 29–January 10: Heads south to Georgia, stopping (often to preach) in Chester, Wilmington, Newcastle, Joppa, Annapolis, Upper Marlboro, Port Tobacco, Seals Church, Williamsburg, Bell's Ferry, Bath, New Bern, New Town (Wilmington, NC), Charleston, Beaufort, and other towns.

1740

January 11–April 3: Based in Savannah, buys land for orphanage. A brief trip to Charleston in March.

April 4–13: Travels by boat to Pennsylvania.

April 13–23: In Philadelphia area, also preaches in Wilmington (DE), Abington, Germantown, Whitemarsh, Greenwich (NJ), and Gloucester (NJ).

This is probably when Whitefield and Franklin talk about the orphanage and Franklin is moved to donate coppers, silver, and gold. The dust-up of William Seward and the dance hall occurs.

April 23–May 7: Heads to New York and back to Philadelphia, preaching also in Neshaminy, Montgomeryville, Amwell, New Brunswick, Woodbridge, Elizabeth, Long Island, Freehold, Perth Amboy, Burlington, and Bristol.

Preaches in the church of Moravian missionary Peter Bohler.

May 8–16: In Philadelphia and western suburbs: Pennypack, Darby, Chester, Wilmington, and Nottingham.

May 16–June 4: Boards sloop, waits at Reedy Island for fair weather, docks at Lewes, sails south.

June 5–30: Resettles in Savannah.

July 1–25: Visits Charleston and environs: Beaufort, John's Island, returning to Savannah via Ponpon, Good Hope.

Faces opposition from church leaders in Charleston.

July 25–August 21: Settles in Savannah.

August 22–25: To Charleston and off by boat to New England.

September 14: Arrives in Newport, RI. Preaches there. Heads to Boston via Bristol.

September 19–October 12: Preaches in Boston and suburbs: Roxbury, Marblehead, Salem, Ipswich, Newbury, Hampton (NH), Portsmouth (NH), York (ME), Hampstead (NH), Malden, Reading, and Cambridge.

(September 24) *Visits Harvard College.*

October 13–20: Westward trek toward Springfield, preaching also in Concord, Sudbury, Marlborough, Worcester, Leicester, Brookfield, Hadley, Northampton, Hatfield, and Westfield.

(October 17–20) *Visits Jonathan and Sarah Edwards in Northampton.*

October 21–30: Moves south and west through Connecticut, preaching in Suffield, Windsor, Hartford, Wethersfield, Middletown, Wallingford, New Haven, Milford, Stratford, Fairfield, Norwalk, Stamford, Rye (NY), and Kingsbridge.

(October 25) *Meets with students at New Haven (Yale) College.*

October 31–November 4: In New York.

November 5–8: To Philadelphia, via Baskin Ridge, New Brunswick, and Trenton.

November 9–16: In Philadelphia.

Preaches in building constructed for him (but still roofless).

Possible conversation with Franklin on spiritual matters.

November 17–25: Goes south and west around Philadelphia,

preaching in Gloucester, Greenwich, Pilesgrove, Cohansey (Bridgeton, NJ), Salem, New Castle (DE), White Clay Creek (Newark, DE), Nottingham (PA), St. George's (DE), and other towns.

November 25–December 13: Reedy Island, awaiting good weather, then sails to Savannah via Charleston.

Writes to Franklin while at Reedy Island.

December 14–31: Relaxing (and Christmassing) at the orphanage.

1741

January 1–3: To Charleston via Port Royal.

January 4–23: In and around Charleston.

January 24–March 11: Sails for England.

Encounters

The Meetings and Correspondence of George and Ben

November 1739: First meeting, presumably on publishing business.

November 1739–December 1740: Nearly every week Franklin publishes something in the *Gazette* on Whitefield's American tour.

April 1740: Whitefield tells Franklin about the orphan house building project. This is possibly when Franklin, resistant at first, is moved to donate to orphanage.

May 8–16, 1740: No definite evidence of a meeting, but both were in Philadelphia.

November 1740: A probable meeting and a possible spiritual conversation.

November 26, 1740: Whitefield writes to Franklin: "I do not despair of your seeing the reasonableness of Christianity."

September 6–19, 1745 (probably): Whitefield, invited to stay in the Franklin home, does.

April–May, 1746: Whitefield sends Franklin his financial accounts for publication.

Summer 1746: Whitefield ministers in Philadelphia, maybe stays
   with Franklin.
July 31, 1746: Franklin publishes "Appreciation of George
   Whitefield" editorial.
June 23, 1747: Whitefield thanks Franklin for help in fundraising for
   the orphan house.
Summer 1747: Whitefield ministers in Philadelphia, may stay with
   Franklin.
August 6, 1747: Franklin writes to brother John about Whitefield,
   "He is a good man."
May 27, 1748: Whitefield writes a note to Franklin and a brief report
   from Bermuda.
June 1748: Franklin passes along to sister Jane a note from George to
   one of her friends.
July 6, 1749: Franklin writes to Whitefield, thanking him for some
   gifts and responding to George's new activities preaching among
   the leaders of society.
[1749–50]: Franklin must have sent Whitefield plans for the new
   academy.
February 26, 1750: Whitefield writes to Franklin about the academy,
   insisting that there be more Christian curriculum.
1751: Franklin starts the academy.
1751–52: Whitefield takes his fourth voyage to America, a quick trip
   to Georgia, does not visit Franklin.
August 17, 1752: Whitefield commends Franklin on scientific fame,
   urges him to study Jesus.
1754–55: Whitefield in America for fifth trip. Possible connections
   with Franklin in Philadelphia and Boston.
September 2, 1754: John Franklin thanks Ben for the account
   Deborah sent about Whitefield.
January 17, 1755: Whitefield writes to Franklin from Virginia,
   inviting him to Bethesda. "Believe on Jesus, and get a feeling
   possession of God in your heart."

July 2, 1756: Franklin writes to Whitefield with an idea to start a
    new colony together on the Ohio River.

1757–63: Both are in England, with trips to Scotland, Holland, and
    Ireland, but they probably don't connect.

1763–65: Both are in America, missing connections at first.

November 28, 1763: Franklin sends a nice note, with a package, to
    Whitefield, after failing to connect in Philadelphia.

June 19, 1764: Franklin responds sweetly to Whitefield's prayers and
    issues a sort of faith statement: "Can I doubt that [God] loves
    me?"

1765–69: Both are in England.

February 13, 1766: Franklin appears before Parliament, with
    Whitefield present.

February 27, 1766: Ben writes to Deborah, "Mr. Whitfield called
    today."

March 1766: Whitefield writes letter to his network of supporters
    praising Ben's Parliamentary testimony.

March 2, 1767: Franklin refers to Whitefield in a letter to sister Jane.

1767–68: Whitefield confers with Franklin about starting Bethesda
    College.

January 21, 1768: Whitefield writes to Franklin seeking another get-
    together. He also muses about death.

December 6, 1768: Franklin writes to Whitefield about the
    recommendation of a friend.

Sometime before September 2, 1769: Franklin writes to Whitefield
    warning about growing tensions in America.

1769–70: Whitefield's final tour of America; he dies in New England,
    September 1770.

March 5, 1771: Franklin writes to Georgia legislature about
    Whitefield's integrity.

Notes

Chapter 1

1. Benjamin Franklin, *Autobiography*, ed. Joyce E. Chaplin (New York: W. W. Norton, 2012), 80.
2. For some of the ideas on "gentlemen," the author is indebted to Gordon S. Wood, *The Americanization of Benjamin Franklin* (New York: Penguin, 2005), 17–60.
3. George Whitefield, Letter CCXXXVIII (November 26, 1740), *Works of George Whitefield*, vol. 1 (Shropshire, England: Quinta Press, 2000), 255–56.
4. Arnold Dallimore, *George Whitefield: The Life and Times of the Great Evangelist of the Eighteenth-Century Revival*, vol. 2 (Carlisle, PA: Banner of Truth Trust, 1980), 450.
5. Franklin, *Autobiography*, 101.
6. Benjamin Franklin, Letter to John Franklin, August 6, 1747, http://franklin papers.org/franklin//framedVolumes.jsp.

Chapter 2

1. Dante Alighieri, *The Divine Comedy*, translated by Henry Wadsworth Longfellow, public domain, *Inferno*, canto 26.
2. Augustus Jessopp, *John Donne: Sometime Dean of St. Paul's A.D. 1621–1631, Parts 1621–1631* (Boston: Houghton Mifflin, 1897), 150–61.
3. George Herbert, *The English Poems of George Herbert: Together with His Collection of Proverbs Entitled Jacula Prudentum* (London: Rivingtons, 1871), 203–10.
4. George Whitefield, *Journals* (Shropshire, England: Quinta Press, 2000), 398.
5. Thomas Paine, *Common Sense*, public domain.
6. Mayflower Compact cited in Rod Gragg, *Forged in Faith* (New York: Howard, 2010), 30.
7. "John Winthrop Delivers 'City Upon a Hill' Sermon Aboard the Arbella, Heading En Route to Colonial America, 1630," http://worldhistoryproject

.org/1630/john-winthrop-delivers-city-upon-a-hill-sermon-aboard-the
-arbella-heading-en-route-to-colonial-america.

8. Ibid.

9. For some ideas and information in this chapter, the author is indebted to Charles L. Sanford, "An American Pilgrim's Progress," *American Quarterly* 6, no. 4 (Winter 1954): 297–310.

Chapter 3

1. Benjamin Franklin, *Autobiography*, ed. Joyce E. Chaplin (New York: W. W. Norton, 2012), 13.

2. Ibid., 15.

3. Ibid.

4. Ibid.

5. Ibid., 14.

6. Ibid., 17.

7. Ibid.

8. George Whitefield, *Journals* (Shropshire, England: Quinta Press, 2000), 41.

9. Ibid.

10. Ibid., 41–42. Italics his.

11. Franklin, *Autobiography*, 15.

12. Ibid., 15–16.

13. Ibid., 78.

14. Whitefield, *Journals*, 42.

15. Franklin, *Autobiography*, 17–18.

16. Ibid., 18.

Chapter 4

1. Benjamin Franklin, *New-England Courant*, April 2, 1722 (Silence Dogood Letter no. 1), www.historycarper.com.

2. Franklin, *New-England Courant*, May 14, 1722 (Silence Dogood Letter no. 4), www.historycarper.com.

3. Franklin, *New-England Courant*, July 23, 1722 (Silence Dogood Letter no. 9) www.historycarper.com.

4. Benjamin Franklin, *Autobiography*, ed. Joyce E. Chaplin (New York: W. W. Norton, 2012), 23.

5. Ibid., 24.

6. Ibid., 26.

7. Ibid.

8. For more on this theme, see Charles L. Sanford, "An American Pilgrim's Progress," *American Quarterly* 6, no. 4 (Winter 1954): 297–310.

9. Daniel J. Boorstin, *The Creators: A History of Heroes of the Imagination* (New York: Random House, 1992), 577–84.

10. George Whitefield, *Journals* (Shropshire, England: Quinta Press, 2000), 40.
11. Franklin, *Autobiography*, 17.
12. Boorstin, *The Creators*, 583.
13. Franklin, *Autobiography*, 26.
14. John Bunyan, *Grace Abounding to the Chief of Sinners* (London: Religious Tract Society, 1905), sec. 8.
15. George Whitefield, "A Recommendatory Preface to the Works of Mr. John Bunyan," January 3, 1767, in *The Works of the Reverend George Whitefield*, vol. 4 (London: Dilly, 1771), 327–28.
16. Ibid., 328.
17. Bunyan, *Grace Abounding*, sec. 12.

Chapter 5

1. The US Census didn't begin until 1790, so early data must be inferred from various other sources, and some guesswork is involved. Also, many cities (like Philadelphia) were still establishing their boundaries. For instance, Germantown is now part of Philadelphia, but when Whitefield preached there, it was a separate town. For estimates of metropolitan areas in the 1700s, The author is using the calculations of this Web site: http://www.peakbagger.com/pbgeog/histmetropop.aspx#tables. Even if Whitefield exaggerated the attendance figures, as some historians think, it's still a huge portion of the area's population.
2. Benjamin Franklin, *Autobiography*, ed. Joyce E. Chaplin (New York: W. W. Norton, 2012), 100.
3. George Whitefield, *Journals* (Shropshire, England: Quinta Press, 2000), 396. The quotation is from Revelation 3:8 (KJV).
4. There is a Whitefield Society at City Church, meeting in the University of Pennsylvania area.
5. Franklin, *Autobiography*, 28.
6. Ibid.
7. Ibid., 28–29.
8. Ibid., 29.
9. Ibid., 28.

Chapter 6

1. Benjamin Franklin, *Autobiography*, ed. Joyce E. Chaplin (New York: W. W. Norton, 2012), 32.
2. Ibid., 18. See the accompanying note by editor Joyce E. Chaplin. Franklin also references this book in a letter to Samuel Mather, May 12, 1784: "I have always set a greater value on the character of a doer of good, than on any other kind of reputation; and if I have been, as you seem to think, a useful citizen, the public owes the advantage of it to that book."

3. Benjamin Franklin, Letter to Samuel Mather, May 12, 1784, http://franklin papers.org/franklin//framedVolumes.jsp.

4. Ibid.

5. Franklin, Letter to Samuel Mather, July 7, 1773, franklinpapers.org.

6. Ibid.

7. Franklin, *Autobiography*, 42.

8. Ibid.

Chapter 7

1. George Whitefield, *Journals* (Shropshire, England: Quinta Press, 2000), 49.

2. Arnold A. Dallimore, *George Whitefield: God's Anointed Servant*, vol. 1 (Carlisle, PA: Banner of Truth Trust, 1970), 13.

3. George Whitefield, *Journals*, 43.

4. Ibid.

5. Ibid., 42.

6. George Whitefield, Letter DXXIII (June 21, 1743), *The Works of the Reverend George Whitefield*, vol. 2 (London: Dilly, 1771), 27.

7. Ibid.

8. Whitefield, *Journals*, 42.

9. Benjamin Franklin, *Autobiography*, ed. Joyce E. Chaplin (New York: W. W. Norton, 2012), 42.

10. Ibid., 43.

11. Lewis Theobald, *Harlequin Sorcerer: With the Loves of Pluto and Proserpine* (Google eBook) (London: Woodfall, 1752), 10.

12. James Ralph, *The Touch-stone* ("Booksellers of London and Westminster," 1728), 221.

13. Benjamin Franklin, *A Dissertation on Liberty and Necessity, Pleasure and Pain*, 1725, franklinpapers.org.

14. Franklin, *Autobiography*, 50.

Chapter 8

1. A. M. Nagler, *A Sourcebook in Theatrical History* (New York: Dover Publications, 1952), 115.

2. Ibid., 128–29.

3. Ibid., 130.

4. Scott McMillin, ed., *Restoration and Eighteenth-Century Comedy* (New York: W. W. Norton, 1997), 494.

5. Ibid., 496.

6. In this context, our interest in Franklin is as a promoter of the "Whitefield show," a role that Ben performed quite well. (Franklin also provided literary entertainment. The colonies didn't have much of a theater scene until

about 1750, but Franklin's wit, especially in *Poor Richard's Almanac*, was certainly a key part of the pop culture of eighteenth-century America.)

7. McMillin, *Restoration and Eighteenth-Century Comedy*, 324–5.
8. John Gay, *The Beggar's Opera and Companion Pieces*, ed. C. F. Burgess (New York: Meredith Corporation, 1966), 5.
9. Romans 3:10 (KJV).
10. *Eighteenth-Century Plays, with an Introduction by Ricardo Quintana* (New York: Random House, 1952), 325.

Chapter 9

1. "George Whitefield," *Christian History* (blog), *Christianity Today*, August 8, 2008, http://www.christianitytoday.com/ch/131christians/evangelistsandapologists/whitefield.html.
2. Benjamin Franklin, *Autobiography*, ed. Joyce E. Chaplin (New York: W. W. Norton, 2012), 102–3.
3. George Whitefield, *Journals* (Shropshire, England: Quinta Press, 2000), 43.
4. Cicero, *On Rhetoric*, lines 221ff. My translation.
5. Cicero, *On Oratory and Orators,* trans. J. S. Watson (New York: Harper and Bros., 1860), book 3, chapter XIV.
6. Jean Benedetti, *The Art of the Actor* (New York: Routledge, 2007), 71.
7. Aaron Hill, *The Prompter*, no. 118, December 23, 1735.
8. Kevin A. Miller, "George Whitefield: From the Editor—The Original Christian History," *Christian History*, issue 38 (1993): 2.
9. "George Whitefield," *Christian History* (blog).
10. "Controversial George Whitefield," Christianity.com, http://www.christianity.com/church/church-history/timeline/1701-1800/controversial-george-whitefield-11630198.html.
11. Harry S. Stout, *The Divine Dramatist: George Whitefield and the Rise of Modern Evangelicalism* (Grand Rapids, MI: Eerdmans, 1991), 239–40.
12. Ibid., 239.
13. Ibid., xviii.
14. Whitefield, *Journals*, 43.
15. Ibid., 44.
16. Franklin, "Journal of a Voyage, 1726," in *Autobiography*, 226.

Chapter 10

1. Benjamin Franklin, *Autobiography*, ed. Joyce E. Chaplin (New York: W. W. Norton, 2012), 51.
2. Ibid.
3. Benjamin Franklin, *Poor Richard's Almanac*, 1743, http://franklinpapers.org/franklin//framedVolumes.jsp.

Chapter 11

1. George Whitefield, *Journals* (Shropshire, England: Quinta Press, 2000), 44.
2. Ibid.
3. Ibid., 45–6.
4. Ibid., 47.
5. Ibid.
6. Ibid., 46.
7. Ibid.
8. Ibid., 47.
9. Ibid., 48.
10. Ibid.
11. Ibid., 49.
12. James Boswell, *Boswell's Life of Johnson*, ed. Charles Grosvenor Osgood, Project Gutenberg, May 12, 2006, http://www.gutenberg.org/files/1564/1564-h/1564-h.htm.
13. Whitefield, *Journals*, 50.
14. Charles Wesley, "An Elegy on the Late Reverend George Whitefield, M.A.," *Journal of Charles Wesley*, vol. 2 (Grand Rapids, MI: Baker, 1960), 419.
15. George Whitefield, "Sermon LXXV," *Sermons on Important Subjects by the Rev. George Whitefield* (London: Fisher, 1836), 251.
16. Samuel Johnson said, "When at Oxford, I took up Law's *Serious Call to a Holy Life*, expecting to find it a dull book (as such books generally are), and perhaps to laugh at it. But I found Law quite an overmatch for me; and this was the first occasion of my thinking in earnest of religion, after I became capable of rational inquiry." His biographer added, "From this time forward religion was the predominant object of his thoughts; though, with the just sentiments of a conscientious Christian, he lamented that his practice of its duties fell far short of what it ought to be." Boswell, *Boswell's Life of Johnson*.
17. William Law, *A Serious Call to a Devout and Holy Life*, Christian Classics Ethereal Library, July 13, 2005, http://www.ccel.org/ccel/law/serious_call.ii.html.
18. John Gillies, *Memoirs of the Life of the Reverend George Whitefield, M.A.* (London: Dilly, 1772), 19.
19. Whitefield, *Journals*, 20.

Chapter 12

1. Benjamin Franklin, *Poor Richard's Almanac*, Melons, 1733; Haste, 1753; Gains, 1745; Fleas, 1733. The publication was known as *Poor Richard Improved* from 1748 on. http://franklinpapers.org/franklin//framedVolumes.jsp.
2. Franklin, *Poor Richard's Almanac*, 1736, franklinpapers.org.
3. Benjamin Franklin, *Autobiography*, ed. Joyce E. Chaplin (New York: W. W. Norton, 2012), 55.

4. Ibid., 55–56.

5. Ibid., 56.

6. Edmund S. Morgan, *Benjamin Franklin* (New Haven, CT: Yale University Press, 2002), 40.

7. Adam B. Seligman, *Innerworldly Individualism: Charismatic Community and Its Institutionalization* (New Brunswick, NJ: Transaction Publishers, 1994), 165.

8. Samuel Mather, *The Life of Dr. Cotton Mather* (Minneapolis: Curiosmith, 2012), 45.

9. *Benjamin Franklin*, PBS, http://www.pbs.org/benfranklin/pop_junto questions.html.

10. Ibid.

11. Ibid.

12. Ibid.

13. John Wesley, questions gathered from "A Scheme of Self-Examination" and "Rules of the Band Societies."

14. George Whitefield, *Journals* (Shropshire, England: Quinta Press, 2000), 51.

15. August Hermann Francke, *Nicodemus, or A Treatise Against the Fear of Man*, 3rd ed. Bath, UK: S. Hazard, 1801), ii.

16. *The Country-Parson's Advice to His Parishioners: In Two Parts* (Google eBook) (London: Benj. Tooke, 1680), https://play.google.com/store/books/details/The _Country_parson_s_Advice_to_His_Parishioners?id=6gk8AQAAMAAJ, 79–80.

17. Ibid., 80–81.

Chapter 13

1. "Benjamin Franklin's Epitaph," http://www.librarycompany.org/bfwriter /images/large/1.10.jpg.

2. George Whitefield, Letter MLXXIII (January 17, 1755), *Works*, vol. 3 (London: Dilly, 1771), 120.

3. Benjamin Franklin, "Articles of Belief and Acts of Religion," 1728, http://franklin papers.org/franklin//framedVolumes.jsp.

4. George Whitefield, Letter DCCCCXXVI (August 17, 1752), *Works*, vol. 2 (London: Dilly, 1771), 445.

5. *The Country-Parson's Advice to His Parishioners: In Two Parts* (Google eBook) (London: Benj. Tooke, 1680), https://play.google.com/store/books/details/The _Country_parson_s_Advice_to_His_Parishioners?id=6gk8AQAAMAAJ, 43.

6. George Whitefield, *Journals* (Shropshire, England: Quinta Press, 2000), 51.

7. Ibid. He cites Henry Scougal, *The Life of God in the Soul of Man*, ccel.org, 38–39. Whitefield paraphrases the original, which reads: "I cannot speak of religion, but I must lament, that, among so many pretenders to it, so few understand what it means: some placing it in the understanding, in orthodox notions and opinions; and all the account they can give of their religion

is, that they are of this or the other persuasion, and have joined themselves to one of those many sects whereinto Christendom is most unhappily divided. Others place it in the outward man, in a constant course of external duties, and a model of performances: if they live peaceably with their neighbors, keep a temperate diet, observe the returns of worship, frequenting the church and their closet, and sometimes extend their hands to the relief of the poor, they think they have sufficiently acquitted themselves. Others again put all religion in the affections, in rapturous heats and ecstatic devotion; and all they aim at, is, to pray with passion, and think of heaven with pleasure, and to be affected with those kind and melting expressions wherewith they court their Saviour, till they persuade themselves that they are mightily in love with him; and from thence assume a great confidence of their salvation, which they esteem the chief of Christian graces. Thus are those things which have any resemblance of piety, and at the best are but means of obtaining it, or particular exercises of it, frequently mistaken for the whole of religion. . . . But certainly religion is quite another thing, and they who are acquainted with it will entertain far different thoughts, and disdain all those shadows and false imitations of it. They know by experience that true religion is a union of the soul with God, a real participation of the divine nature, the very image of God drawn upon the soul, or, in the apostle's phrase, 'It is Christ formed within us.'"

8. Ibid.
9. Whitefield, *Journals*, 60.
10. Whitefield, *Journals*, 63, footnote 2.
11. Ibid.
12. Whitefield, *Journals*, 64.
13. George Whitefield, Sermon LXII, "Repentance and Conversion," *Sermons on Important Subjects by the Rev. George Whitefield* (London: Fisher, 1836), 75.
14. John Wesley, *The Heart of John Wesley's Journal*, ed. Percy Livingstone Parker (New Canaan, CT: Keats, 1979), 43.
15. Charles Wesley, *Journal of Charles Wesley*, vol. 1 (Grand Rapids, MI: Baker, 1960), 91.
16. John Wesley, "The Almost Christian," sermon 2, UMCMission.org, http://www.umcmission.org/Find-Resources/John-Wesley-Sermons/Sermon-2-The-Almost-Christian.
17. Whitefield, Sermon LXII, 70, 72–73
18. Ibid., 74.
19. Henry Scougal, *The Life of God in the Soul of Man*, Christian Classics Ethereal Library, http://www.ccel.org/ccel/scougal/life/, 40–41.
20. Benjamin Franklin, *Autobiography*, ed. Joyce E. Chaplin (New York: W. W. Norton, 2012), 56.
21. Ibid., 101.

Chapter 14

1. Benjamin Franklin, *Autobiography*, ed. Joyce E. Chaplin (New York: W. W. Norton, 2012), 67.
2. Ibid.
3. Ibid., 99.
4. *The Pennsylvania Gazette*, February 4, 1735, http://www.accessible-archives .com/collections/the-pennsylvania-gazette/.
5. Franklin, *Autobiography,* 99.
6. Edmund S. Morgan, *Benjamin Franklin* (New Haven, CT: Yale University Press, 2002), 55.
7. George Whitefield, *Journals* (Shropshire, England: Quinta Press, 2000), 71.
8. George Whitefield, Letter XIII (June 20, 1736), *Works*, vol. 1 (London: Dilly, 1771), 26.
9. George Whitefield, *Works*, vol. 5 (London: Dilly, 1771), 134.
10. Whitefield, Letter XVI (June 30, 1736), *Works*, vol. 1, 28–29.
11. Whitefield, *Works*, vol. V, 134–5.
12. Whitefield, Letter XVI, 28–29.
13. Whitefield, *Journals*, 87.
14. Ibid.
15. James Paterson Gledstone, *George Whitefield, M.A.: Field Preacher* (London: Hodder and Stoughton, 1900), 42.
16. Whitefield, *Journals*, 90.
17. Ibid., 91.
18. Whitefield, Letter XX (February 10, 1737), *Works*, vol. 1, 35.
19. Whitefield, Letter XXVII (October 25, 1737), *Works,* vol. 1, 40–41.
20. Whitefield, Letter XX.
21. Whitefield, *Journals*, 99.
22. Ibid.
23. Frank Lambert, "Pedlar in Divinity: George Whitefield and the Great Awakening, 1737–1745," *Journal of American History* 77, no. 3 (December 1990): 816–17.
24. Franklin, *Autobiography*, 103.
25. Whitefield, *Journals*, 110.

Chapter 15

1. Benjamin Franklin, *Autobiography*, ed. Joyce E. Chaplin (New York: W. W. Norton, 2012), 51–52. All the early material on George Webb comes from this source.
2. For Webb's involvement in the Junto and his betrayal of Ben's secret, see *Autobiography*, 58–59.
3. Ibid., 221.

4. Samuel Austin Allibone, *Poetical Quotations from Chaucer to Tennyson* (Philadelphia: Lippincott, 1875), 514.

5. Franklin, *Autobiography*, 78.

6. Franklin, *Autobiography*, 93–94.

7. Bryan F. LeBeau, *Jonathan Dickinson and the Formative Years of American Presbyterianism* (Lexington: University Press of Kentucky, 1997), 46 (note 5). LeBeau gives a thorough treatment of the Hemphill affair on pages 45–63.

8. *The Pennsylvania Gazette*, April 10, 1735, http://www.accessible-archives .com/collections/the-pennsylvania-gazette/.

9. This analysis of Franklin's religious search comes partly from Herbert W. Schneider in his article "Ungodly Puritans," included in *Benjamin Franklin and the American Character*, ed. Charles L. Sanford (Boston: D. C. Heath, 1955), 77–83, and excerpted from Schneider's *The Puritan Mind* (New York: Holt, 1930).

10. LeBeau, *Jonathan Dickinson and the Formative Years of American Presbyterianism*, 55.

Chapter 16

1. George Whitefield, *Journals* (Shropshire, England: Quinta Press, 2000), 159.

2. Ibid., 139.

3. George Whitefield, *Sermons of George Whitefield*, ed. Evelyn Bence (Peabody, MA: Hendrickson, 2009), 42.

4. Ibid, 44–5.

5. Whitefield, *Journals*, 90.

6. Ibid., 633.

7. Ibid., 183.

8. George Whitefield, Letter XL (June 10, 1738), *Works*, vol. 1 (London: Dilly, 1771), 55–56.

9. Whitefield, *Journals*, 178.

10. It's hard to determine exactly what an amount of money in the past would be worth in modern times, but thirteen hundred pounds in 1738 would probably equate to, at minimum, a quarter-million US dollars today, and possibly a million or more.

11. Benjamin Franklin, *Autobiography*, ed. Joyce E. Chaplin (New York: W. W. Norton, 2012), 101.

12. *The Pennsylvania Gazette*, April 24, 1740, http://www.accessible-archives.com /collections/the-pennsylvania-gazette/.

13. Whitefield, Letter XL, 55–56.

14. John Gillies, *Memoirs of the Life of the Reverend George Whitefield* (London: Dilly, 1772), 38.

15. Whitefield, Letter XLII (December 30, 1738), *Works*, vol. 1, 58.

16. Whitefield, *Journals*, 293.

17. Gillies, *Memoirs of the Life of the Reverend George Whitefield*, 37–38.

Chapter 17

1. *The Pennsylvania Gazette*, July 26, 1739, http://www.accessible-archives.com /collections/the-pennsylvania-gazette/.
2. *The Pennsylvania Gazette*, November 8, 1739.
3. Ibid.
4. *The Pennsylvania Gazette*, November 15, 1739.
5. George Whitefield, *Journals* (Shropshire, England: Quinta Press, 2000), 396.
6. Ibid., 395.
7. Ibid., 396.
8. Ibid., 399.
9. Benjamin Franklin, *Autobiography*, ed. Joyce E. Chaplin (New York: W. W. Norton, 2012), 100.
10. Whitefield, *Journals*, 444.
11. Franklin, *Autobiography*, 101.
12. Ibid.
13. Whitefield, *Journals*, 460.
14. Ibid.
15. Ibid., 459–60.
16. *The Pennsylvania Gazette*, May 15, 1740.
17. George Whitefield, Letter CCXXXVIII (November 26, 1740), *Works*, vol. 1 (London: Dilly, 1771), 255–56.

Chapter 18

1. George Whitefield, Letter LXIX (November 10, 1739), *Works*, vol. 1 (London: Dilly, 1771), 81.
2. Ibid.
3. *The Pennsylvania Gazette*, May 1, 1740, http://www.accessible-archives.com /collections/the-pennsylvania-gazette/.
4. *The Pennsylvania Gazette*, May 8, 1740.
5. Ibid.
6. *The Pennsylvania Gazette*, June 10, 1731.
7. Ibid.
8. William Seward, *Journal of a Voyage* (Shropshire, England: Quinta Press, 2009), 30–31.
9. Walter Isaacson, *Benjamin Franklin: An American Life* (New York: Simon and Schuster, 2003), 112.
10. George Whitefield, *Journals* (Shropshire, England: Quinta Press, 2000), 492–93.
11. *The Pennsylvania Gazette*, April 10, 1740.
12. Frank Lambert, "Pedlar in Divinity: George Whitefield and the Great Awakening, 1737–1745," *Journal of American History* 77, no. 3 (December 1990): 821, 836.

13. Whitefield, Letter CLXIX (March 26, 1740), *Works*, vol. 1, 179.
14. Whitefield, Letter CXCII (May 24, 1740), *Works*, vol. 1, 207.
15. Whitefield, Letter CXCIX (June 25, 1740), *Works*, vol. 1, 214–15.
16. Whitefield, Letter CCXIV (August 25, 1740), *Works*, vol. 1, 231–32.
17. Whitefield, Letter CCXXI (September 25, 1740), *Works*, vol. 1, 239.
18. Whitefield, Letter CCXXIX (November 9, 1740), *Works*, vol. 1, 247–48.
19. Whitefield, Letter CCXXXVI (November 24, 1740), *Works*, vol. 1, 254.
20. Luke Tyerman, *The Life of the Rev. George Whitefield*, vol. 1 (London: Hodder and Stoughton, 1877), 412.
21. Whitefield, Letter CXCII (May 24, 1740), *Works*, vol. 1, 207.
22. Ibid.
23. *The Pennsylvania Gazette*, October 2, 1740.

Chapter 19

1. John R. Williams, "The Strange Case of Dr. Franklin and Mr. Whitefield," *Pennsylvania Magazine of History and Biography* 102, no. 4 (October 1978): 403.
2. *The Pennsylvania Gazette*, October 9, 1740, http://www.accessible-archives.com/collections/the-pennsylvania-gazette/.
3. George Whitefield, *Journals* (Shropshire, England: Quinta Press, 2000), 505–6.
4. Ibid., 506, footnote.
5. Jonathan Edwards, *A Faithful Narrative of the Surprising Work of God*, sec. 1, http://www.jonathan-edwards.org/Narrative.html.
6. Edwin S. Gaustad, ed., *A Documentary History of Religion in America to the Civil War* (Grand Rapids, MI: Eerdmans, 1982), 216.
7. Iain H. Murray, *Jonathan Edwards: A New Biography* (Carlisle, PA: Banner of Truth Trust, 1987), 157.
8. Whitefield, *Journals,* 521.
9. Ibid., 522.
10. J. B. Wakeley, *Anecdotes of the Rev. George Whitefield* (London: Hodder and Stoughton, 1879), 184–85.
11. Chris Armstrong, "The Trouble with George," *Christian History,* issue 77 (2003): 19.
12. Whitefield, Letter CCXIV (August 25, 1740), *Works*, vol. 1 (Shropshire, England: Quinta Press, 2000), 232. The reference is to 1 Corinthians 3:6–8.
13. Daniel Walker Howe, "Franklin, Edwards, and the Problem of Human Nature," *Benjamin Franklin, Jonathan Edwards, and the Representation of American Culture*, eds. Barbara B. Oberg and Harry S. Stout (Oxford: Oxford University Press, 1993), 90.

Chapter 20

1. Benjamin Franklin, *Autobiography*, ed. Joyce E. Chaplin (New York: W. W. Norton, 2012), 80.
2. Walter Isaacson, *Benjamin Franklin: An American Life* (New York: Simon and Schuster, 2003), 163.
3. Ibid., 165.
4. Charles Wesley, *Journal of Charles Wesley*, vol. 1 (Grand Rapids, MI: Baker, 1960), 79.
5. George Whitefield, Letter XCIII (November 10, 1739), *Works*, vol. 1 (London: Dilly, 1771), 105.
6. Harry S. Stout, *The Divine Dramatist: George Whitefield and the Rise of Modern Evangelicalism* (Grand Rapids, MI: Eerdmans, 1991), 164.
7. Whitefield, Letter CLX (February 1, 1740), *Works*, vol. 1, 171.
8. Whitefield, Letter CLXXII (April 4, 1740), *Works,* vol. 1, 182–83.
9. Whitefield, Letter CLXXIII (April 4, 1740), *Works,* vol. 1, 184–85.
10. Whitefield, Letter CCIII (June 26, 1740), *Works*, vol. 1, 219–20. *Note:* Some assume that the June 26 letter must be misdated and should be July 26. In that case, George would have been telling Seward about a rejection letter he had just received from Elizabeth. But it makes more sense both emotionally and chronologically to see this June letter coming after George got a reply to the letter he sent to Elizabeth on February 1. Since he had sent a letter of strong spiritual exhortation, she might have responded with a letter lacking the kind of spiritual commitment he wanted.
11. Wesley, *Journal of Charles Wesley*, 237–40.
12. Arnold Dallimore, *George Whitefield: The Life and Times of the Great Evangelist of the Eighteenth-Century Revival*, vol. 1 (Carlisle, PA: Banner of Truth Trust, 1970), 473–74, 597.
13. Whitefield, Letter CCXII (August 15, 1740), *Works*, vol. 1, 229.
14. Whitefield, *Journals*, 521–22.
15. Mark Galli, "Whitefield's Curious Love Life," *Christian History*, issue 38 (1993): 33.
16. Whitefield, Letter CCCXC (February 2, 1742), *Works*, vol. 1, 403.
17. Franklin, *Autobiography*, 77.
18. Anonymous, but attributed to Charles Chauncy, *A Letter from a Gentleman in Boston to Mr. George Wishart One of the Ministers of Edinburgh, Concerning the State of Religion in New England* (Edinburgh: s.n., 1742), 8.
19. Ibid., 12–13.

Chapter 21

1. There was a broadside printed that was purported to be a letter from

Franklin to Whitefield, dated June 3, 1743. Carrying the title "Give Us But Light," it had some personal remarks and then launched into a discussion of good works. Later analysis identified it as a letter written a decade later to a Reverend Joseph Huey. It appears as such in collections of Franklin's letters.

2. Harry S. Stout, *The Divine Dramatist: George Whitefield and the Rise of Modern Evangelicalism* (Grand Rapids, MI: Eerdmans, 1991), 175.

3. Luke Tyerman, *The Life of the Rev. George Whitefield*, vol. 2 (London: Hodder and Stoughton, 1877), 134.

4. Benjamin Franklin, *Autobiography*, ed. Joyce E. Chaplin (New York: W. W. Norton, 2012), 102 (italics his).

5. George Whitefield, Letter DCCXIX (December 21, 1748), *Works*, vol. 2 (London: Dilly, 1771), 219.

6. Frank Lambert, "Pedlar in Divinity: George Whitefield and the Great Awakening, 1737–1745," *Journal of American History* 77, no. 3 (December 1990): 826.

7. Arnold Dallimore, *George Whitefield: The Life and Times of the Great Evangelist of the Eighteenth-Century Revival*, vol. 2 (Carlisle, PA: Banner of Truth Trust, 1980), 214.

8. Benjamin Franklin, Letter to Joseph Huey, June 6, 1753, http://franklinpapers.org/franklin//framedVolumes.jsp.

9. George Whitefield, Letter to Benjamin Franklin, June 23, 1747, http://franklinpapers.org/franklin//framedVolumes.jsp.

10. Whitefield, Letter to Benjamin Franklin, February 26, 1750, franklinpapers.org.

11. Franklin, Letter to Cadwallader Colden, September 29, 1748, franklinpapers.org.

12. Franklin, Letter to George Whitefield, July 6, 1749, franklinpapers.org.

13. See Franklin, Letter to Thomas Hopkinson, October 16, 1746, and Letter to Jane Mecom, July 28, 1743, franklinpapers.org.

Chapter 22

1. Document dated April 16, 1746, from the *Pennsylvania Gazette*, May 22, 1746, http://www.accessible-archives.com/collections/the-pennsylvania-gazette/.

2. *The Pennsylvania Gazette*, July 31, 1746.

3. Ibid.

4. Harry S. Stout, *The Divine Dramatist: George Whitefield and the Rise of Modern Evangelicalism* (Grand Rapids, MI: Eerdmans, 1991), 196.

5. Benjamin Franklin, Letter to John Franklin, August 6, 1747, http://franklinpapers.org/franklin//framedVolumes.jsp.

6. Peter Collinson, Letter to Benjamin Franklin, July 7, 1752, http://franklinpapers.org/franklin//framedVolumes.jsp.

7. *The Pennsylvania Gazette*, October 19, 1752.

8. George Whitefield, Letter DCCCCXXVI (August 17, 1752), *Works*, vol. 2 (London: Dilly, 1771), 445.

9. Whitefield, Letter MLV (August 15, 1754), *Works*, vol. 3, 105.
10. Whitefield, Letter MLVI (August 17, 1754), *Works*, vol. 3, 106
11. Whitefield, Letter MLIV, (August 7, 1754), *Works*, vol. 3, 105.
12. Whitefield, Letter MLXXIII (January 17, 1755), *Works*, vol. 3, 120.
13. Franklin, Letter to George Whitefield, July 2, 1756, franklinpapers.org.

Chapter 23

1. Benjamin Franklin, Letter to Deborah Franklin, November 22, 1757, http://franklinpapers.org/franklin//framedVolumes.jsp.
2. James Paterson Gledstone, *George Whitefield, M.A.: Field Preacher* (London: Hodder and Stoughton, 1900), 225.
3. David Hume, Letter to Benjamin Franklin, May 10, 1762, http://franklin papers.org/franklin//framedVolumes.jsp.
4. George Whitefield, Letter MCCXL (August 15, 1760), *Works*, vol. 3 (London: Dilly, 1771), 268–69.
5. Whitefield, Letter MCCCXII (June 25, 1764), *Works*, vol. 3, 317.
6. Franklin, Letter to George Whitefield, November 28, 1763, franklinpapers.org.
7. Franklin, Letter to George Whitefield, June 19, 1764, franklinpapers.org.
8. Ibid.
9. Franklin, Letter to William Strahan, June 25, 1964, franklinpapers.org.
10. Franklin, Letter to Sally Franklin, Nov 8, 1764, franklinpapers.org.
11. John Gillies, *Memoirs of the Life of the Reverend George Whitefield, M.A.* (London: Dilly, 1772), 189.
12. Arnold Dallimore, *George Whitefield: The Life and Times of the Great Evangelist of the Eighteenth-Century Revival*, vol. 2 (Carlisle, PA: Banner of Truth Trust, 1980), 450.
13. Franklin, Letter to Deborah Franklin, February 27, 1766, franklinpapers.org.
14. Franklin, Letter to Jane Mecom, March 2, 1767, franklinpapers.org.
15. Whitefield, Letter to Benjamin Franklin, January 21, 1768, franklin papers.org.
16. Ibid.
17. Franklin, Letter to George Whitefield, December 6, 1768, franklinpapers.org.
18. Whitefield, Letter MCCCXCVIII (November 12, 1768), *Works*, vol. 3, 382.
19. Whitefield, Letter MCCCCVII (March 17, 1769), *Works*, vol. 3, 387.
20. Luke Tyerman, *The Life of the Reverend George Whitefield*, vol. 2 (London: Hodder and Stoughton, 1877), 558.
21. Franklin, Letter to George Whitefield, before September 2, 1769. franklin papers.org.
22. Ibid.
23. Harry S. Stout, *The Divine Dramatist: George Whitefield and the Rise of Modern Evangelicalism* (Grand Rapids, MI: Eerdmans, 1991), 230–31.

24. Phillis Wheatley, *The Poems of Phillis Wheatley* (Chapel Hill: University of North Carolina Press, 1989), 133.

25. *The Pennsylvania Gazette,* October 11, 1770, http://www.accessible-archives .com/collections/the-pennsylvania-gazette/.

26. Franklin, Letter to Noble Wimberly Jones, March 5, 1771, franklinpapers.org.

Chapter 24

1. Benjamin Franklin, *Autobiography*, ed. Joyce E. Chaplin (New York: W. W. Norton, 2012), 101.

2. Harry S. Stout, *The Divine Dramatist: George Whitefield and the Rise of Modern Evangelicalism* (Grand Rapids, MI: Eerdmans, 1991), 220.

3. Franklin, Letter to Noble Wimberly Jones, March 5, 1771, http://franklin papers.org/franklin//framedVolumes.jsp.

4. Harry S. Stout, "Heavenly Comet," *Christian History*, issue 38 (1993).

5. Paul Johnson, *A History of Christianity* (New York: Touchstone, 1976), 427.

6. Ibid.

7. *The Pennsylvania Gazette*, June 12, 1740, http://www.accessible-archives.com /collections/the-pennsylvania-gazette/.

8. Franklin, Letter to Ezra Stiles, March 9, 1790, *In God We Trust*, ed. Norman Cousins (New York: Harper, 1958), 41–42.

BIBLIOGRAPHY

NOTE: Quotations from some works from the eighteenth century and earlier have been lightly edited, adjusting capitalization and spelling to conform to modern styles.

Books

Eighteenth-Century Plays, with an Introduction by Ricardo Quintana. New York: Random House, 1952.

Andrews, J. R. *The Life of George Whitefield.* 1879. Reprinted by Quinta Press, 2000.

Barnett, Dene. *The Art of Gesture: The Practices and Principles of 18th-Century Acting.* Heidelberg: Carl Winter Universitatsverlag, 1987.

Benedetti, Jean. *The Art of the Actor.* New York: Routledge, 2007.

Boorstin, Daniel J. *The Creators: A History of Heroes of the Imagination.* New York: Random House, 1992.

Bowen, Catherine Drinker. *The Most Dangerous Man in America: Scenes from the Life of Benjamin Franklin.* New Delhi: Affiliated East-West Press, 1987.

Chaplin, Joyce E., ed. *Benjamin Franklin's Autobiography.* New York: W. W. Norton, 2012.

Cousins, Norman, ed. *In God We Trust: The Religious Beliefs and Ideas of the American Founding Fathers.* New York: Harper and Brothers, 1958.

Dallimore, Arnold. *George Whitefield: The Life and Times of the Great Evangelist of the Eighteenth-Century Revival.* 2 vols. Carlisle, PA: Banner of Truth Trust, 1970.

DeRitter, Jones. *The Embodiment of Characters: The Representation of Physical Experience on Stage and in Print 1728–1749.* Philadelphia: University of Pennsylvania Press, 1994.

Fay, Bernard. *Franklin, the Apostle of Modern Times.* New York: Little, Brown, 1929.

Gaustad, Edwin S., ed. *A Documentary History of Religion in America to the Civil War.* Grand Rapids, MI: Eerdmans, 1982.

Gaustad, Edwin Scott. *A Religious History of America.* New York: Harper and Row, 1966.

Gillies, John. *Memoirs of the Life of the Reverend George Whitefield, M.A.* London: Dilly, 1772.

Gledstone, James Paterson. *George Whitefield M.A.: Field Preacher.* London: Hodder and Stoughton, 1900.

Gragg, Rod. *By the Hand of Providence.* New York: Howard, 2011.

——— *Forged in Faith.* New York: Howard, 2010.

Hoffer, Peter Charles. *When Benjamin Franklin Met the Reverend Whitefield.* Baltimore: Johns Hopkins Press, 2011.

Huang, Nian-Sheng. *Benjamin Franklin in American Thought and Culture 1790–1990.* Canton, MA: American Philosophical Society, 1994.

Isaacson, Walter. *Benjamin Franklin: An American Life.* New York: Simon and Schuster, 2003.

Jenkins, Simon. *A Short History of England.* London: Profile, 2011.

Johnson, Paul. *A History of Christianity.* New York: Touchstone, 1976.

LeBeau, Bryan F. *Jonathan Dickinson and the Formative Years of American Presbyterianism.* Lexington: University Press of Kentucky, 1997.

McMillin, Scott, ed. *Restoration and Eighteenth-Century Comedy.* New York: W. W. Norton, 1997.

Mahaffey, Jerome Dean. *The Accidental Revolutionary: George Whitefield & the Creation of America.* Waco, TX: Baylor University Press, 2011.

Mansfield, Stephen. *Forgotten Founding Father: The Heroic Legacy of George Whitefield.* Nashville, TN: Cumberland House, 2001.

Morgan, Edmund S. *Benjamin Franklin.* New Haven, CT: Yale University Press, 2002.

Murray, Iain H. *Jonathan Edwards: A New Biography.* Carlisle, PA: Banner of Truth Trust, 1987.

Nagler, A. M. *A Sourcebook in Theatrical History.* New York: Dover Publications, 1952.

Oberg, Barbara B. and Harry S. Stout, eds. *Benjamin Franklin, Jonathan Edwards, and the Representation of American Culture.* Oxford: Oxford University Press, 1993.

Philip, Robert. *The Life and Times of the Reverend George Whitefield.* London: George Virtue, 1842.

Sanford, Charles L., ed. *Benjamin Franklin and the American Character.* Boston: D.C. Heath, 1955.

Schiff, Stacy. *A Great Improvisation: Franklin, France, and the Birth of America.* New York: Holt, 2005.

Seligman, Adam B. *Innerworldly Individualism: Charismatic Community and Its Institutionalization.* New Brunswick, NJ: Transaction Publishers, 1994.

Stout, Harry S., *The Divine Dramatist: George Whitefield and the Rise of Modern Evangelicalism.* Grand Rapids, MI: Eerdmans, 1991.

Tyerman, Luke. *The Life of the Rev. George Whitefield.* 2 vols. London: Hodder and Stoughton, 1877.

Wentz, Richard E. *Religion in the New World: The Shaping of Religious Traditions in the United States.* Minneapolis, MN: Fortress, 1990.

Wesley, Charles. *Journal of Charles Wesley*. 2 vols. London: John Mason, 1849. Reprint, Grand Rapids, MI: Baker, 1960.

Wesley, John. *The Heart of John Wesley's Journal*. Edited by Percy Livingston Parker. New Canaan, CT: Keats, 1979.

Whitefield, George. *Sermons of George Whitefield*. Edited by Evelyn Bence. Peabody, MA: Hendrickson, 2009.

Wood, Gordon S. *The Americanization of Benjamin Franklin*. New York: Penguin, 2005.

Wright, Louis B., *Everyday Life in Colonial America*. New York: G.P. Putnam's Sons, 1965.

Articles

Aldridge, Alfred Owen. "Benjamin Franklin and the *Pennsylvania Gazette*." *Proceedings of the American Philosophical Society* 106, no. 1 (February 15, 1962): 77–81.

Aldridge, Marion D. "George Whitefield: The Necessary Interdependence of Preaching Style and Sermon Content to Effect Revival." *Journal of the Evangelical Theological Society* 23, no. 1 (March 1980): 55–64.

Bosco, Ronald A. "'He That Best Understands the World, Least Likes It': The Dark Side of Benjamin Franklin." *Pennsylvania Magazine of History and Biography* 111, no. 4 (October 1987): 525–54.

Fea, John. "Religion And Early Politics: Benjamin Franklin and His Religious Beliefs." *Pennsylvania Heritage* 37, no. 4 (Fall 2011).

Gragg, Larry. "A Mere Civil Friendship." *History Today* 28, no. 9 (September 1978).

Lambert, Frank. "Subscribing for Profits and Piety: The Friendship of Benjamin Franklin and George Whitefield." *William & Mary Quarterly* 50, no. 3 (July 1993): 529–54.

———. "Pedlar in Divinity: George Whitefield and the Great Awakening, 1737–1745." *Journal of American History* 77, no. 3 (December 1990).

Mahaffey, Jerome Dean. "George Whitefield's Homiletic Art: Neo-sophism in the Great Awakening." *Homiletic* 31, no. 1 (2006).

Miller, C. William. "Franklin's *Poor Richard Almanacs*: Their Printing and Publication." *Studies in Bibliography* 14 (1961): 97–115.

Sanford, Charles L. "An American Pilgrim's Progress." *American Quarterly* 6, no. 4 (Winter 1954): 297–310.

Stout, Harry S. "George Whitefield and Benjamin Franklin: Thoughts on a Peculiar Friendship." *Proceedings of the Massachusetts Historical Society*, 3rd ser., 103 (1991): 9–23.

Wiliams, John R. "The Strange Case of Dr. Franklin and Mr. Whitefield." *Pennsylvania Magazine of History and Biography* 102, no. 4 (October 1978).

Zuckerman, Michael. "Food for Thought: America's Accessible Founder." *Pennsylvania Legacies* 6, no. 1 (May 2006): 36–37.

Older Works Accessed Online

The Country-Parson's Advice to His Parishioners. Google eBook. London: Benj. Tooke,
    1680.
Boswell, James. *Boswell's Life of Johnson.* Edited by Charles Grosvenor Osgood.
    Project Gutenberg. May 12, 2006. http://www.gutenberg.org/files/1564/1564
    -h/1564-h.htm.
Bunyan, John. *Grace Abounding to the Chief of Sinners.* London: The Religious Tract
    Society, 1905.
Francke, August Hermann. *Nicodemus, or A Treatise Against the Fear of Man.* 3rd ed.
    Bath: S. Hazard, 1801.
Law, William. *A Serious Call to a Devout and Holy Life.* London: Innys, 1729.
    Accessed through Christian Classics Ethereal Library, www.ccel.org.
Mather, Samuel. *The Life of Dr. Cotton Mather.* Minneapolis, MN: Curiosmith, 2012.
Ralph, James. *The Touch-stone.* London: Booksellers of London and Westminster,
    1729.
Scougal, Henry. *The Life of God in the Soul of Man.* Accessed through ccel.org.
Seward, William. *Journal of a Voyage.* 1740. Accessed through Quinta Press.

Other Sites and Sources

Christian History magazine. Worcester, PA: and Carol Stream, IL: Christian History
    Institute, 1982–2014. Especially issues 23, 38, 41, 77, 89, II-1 and IV-4.
"Silence Dogood" letters from *New-England Courant*, found at www.historycarper
    .com.
Pennsylvania Gazette and other colonial newspapers available at www.accessible
    -archives.com.
Franklin writings and correspondence at www.franklinpapers.org.
Whitefield writings, including his *Journals* and *Works* (sermons and correspondence),
    at www.quintapress.com.
The Quinta Press collection includes:
George Whitefield's Journals. Shropshire, England: Quinta Press, 2000.
The Works of the Reverend George Whitefield, M.A., vol. 1–5. London: Edward and
    Charles Dilly, 1771.
Wakeley, J. B., *Anecdotes of the Rev. George Whitefield, M.A.,* London: Hodder and
    Stoughton, 1879.
Sermons on Important Subjects by the Rev. George Whitefield, M.A. London: Henry
    Fisher, Son, and P. Jackson, 1836.

ABOUT THE AUTHOR

Randy Petersen has written more than sixty books on a wide range of themes, including history, the Bible, relationships, psychology, Christian growth, and sports. He holds a BA in Ancient Languages from Wheaton College (Illinois) and an MA in Theater from Villanova University (Pennsylvania).

Living most of his life in the Philadelphia area, Randy has attended concerts on the Franklin Parkway, roamed through the Franklin Institute, and gotten stuck in traffic on the Ben Franklin Bridge. Any writer in this region can claim a great heritage from Franklin, "the Printer."

Randy's interest in "the Preacher," George Whitefield, came alive in the late 1980s, during his work with *Christian History* magazine (which recycled the name of an eighteenth-century periodical published by Whitefield). As a leader and occasional preacher in Hope United Methodist Church of Voorhees, New Jersey, Randy can savor an additional connection with the Methodist pioneer Whitefield. And as a director/actor/playwright, he appreciates the theatricality Whitefield brought to his ministry.

Formerly on the staff of *Eternity* magazine, Randy managed publications targeted to church and ministry leaders. As an independent writer, he has produced a wide range of educational curriculum for youth and adults. He also contributed to the *Quest Study Bible* (Zondervan), helped edit the *Revell Bible Dictionary*, and wrote copy for the groundbreaking *iLumina Bible* software (Tyndale House). He blogs regularly for the American Bible Society.

Among his historical works are: *The 100 Most Important Dates in Christian History* (with Ken Curtis and Stephen Lang, published by Revell), *100 Bible*

Verses that Changed the World (with his father, William J. Petersen, also Revell), and *The One-Year Book of Women in Christian History* (with Robin Shreeves, Tyndale House).

Randy has taught public speaking at Camden County College (New Jersey) and acting at Eastern University (St. David's, Pennsylvania). He has written and directed plays, acted, and taught acting at scholastic, community, and professional theaters throughout the Philadelphia area—including the development of an acting workshop for teenagers at Urban Promise of Camden, New Jersey. Among his greatest delights is his role as player-manager of a church softball team, which will actually win a game any day now.

INDEX

A

acting, Whitefield and, 67–70

Adams, John, 175, 211, 221

adult relationships, George's upbringing
and, 24

advertising by Whitefield, 7–8, 120

Albany Plan, 202, 219

"Almost a Christian," 107

America, discovery as religious mission,
13–15

The American Weekly Mercury, 77

Andrews, Jedediah, 126–127

Anglican church, 119
  conflict between education and
    experience, 98
  and Georgia orphanage, 140
  Henry VIII and, 14
  Whitefield and, 5, 220

apprentice, 30

Aristotle, writing on arts, 69

"Articles of Beliefs and Acts of Religion"
  (worship liturgy), 101

atheists, vs. deists, 195

author, image of, 46

autobiography, 33. *See also* Franklin,
  Benjamin, *Autobiography*
  by Whitefield, 33

B

Baptists, 14, 40, 119

The Beggar's Opera, 63–64

Bethesda orphanage, 148. *See also* orphanage
  college charter, 213

Bible
  Genesis 24, 180
  1 Kings 13, 135
  Psalm 1:1-2, 71
  Psalm 118:10-12, 51
  Ecclesiastes 4:9, 114
  Matthew 13:1-30, 170
  Matthew 25:40, 139
  Luke 18:9-14, 141
  John 3:3, 101
  Acts 2:46, 92
  Romans 4:16-22, 180
  Romans 6:23, 102
  1 Corinthians 1:23, 128
  1 Corinthians 2:14-15, 177
  2 Corinthians 5:17, 103
  1 Timothy 4:12, 115
  Hebrews 11:6, 225
  James 1:27, 139

Bible Moths, 95

blessings from God, 105

Boorstin, Daniel, 33, 34

Boston, 164
  Franklin departure from, 31–32
  Quakers in, 16
  soldiers in, 214
  Whitefield preaching in, 165

Boston Evening Post, 184

Boston Massacre, 214

bourgeoisie, *The London Merchant* and, 65

Braddock, General, troop transport to
  Ohio Valley, 204

Bradford, Andrew, 76

The American Weekly Mercury, 77
Bristol, England, Whitefield preaching in, 117, 141–142
British Empire, Julian calendar switch to Gregorian, 19
bullying of Whitefield, 51
Bunyan, John, 35–36
  Grace Abounding to the Chief of Sinners, 37
  Pilgrim's Progress, 17, 27, 32
  Pilgrim's Progress, and Franklin, 34–37
business
  Franklin/Whitefield partnership, 3
  Franklin's sense of, 45
  opportunities in new world, 17
Busy-Body (Franklin pseudonym), 77, 85
byline, power of, 45

C
Caesar in Egypt, 55
calendar, switch from Julian to Gregorian, 19
Calvin, John, 15, 92
Cambridge, Whitefield visit to, 166
candle-making business, 21
celebrity, 7–10
censure of printers, 157
character, 224
Charles I (king of England), 15, 17
Charles II (king of England), 17, 60
Charleston, Whitefield's farewell sermon, August 1740, 159
Chauncy, Charles, opposition to Whitefield, 181–182
Christ Church (Philadelphia), 40, 126
  for lightning experiment, 199
  Whitefield preaching in, 146
Christian Perfection (Law), 95
Christianity, Whitefield on reasonableness of, 153
church establishment, 5
  and society, 128
  Whitefield's rejection of aristocratic spirit, 64
"The Church Militant" (Herbert), 13

Church of England, 14, 87–88. *See also* Anglican church
Cibber, Colley, 55, 61
Cicero, 114
  and speech-making, 67
citizenship, Franklin's promotion of, 184
"city upon a hill," 15, 16
City Watch program, 112–113
class system. *See also* social classes
  knowledge for breaking, 111
codes of conduct, from Franklin, 173
Cole (minister in Gloucester), ridicule of, 51–52
college. *See also* Oxford University
  Franklin thoughts on, 192–193
  Harvard College, 164, 166
  Princeton University, 201
  University of Pennsylvania, 39, 193
College of New Jersey, 201
Collier, Jeremy, *A Short View of the Immorality and Profaneness of the English Stage*, 61
Collins, John, 79
Collinson, Peter, 199
colonial unity, 202
Columbus, Christopher, 11
  focus on evangelism, 13
common-law marriage, 81
Common Sense (Paine), 14
communication, Franklin and, 220
communication styles, 2–3
Communion on Christmas, Whitefield and, 84
community, Franklin's work for, 75
The Confessions of St. Augustine, 33
Congreve, William, 61
The Conscious Lovers (Steele), 62
Continental Congress, 219
controversy, safe way to deal with, 29
conversion experience
  as process, 103
  versions of, 104–109
correspondence, 4
  openness in, 8
The Country Parson's Advice to His Parishioners, 99, 102

creativity, 224
crime in London, 63
Crooked Billet (Philadelphia), 43
currency, paper, 113
  Franklin's printing of, 75

D
dancing hall in Philadelphia
  Franklin and debate over, 157–159
  Whitefield opposition to, 156–159
Dante, *Inferno*, 11
Davenport, James, 183
death, Whitefield's awareness of, 213
Declaratory Act (Parliament), 212
dedication to church, as J. Franklin's plan
  for Ben, 20–21
deism, 215
  vs. atheism, 195
Dekker, Thomas, 60
Delamotte, Elizabeth
  marriage, 179
  Whitefield and, 176–177
Delamotte family, 175–179
Denham, Thomas, 49, 53, 73
  death, 75
denominations, 5
  in America, 134
  in Philadelphia, 40
  Whitefield's appeal to multiple, 40, 119,
    221
devotion, 87
diplomat, Franklin as, 201–202
Dissenters, 14
dissenting movements in England, 119
*A Dissertation on Liberty and Necessity,
  Pleasure and Pain* (Franklin), 56
Donne, John, 12
Drury Lane Theatre (London), 54

E
education
  of Franklin, 3, 21
  of Whitefield, 3, 23
  as Whitefield/Franklin conversation
    topic, 192–193

Edwards, Jonathan, 25, 164, 166–168
  *A Faithful Narrative of the Surprising Work
    of God*, 167
  role in American evangelicalism,
    170–171
  Whitefield and, 179
Edwards, Sarah, 168, 169–170, 179
electricity, 198–200
emotions, gospel and, 105
England
  in 1724, 50
  Charles I deposed by Parliament, 17
  dissenting movements in, 119
  opposition to Whitefield in 1738, 139
English, North America exploration,
  12–13
Enlightenment, and theological training,
  166
entertainment, in London, 55
established church, 5
  and society, 128
  Whitefield's rejection of aristocratic
    spirit, 64
evangelism, 221, 222
Everyman (medieval play), 35
extemporaneous preaching, by Whitefield,
  121–122

F
faith, 18
  Franklin's views, 209–210
  saved by, 128
  as Whitefield/Franklin conversation
    topic, 195
family, as Whitefield/Franklin
  conversation topic, 188
father figures, 23–25
Fielding, Henry, 55
fire protection, in Philadelphia, 112
First Presbyterian Church (Philadelphia),
  126
Folger, Peter, 47
folk wisdom, in *Poor Richard's Almanac*, 89
France
  diplomacy with, 219

war with, 188–190, 205

Francke, August, 95

Nicodemus, or A Treatise Against the Fear
of Man, 27, 97–98, 102

Franklin, Abiah Folger, 20

Franklin, Anne Child, 20

Franklin, Benjamin, 55. *See also* Whitefield
and Franklin: relationship

approach to Bunyan, 36

birth, 19

business sense, 45

childhood environment, 17, 20

choices and consequences, 62–63

and church authorities, 5

and dance hall debate, 157–159

education, 73–81

experiment on size of Whitefield
audience, 41

father figure, 23–25

humility of, 101

identity crisis, 53

lobbying for Stamp Act repeal, 211

marriage, 181

misrepresentation charge on
Whitefield's success, 157

organization creation, 111

parenthood, 80–81

before Parliament to argue for Stamp Act
repeal, 9

reading of London papers on Whitefield,
129

relationships with women, 172–175, 176

religious culture at birth, 16

retirement, 193

in science, 198–200

significance to America, 219–223

theft of materials, 20

timeline, 229–238

as tradesman, 65

understanding of importance of image, 34

visit with brother, James, 46–47

in working class, 6

Franklin, Benjamin, *Autobiography*, 29, 33,
34

Ben's tribute to father, 23–24

on religious development, 91

writing, 44

Franklin, Benjamin: travel

to Albany, New York, 201–202

departure from Boston, 31–32

to England, 1765, 210

to London, 48–49, 174–175, 205

London to Philadelphia, 72

to Paris, 174

postal inspection tour, 208

return to America, 1762, 208

Franklin, Benjamin: views

attitude on good life, 109

concern for reputation in London, 208

faith development, 2

of God, 56, 74, 90–91, 209

on reading, 27

on religion, 154, 224

on Whitefield, 9–10, 186–187

on Whitefield influence, 4

Franklin, Benjamin: writings

"Apology for Printers," 157

"Appreciation of George Whitefield"
(editorial), 197–198

A Dissertation on Liberty and Necessity,
Pleasure and Pain, 56

early epitaph written by, 100, 203

early writings, 28–30

Poor Richard Improved, 194

Poor Richard's Almanac, 1, 9, 65, 89,
146–147

"Short Hints towards a Scheme for
Uniting the Northern Colonies," 202

Thirteen Weeks to Self-Actualization, 26

Franklin, Deborah, 202

Franklin's letter to, 207

marriage to Ben, 181

Franklin, James (brother), 21–22

Ben's relationship with, 78

jailing for criticism of government, 31

view of Ben, 28

worries about Ben, 30

Franklin, John, 188

Franklin, Josiah (father), 20

emigration from England, 17

and Keith's recommendation, 46
Franklin, William (son)
  birth question, 80–81
  as governor of New Jersey, 213
Franklin family, 20–22
  Ben on dinners, 24
freedom, 18
freedom of religion, Penn and, 40
Frelinghuysen, Theodore, 167
French and Indian War, 190
friendships, 187. *See also* Whitefield and
  Franklin: relationship
  of Franklin, 79–80
fund-raising by Whitefield, 138

G
Galloway, Joseph, 212
Garrick, David, 61, 66
Gay, John, 63
gentlemen
  in colonial America, 6
  and work, 25
Georgia, 17. *See also* orphanage
  1738 conditions, 133
  delays in Whitefield's travels to, 117–119
  orphanage, 25, 137–139
  Whitefield in, 135–137
  Whitefield travel to, 131–142
  Whitefield's call to, 116
gesture, in acting, 69
Gildon, Charles, *The Rules of Oratory
  Applied to Acting*, 68, 69
Gillies, John, 88, 141
"Glorious Revolution" of 1688, 61
Gloucester, England, Whitefield preaching
  in, 117
God
  Franklin's views, 56, 74, 90–91, 209
  plans for Whitefield, 83
  truth of, 98
God's plan, 18
good works, role of, 26
grace, 26, 36, 107, 161
Grace Abounding to the Chief of Sinners
  (Bunyan), 35, 37

grammar school in England, 66–67
Great Awakening, 1, 10, 166–168, 186,
  221, 222
Great Migration, 15–17
Gregorian calendar, switch from Julian to,
  19
Gwyn, Nell, 60

H
Habersham, James, 148, 196, 201
Hall, David, 193
hard work, value of, 25
Harlequin Sorcerer, 55
Harris, Gabriel, 189
  Whitefield's note to, 118
Harris, Howell, 140, 180
Harvard College, 164, 166
Hastins, Lady Selina (Countess of
  Huntingdon), 6, 194, 207
"heart strangely warmed," J. Wesley on,
  105
heart, transformation of, 105
Henphill, Samuel, 127–130
Henry, Patrick, 211
Henry VIII (king of England), 14
Herbert, George, *The Temple*, 13
Hill, Aaron, *The Prompter* (newsletter),
  69
holiness, 168
Holy Club at Oxford, 26, 94–96
  passion and, 136
  Whitefield and, 96–99, 102
The Holy War (Bunyan), 35
hope, 209
Hopkinson, Thomas, 149–150
hospitality, 187
Howe, Daniel Walker, 171
humanism, 10
Hume, David, 206–207, 220
humility, 113, 118
  of Franklin, 101, 153
Huntingdon, Lady Selina (Selina Hastins),
  6, 194, 207
Hutchinson, Anne, 16
Hutton, James, 121, 184

I

identity, Whitefield development of, 131
image
    Ben and George intentional construction
        of, 84–85
    power of, 46
immigration to Philadelphia, 110
indentured servant, Webb as, 124
individualists, vs. teamwork, 111
Inferno (Dante), 11
integrity, as Franklin's priority, 91
intelligence of Franklin, 91
Iroquois, Franklin's views on, 202
Isaacson, Walter, 176

J

James, Elizabeth, marriage to Whitefield,
    180
Jamestown colony (Virginia), 14, 17
jealousy, of Keimer, 75
Jesus
    Franklin's views, 2, 101, 210, 224–225
    Hemphill on, 127
    trust in, 106–107
    Whitefield view on, 2
Johnson, Paul, 221
Johnson, Samuel, 86, 87
"Join or Die" with snake, in political
    cartoon, 111–112
Jonson, Ben, 59
journaling, by Whitefield, 8, 131–132,
    150, 168
Julian calendar, switch to Gregorian, 19
Junto, 91–94
    Franklin's questions for, 93–94
    science discussions, 198
    Webb in, 125
justification by faith, 167

K

Keimer, Samuel
    Franklin as print shop foreman, 75
    newspaper publishing, 125
    *Universal Instructor in all Arts and
        Sciences: and Pennsylvania Gazette*, 77

Keith, William, 46
    betrayal of Franklin, 53
    letters of credit promised, 48–49
Ken, Thomas, 26
Kensington Common, Whitefield
    preaching in, 143
King's Theatre (London), 54
kite experiment, 199–200
knowledge, social value of, 111

L

laborer, Franklin's view of, 21
Lambert, Frank, 189
Law, William, 119
    *A Practical Treatise upon Christian
        Perfection*, 26, 95
    A Serious Call to a Devout and Holy Life,
        26, 87–88, 95
Leather Apron Club, 92
Lenten fast, by Whitefield, 104
letters of credit, Keith's promise of, 48–49
Library Company, Franklin's formation
    of, 111
The Life and Death of Mr. Badman (Bunyan),
    35
The Life of God in the Soul of Man (Scougal),
    102–103
lightning rod, 200
Lillo, George, *The London Merchant*, 64–65
Lincoln's Inn Fields (London), 54, 63
literary club, formation with Franklin, 45
literary form, Franklin's creation of, 33
Little Haymarket Theatre (London), 54
Locke, John, 167, 207
London
    crime in, 63
    entertainment in, 55
    Franklin in, 48–49, 53–54
    growth, 63
    play lampooning Whitefield, 207–208
    theaters in, 54–55
    Webb in, 124
The London Merchant (Lillo), 64–65
Longden, Capel (George's stepdad), 50–51
love

from God, 108
of God, Whitefield emphasis on, 136
Whitefield and, 176
loving actions, 224
lower class
dignity of, 64
impact of Whitefield's message on, 151
Luther, Martin, 12, 107
Lutherans, 40, 95

M
Marlowe, Christopher (Kit), 59
marriage, romance in, 180–182
Massachusetts Bay Colony, 15
Mather, Cotton, 16, 92, 93
Ben's visit with, 47
Essays to Do Good, 48
questions to be asked in religious
societies, 93
*Religious Societies: Proposals for the Revival
of Dying Religion*, 92
writings, 47–48
Mather, Samuel, 47
Franklin's letter to, 48
Mayflower, 14–15
Mayflower Compact, 15
Mecom, Jane (Franklin's sister), 188
Mennonites, 40
Mercury, Franklin's writings in, 77
Meredith, Hugh, Franklin's partnering
with, 76
Methodists, 26, 64, 95
Delamotte family rejection of, 179
in England, 221
in Georgia, 133–134
J. and C. Wesley and, 119
life style, 155
message, 114
plan for prayer, study, accountability,
and exhortation, 99
Whitefield and, 40
metropolitan areas, statistics estimates, 249n
mistreatment of Franklin, 79
mockery, true believers need to withstand, 98
Moorfields in Britain, 185

morality, 57
Franklin's views, 90–91
and theater, 59
Moravians, 40, 95
John Wesley and, 105
Morgan, Edmund S., 92, 113

N
near-death experience of Franklin, 73–74
"The Necessiity and Benefit of Religious
Society," 114–115
new birth, 108
denominations and, 221
emotional experience of receiving, 105
opposition to Whitefield doctrine, 119,
140
Whitefield and, 12, 104, 225
Whitefield encouragement of study, 200
New England Courant, 30–31
Ben as sole publisher, 31
"New Lights," vs. "Old Lights," 167
new world, 12
New York, 32
newspaper publishing, 76–77
potential impact, 78
Nicodemus, 101
Nonconformists, 14
Nova Scotia, French fort, 190–191

O
Of the Imitation of Christ (Thomas à
Kempis), 95
Oglethorpe, James, 116, 117
Ohio, Franklin's dream for, 204
ordination of Whitefield, 113–114, 140
organizations, Franklin's creation of, 111
orphanage, 25, 137–139
Franklin opinion on, 149
fund-raising, 144–145, 191–192
property purchase, 148
public audit of accounts, 196
public questions about, 196
Whitefield and, 39
as Whitefield/Franklin conversation
topic, 191–192

Whitefield's efforts for approval and
    funding, 140
Whitefield's last visit, 215
"ounce of prevention," 112
outdoor meetings, 140–141
    J. Wesley and, 164
overseas travel, danger of, 205
Oxford University
    class consciousness at, 86
    Holy Club, 26, 94–96
    religious activities at, 87
    "servitor" program at, 83
    Webb attendance at, 124

P

Paine, Thomas, *Common Sense*, 14
Palmer, Samuel, 56
paper currency, 113
    Franklin's printing of, 75
Parliament,, Franklin testimony before,
    211
passion, 167
    Holy Club and, 136
    Whitefield revival and, 181
    in Whitefield's oratory, 69
Paul (apostle), 107
Pembroke College, Whitefield enrollment,
    86
Penn, Thomas, 194
Penn, William, 39
    and freedom of religion, 40
Pennsylvania Assembly, Franklin as
    representative, 205
The Pennsylvania Gazette, 3, 77, 219
    ad for Whitefield sale items, 144
    attacks on Whitefield in, 184
    defense of Whitefield, 148–149
    Franklin's writings on Hemphill,
        127–128
    news on Whitefield travels, 164
    pseudonyms in, 112
    on Whitefield, 215
    Whitefield's impact, 220
    on Whitefield's ministry, 138, 143–144
    on Whitefield's Philadelphia trip, 145

and Whitefield's reputation, 196
    on Whitefield's travels, 165
Pepperell, Colonel, 190
perfectionism, Wesley vs. Whitefield,
    161–162
personal ethics of Franklin, 74
personal spiritual experience, 98, 140,
    223. *See also* new birth
Philadelphia
    Ben's travel from London to, 72
    Ben's travel to, 32
    communal spirit, 30
    denominations in, 40
    Franklin's first day in, 42–43
    immigration to, 110
    impact of Franklin, 38–44
    opposition to Whitefield, 147, 148
    as Whitefield's base of operations, 39,
        187
philosophy of life of Franklin, 91–94
Pietist movement, 95, 119
Pilgrims, 14
Pilgrim's Progress (Bunyan), 17, 27, 32
    Franklin and, 34–37
pleurisy, Franklin ill with, 73
Plutarch, *Lives*, 27
political cartoon, "Join or Die" with snake,
    111–112
Poor Richard, 30, 89–90
Poor Richard's Almanac, 1, 9, 65, 146–147
    folk wisdom in, 89
postmaster, Franklin as, 202
power of byline, 45
Presbyterians, 14, 40, 126
pricing strategies of Whitefield, 189
pride, 115
    Whitefield's concern about, 120
Princeton University, 201
Pringle, John, 217
print shop
    equipment cost, 48
    Franklin as Keimer's foreman, 75
printer, Franklin as, 3
printing of Whitefield sermons, 121, 146
    distribution of business, 161

by Franklin and Bradford, 152
printing press, 22
prison reform, and Georgia, 116
prisons, Wesleys' visits to, 116
The Prompter (newsletter), 69
prostitution, women in theater and, 60
Protestant Reformation, 14
pseudonyms, 112
    Busy-Body, 77, 85
    Franklin's use of, 30
    Obadiah Plainman, 151, 157
    Poor Richard, 30, 89–90
    Tom Trueman, 152, 157
publishing, as Whitefield/Franklin
    conversation topic, 188–190
"Puritan work ethic," 16
Puritans, 14
    Franklin and, 129
    Franklin's opposition to rigid theology,
        154
    and theater, 60
    on work, 25

Q
Quaker Meeting House, Franklin in, 43
Quakers, 14, 40
    in Boston, 16
    in England, 119
    Whitefield speaking at meeting, 146

R
Raikes, Robert, 189
Ralph, James, 45, 48–49, 54, 55, 57
Ray, Catherine, 173, 202
Read, Deborah, 42, 80–81. *See also*
    Franklin, Deborah
Read, John, 42
rebirth. *See* new birth
relationships. *See also* Whitefield and
    Franklin: relationship
    Franklin's education on, 78
religion, alteration in, 222–223
The Religion of Nature Delineated
    (Wollaston), 56
religious activities, at Oxford, 87

religious emigration, 15
religious exiles, 14–15
religious freedom, 14, 16, 18
religious "small groups," 92. *See also* Holy
    Club at Oxford
*Religious Societies: Proposals for the Revival of
    Dying Religion*, 92
religious traditions, Whitefield contact
    with varied, 137
responsibility, 57
    Franklin's sense of, 91–92
"Restoration comedies," 60
retirement, as Whitefield/Franklin
    conversation topic, 193–195
rhetoric, 67
Rich, John, 55
righteous living, methodical approach to,
    26
righteousness, 107, 155, 159
romance, in marriage, 180–182
The Rule and Exercises of Holy Living
    (Taylor), 95
The Rules of Oratory Applied to Acting
    (Gildon), 68, 69

S
St. Mary de Crypt school, 114
Salem witch trials, 16, 47
sanctification, 26
Savannah, Georgia, Whitefield's arrival in
    1738, 132
saved by faith, 128
Savonarola, 12
schools in Georgia, 136
science, Franklin and, 198–200
Scougal, Henry, 108
    The Life of God in the Soul of Man,
        102–103, 254n
self-examination, Wesley's questions on,
    96
self-improvement plan of Franklin, 26
Separatists, 14
A Serious Call to a Devout and Holy Life
    (Law), 87–88, 95
"servitor" program

at Oxford, 83
Whitefield in, 86
Seven Years' War between England and France, 205
Seward, William, 120, 145–146, 157–158, 178
death, 184
and publishing by Whitefield, 189
sexual mores, Franklin and, 173
Shakespeare, William, 59
Sheppard, Jack, 63
A Short View of the Immorality and Profaneness of the English Stage (Collier), 61
sick, Whitefield's visits to, 132
"Silence Dogood," 28–30
sin, 102
sincerity, as Franklin's priority, 91
small groups, 95
in Methodism, 183
religious, 92
smallpox, 47
social awareness, 74–75
social classes, 5–7
in America, Whitefield message to, 150–151
Franklin's view of, 152
upward mobility, 194
and value of person, 64
social networking, 94
social structures in Philadelphia, 110–111
society, beneficial effect of Whitefield's message, 149
South Carolina Gazette, 184
sower, parable of, 170
speech-making, Cicero and, 67
Spirit of God, Whitefield and, 104
spiritual discipline, George on lack of, 83
spiritual life, personal nature of, 223
Stamp Act (Parliament), 210–211
Steele, Richard, 61
The Conscious Lovers, 62
Stevenson, Margaret, 174, 205
Stevenson, Polly, 174, 176
Stout, Harry S., 70, 176, 198, 218, 221

Strahan, William, 209
subscriptions for orphanage donations, 192
success, 1
success saga, 33

T
taxation without representation, 211
Taylor, Jeremy, The Rule and Exercises of Holy Living, 95
teamwork, vs. individualists, 111
tears, of Whitefield, 69
The Temple (Herbert), 13
Tennent family, 183
Tennent, Gilbert, 148, 167, 180
Tennent, John, 167
Tennent, William, 167
Tennent, William Jr., 167
theater
in 1600s and 1700s, 61
in London, 54–55
and morality, 59
play lampooning Whitefield, 207–208
productions in Bristol, 67
upper class perspective on, 59–60
Whitefield's repudiation of, 108
theism, 209
Thomas à Kempis, 26
Of the Imitation of Christ, 95
Tillotson, Archbishop, 160
tithe, 20–21
Tower Church of London, 115
tradesmen, group formation in Philadelphia, 92
A Treatise Against the Fear of Man (Francke), 102
true religion, Whitefield on, 103
trust
in Jesus, 106–107
in others by Franklin, 79
truth, 84–86
as Franklin's priority, 91

U
Union Fire Company, 112
unity of colonies, 202

Universal Instructor in all Arts and Sciences: and Pennsylvania Gazette, 77
University of Pennsylvania, 39, 193
upper class, in colonial America, 6
U.S. Census, 249*n*

V

violence
    in America, 214
    against Whitefield, 185
Virginia Company, 12, 14, 17
volunteer fire company, 112
von Zinzendorf, Nicholas, 95

W

wagon train, Franklin and, 203–204
War with France, as Whitefield/Franklin
    conversation topic, 188–190
Watts, Isaac, 197
Webb, George
    "Batchelor's Hall" (poem), 125–126
    in Keimer's print shop, 123–124
    search for work from Franklin, 125
The Weekly History (magazine), 189
Wesley, Charles, 26, 27, 94
    books for Whitefield, 102
    conversion experience, 105–106
    with Delamottes family, 176
    eulogy for Whitefield, 215
    extemporaneous preaching, 122
    first impressions of Whitefield, 86–87
    first meeting with Whitefield, 97
    Franklin quoting from, 197
    in Georgia, 116, 133–134
    illness, 162
    letter to Whitefield, 162–163
    rejection of established church
        aristocratic spirit, 64
Wesley, John, 26, 87, 94, 170
    conversion experience, 105–106
    flight from Georgia, 135
    formation of Methodist societies, 183
    in Georgia, 116, 133–134
    "heart strangely warmed," 137
    infatuation with Georgian woman, 134

message to Whitefield, 136
rejection of established church
    aristocratic spirit, 64
rift with Whitefield, 161
travel to Georgia, 105
and Whitefield, 134, 163, 214
West, European views of, 11
Wheatley, Phillis, 215
Whitefield and Franklin: relationship,
    183–195
    concern for Whitefield's health, 198
    concerns in common, 171
    conversations, 187–193
    distancing from Whitefield, 160
    early view of Whitefield, 147
    first meeting, 145–147
    Franklin support for Whitefield, 152
    Franklin's defense of Whitefield, 4,
        148–149
    friendship, 2–3, 217–218
    letter about Ohio, 204
    like family, 212–213
    lodging offer for Whitefield, 186
    meetings and correspondence, 243–245
    mixed connections, 1757 to 1763,
        206–210
    renewed, 185–187
    Whitefield defense of Franklin, 9
    Whitefield letter of support for Franklin,
        212
    Whitefield's efforts to convert, 109, 185,
        209, 224
    Whitefield's first meeting, 145–147
Whitefield, Elizabeth (mother), 22
    hopes for George, 24, 50
Whitefield, Elizabeth (wife), travel to
    America, 188
Whitefield, George
    accusations of charitable funds misuse, 9
    birth, 19
    C. Wesley's first impression, 86–87
    C. Wesley's first meeting, 97
    childhood, 22–23, 51
    death, 215
    death of wife, 213

education, 23, 66–72
and Elizabeth Delamotte, 176–177
enrollment in Pembroke College, 86
father figure, 23–25
as good influence on society, 4–5
health, 160, 214
Herbert influence on, 13
independence from J. Wesley, 134
isolation, 103
journals, 8, 131–132, 150, 168
in London, 113
London newspapers on, 129
loneliness, 87
as loner, 97
love of acting, 67–68
marriage to E. James, 180
mourning sins of youth, 36
network of letter writers, 189–190
Philadelphia's response to, 39–41
practice of discipline, 102
reading by, 26–27
reading of *Pilgrim's Progress*, 36
romance in England, 161
as school dropout, 82
significance to America, 219–223
social class status, 6
struggle with identity formation, 52–53,
    84
theater impact on, 62
timeline, 229–238
use of press, 120
views on theater, 70, 71–72
and women, 175–179
Whitefield, George: ministry and faith
as Anglican minister, 5
belief in Jesus as God incarnate, 2
call to ministry, 113
Communion on Christmas, 84
conversion experience, 26
extemporaneous preaching by, 121–122
Franklin on preaching style, 66
Franklin's experiment on audience size, 41
and Great Awakening, 166–168
indifference to denominations, 40, 119,
    221

on new birth, 12
ordination, 140
preaching abilities, 114
rejection of established church
    aristocratic spirit, 64
rise to prominence, 65
and sin, 83
as young preacher, 115
Whitefield, George: opposition, 183
in 1739, 160
in England, 139
George's response, 160
to new birth doctrine, 119, 140
in *The Pennsylvania Gazette*, 184
in Philadelphia, 147, 148
reconciliation efforts, 186
Whitefield, George: sermons, 82
publication, 145
request for printed copies, 121
Whitefield, George: travels
to America (1754), 200–203
to America (1763), 208
to America (1769), 214–216
American tour, 239–242
to Boston, 185
to England, 1765, 210
to England, December 1738, 139
to Georgia, 131–142, 201
to Georgia, and letter to Elizabeth,
    177–178
to Georgia, delays, 117–119
to New England, 163–164, 165, 179, 201
to Philadelphia, 145, 149
Philadelphia as base of operations, 39,
    187
Philadelphia to Georgia, 148, 152
Savannah arrival in 1738, 132
Whitefield, Thomas, 22
Whitefield family, and religious, 52
Wilks, Robert, 54
William and Mary, 60–61
Winthrop, John, 15
Wollaston, William, *The Religion of Nature
    Delineated*, 56
women

Franklin relationships with, 172–175,
  176
on stage, 60
Whitefield and, 175–179

Whitefield's ability to play role, 71
work ethic, 25
working class, 6
worldly pursuits, 155–156